Parenting
with the Spirit

"Have you ever wished your child was born with an instruction manual? You're in luck . . . Marlene has written that guide that every parent has longed for! Sister Ellingson is a very experienced and loving mother of thirteen, grandmother of twenty-six. She really knows the ropes! Her approach is loving, gentle and gospel centered. Apply the principles she teaches, through example and story, and you are well on your way to happy family life!"

—DIANE HOPKINS, author of *Happy Phonics,* an award-winning phonics program; and owner of *Love to Learn*™

"What a treat for Janet and myself to read through your book of ideas and support for parents and grandparents. You keep 'hitting the nail on the head!' I found it easy to read, easy to understand and full of hope and not 'thou shalt nots.'"

—GARRY R. FLAKE, former director of LDS Charities

"I have known and watched Marlene and her family for many years. From the beginning, I have been impressed by the patience, love, and teaching that Marlene does as a mother. Likewise, her husband, Mark, has always been a very involved and instructing father to their children. Together they have raised a wonderfully caring and amazing family that has influenced the world for good in a million ways. I know that families the world over will be blessed by her wonderful book!"

—RACHEL KEPPNER, mother and author of the blog *Old-Fashioned Motherhood*

"This book is different from other parenting books because it is full of stories and clear-cut advice for specific situations through real-life examples!"

—TAMI RICHARDSON, mother of six

"As a mom of three little boys, I struggle. There are so many times I end the day upset or feeling awful about how it went, but this book has changed how I parent and I love it! I have seen how it has changed my perspective and changed the way I mother. My new favorite baby shower gift!"

—BECKY ADAIR, mother of three

Parenting with the Spirit

The Answer is MORE Love

Marlene R. Ellingson

CFI

An imprint of Cedar Fort, Inc.

Springville, Utah

To Mark

I love you with all my heart.

© 2018 Marlene R. Ellingson
Artwork by Katie Ellingson

This is not an official publication of The Church of Jesus Christ of Latter-day Saints. The opinions and views expressed herein belong solely to the author and do not necessarily represent the opinions or views of Cedar Fort, Inc. Permission for the use of sources, graphics, and photos is also solely the responsibility of the author.

ISBN 13: 978-1-4621-2231-8

Published by CFI, an imprint of Cedar Fort, Inc.
2373 W. 700 S., Springville, UT 84663
Distributed by Cedar Fort, Inc., www.cedarfort.com

LIBRARY OF CONGRESS CATALOGING-IN-PUBLICATION DATA

Names: Ellingson, Marlene R., 1961- author.
Title: Parenting with the spirit : the answer is more love / Marlene R.
   Ellingson.
Description: Springville, Utah : CFI, [2018] | Includes bibliographical
   references and index.
Identifiers: LCCN 2018025034 (print) | LCCN 2018027186 (ebook) | ISBN
   9781462129119 (epub, pdf, mobi) | ISBN 9781462122318 (perfect bound : alk.
   paper)
Subjects: LCSH: Parenting--Religious aspects--Church of Jesus Christ of
   Latter-day Saints.
Classification: LCC BX8643.C56 (ebook) | LCC BX8643.C56 E45 2018 (print) |
   DDC 248.8/45--dc23
LC record available at https://lccn.loc.gov/2018025034

Cover design by Shawnda T. Craig
Cover design © 2018 Cedar Fort, Inc.
Edited by Emily Chambers and Sydnee Hyer
Typeset by Kaitlin Barwick

Printed in the United States of America

10 9 8 7 6 5 4 3 2

Printed on acid-free paper

Contents

Introduction

A Timeless Approach, Using the Spirit and More Love

When I was a young mom, I found myself dreading my scripture reading. It seemed that every time I read, there before me was yet another thing that I wasn't doing right. I was filled with guilt and discouragement. But gradually, I came to look at it in a different way. Here were principles of truth. By reading them, I was filling my mind and heart with the ideal. I was actually immersing myself in power to become what I wanted to be.

Mothers and fathers often feel guilt. We want to be better parents to our darlings than we are now. May this book fill our hearts with hope and possibilities, rather than discouragement or regret.

Raising our thirteen children, Mark and I have been blessed with lots and lots of trial and error. When one approach didn't work, we tried something else. Then, that way wasn't always right for the next child! Mark likes to joke that now we know thirteen different ways to potty-train a child! As our family grew and my youngest started school, I asked myself, *What do I want to do with my free time at last?* I decided I wanted to help families. So I started collecting ideas. With every issue I thought of, I asked my network of mothers, sisters, daughters, and friends to tell me their approach. I wrote down any story that went along with it, in order to share it with other moms. This book does not have room for all those ideas, but I have included some of them, and more importantly, I've tried to share the principles behind them in hopes that your family will be blessed by our sharing them.

More Love

What do I mean by "The Answer Is More Love?" Of course, we all love our children. Some are harder to love than others at different times, but we pray with all our hearts to be filled with more love for them, as taught in the scriptures (Moroni 7:48). Elder Massimo De Feo taught, "Love indeed is the true sign of every true disciple of Jesus Christ."[1] Constantly working toward using more love as we teach and guide our children is a Christlike approach to parenting.

My Dad taught me tons about love from an accidental fire incident. I must have been about thirteen or fourteen years old when one day I was making no-bake cookies on the stove. A fire suddenly started in the pan of oil! Thinking, *fire—water*, I quickly dumped water into the pan, which of course made the fire burst out larger. Screaming, I ran out, and Dad came in and grabbed the pan, taking it outside to put out the fire. It was all very traumatic for a young girl, and I felt bad, but I got over it quick enough. I was vaguely aware that Dad had gotten hurt somehow, since a nurse from our ward came over to help him treat the burn. Still, when I talked to Dad about it, apologizing for my foolishness, he just expressed praise and thanks to the Lord for preserving his hands, since he needed them to do dental work each day. And he praised the Lord for sending an angel like this sister to help him heal.

It wasn't until many years later, when thinking back on the incident, that I put two and two together and realized I was that cause of some intense suffering for Dad! My mishap caused him great pain. Also, there must have been the headache of an insurance claim and repairs in the kitchen of the smoke damage that surely occurred—but I have little to no memory of that either. What is the miracle to me is that Dad and Mom never made me feel guilty! They didn't blame or lecture or even associate any of this trial as being my fault, which it was. Instead, leaving my self-esteem intact at a tender age, they disassociated the burn from a careless young girl who should have known better. Nor did they discourage me from cooking, but quite the contrary. What amazing parents, to absorb the emotion of the pain and trial and let the mistake just be forgotten. I love them for letting only praise of the Lord's goodness be remembered.

Mark and I have tried to live up to this amazing example of unconditional love. We have fallen short, but we have been blessed for trying to reach the ideal. A prophet taught parents about using love in raising our children: "I implore you to teach and control by the spirit of love and forbearance until you can conquer. If children are defiant and difficult to control, be patient with them until you can conquer by love, and you will have gained their souls, and you can then mould [sic] their characters as you please."[2]

The Spirit

As we grow in our love, our hearts will be softened and ready for the Spirit to guide us in raising our children. More love is the key to effective parenting, and more love may mean extra time or a new idea. It could mean a stricter curfew, or a consequence enforced. The Spirit helps us decide the best way to show more love. Our Father in Heaven parents each of us in a way tailored just for us, with individual gifts, challenges, and missions. He loves us with blessings, tender mercies, miracles, answers, forgiveness through His Son, and promptings from the Holy Ghost. Or He loves us with trials and stretching. Just like He treats us each differently, we can know how to parent each child differently with help from the Spirit. President Russell M. Nelson taught us about "our right to have the manifestations of the Spirit every day of our lives."[3]

It is our love for our children that springboards the promptings of the Spirit. If we love them enough to be truly invested in parenting them well, we will search until we find the solutions to their needs and dilemmas. We will be willing to give the time to truly connect with them and reach their hearts using the promptings of the Lord. Let me illustrate with a story:

My young son was so upset. His outburst was getting worse by the minute. As the youngest in the family, he felt picked on and left out. Many times, I had told him to talk nice or else I dished out a consequence. But this time, I tried to tune in to just what was the problem. Then, I had an idea come to me. "Let's rock and talk," I told him. He climbed on my lap in the big rocking chair, and with my arms snug around him, we rocked a few minutes. Then we talked about what had happened. We tried to see his brother's point of view. I told him that I realized it was hard sometimes, but that I knew he could understand and use kinder responses. I tried to encourage and express love. And soon, he was ready to get up and try it all again. "Rock and talk" remained a tool for connecting with him many times! Even when he grew to be too big for my lap, I still convinced him to come there on occasion.

It was a gift from God to receive this prompting by the Spirit that was perfect for this child. Though this plan would not have been effective for another, since this son loved the feeling of soft things such as being covered in a warm blanket or hugged tight, and since he was able to reason quite well, it worked. Father knew this idea was just the right way to show more love to this son as a tool for correction and growth. So He sent me more love with this idea through His Holy Spirit.

May we grow in our love for our families and use that love to hold out for spiritual promptings that will lead us to the best approach for parenting each child. May we seek the Spirit to help us parent each child with more love.

—Marlene

Chapter 1
Be Their Best Mentor

*O*ur children learn the most from what we are. Growing up, I often saw "Children Learn What They Live"[1] on a wall-hanging in my home. It is really true: children learn the very most from what they live each day. In other words, we teach them the most by our very lives. If we are trying our best to live the gospel, that's what they will likely do too. Example is a wonderful gift we give our kids—even the example of acknowledging that we messed up and are trying harder to do better! In fact, sometimes our kids can't hear what we say, because how we live speaks so loudly.[2] To be the best mentor, we must live what we want to teach. They learn the very most from what we are.

A Calm and Happy Mommy

"Are you a queen in your castle or a dragon in the dungeon?" read a handout taped to my wall until it wore out. It reminded me that children long for their mother to be happy. Life is good and all is well in the world if only Mommy is happy!

Unfortunately, Mommy is often dealing with lack of sleep, or hormones gone wild, or frustration from too much clutter. She is often worried about someone who is sick or is going through a difficult phase. She wonders how to make the budget stretch or how to lose some extra pounds (or at least hide them). How do we moms find peace enough to put on a smile and say the cheerful words our families love to hear? Here are some principles to help us be happier:

1. Reservoirs That Are Full

First, we must have our reservoirs filled. Before we can give, we must have something to give. So we need to spend time on our knees receiving help, guidance, and peace from the source of real peace. We need to keep our minds full of words and principles of truth from the scriptures. I know I need that connection with God to be the mom my kids need and I want to be.

At one point, I figured out that I had a "Minimum Daily Requirement" of scriptures—my MDR. At a very busy time in my life, when I had two-year-old identical twin boys, two older girls, and a baby on the way, I found that I simply had to fit at least half a page of the Book of Mormon in my day. I discovered that if I could fit that much in, I would then be blessed with a minute to pause and react better. Many times, my children were clamoring for my attention, and I had just been through something with one of the twins, then the second one did it *too*! *If* I had read recently, I had a moment to realize that this time it was the other one, and he needed a kind reaction too! I was blessed with a chance to compose a better response. To this day, without my MDR, the "natural-man" mommy kicks in, but with it, I am a much calmer mom. When I have spent even a little time in prayer and scriptures, I am filled with peace and a real power from above that helps me be my better self throughout that day.

2. Turning to Prayer

Mothers run across countless daily dilemmas and need answers. In this "profession," there is a direct conduit to God. We can pray over even little things and get the answers we need. And if we do our best to stay in tune, promptings will come even when we're on the move.

I was having a really hard time trying to take the bottle away from my first little toddler. It had become such a power struggle, and she did *not* need it anymore, but anything I tried just hadn't worked. So I made it a matter of prayer, and a new idea came. She and I found a box and had fun together gathering up all the bottles and putting them inside. "Bye, bye, Bottle," we'd say. Then we closed the box tight and put it up high out of reach in her closet. When nap time came, she asked for a bottle as usual. "Remember, they are gone," I told her and pointed to the box up high. She cried a little bit, but then lay down and went to sleep without one. Only once or twice more did she even think of them. My problem was solved, and I had a new gratitude for God's willingness to help with something small but important to me.

3. Creativity in Our Lives

We moms need to create. Elder Dieter F. Uchtdorf taught,

> The desire to create is one of the deepest yearnings of the human soul. No matter our talents, education, backgrounds, or abilities, we each have an inherent wish to create something that did not exist before.
>
> Everyone can create. You don't need money, position, or influence in order to create something of substance or beauty. Creation brings deep satisfaction and fulfillment. We develop ourselves and others when we take unorganized matter into our hands and mold it into something of beauty.[3]

Much of my creating during my early mothering was figuring out how to use the little resources we had to keep my kids happy and occupied and their brains stimulated and talents developing. I remember how proud I was when I sewed some colorful drawstring bags that hid some of their toys, so that when we got them out, they were fresh and newly fun! Even if our creativity is for our children at present, there is time later—even lots of years after they have left home—to listen to our inner yearnings to sing or to play an instrument, to paint or to write.

I had always wanted to be ballerina, and I finally got to take an adult ballet class a few years ago. I took my five-year-old along, and he was bored watching us ladies do exercises at the barre. I'm sure the Lord prompted me with this plan: I brought along one volume of an encyclopedia and five bookmarks. I challenged him to find five "really cool" things and bookmark them to show me afterward. He loved it! There were all kinds of interesting pictures found in those volumes, and they kept him busy the entire class time!

4. A Warm Smile and a Compassionate Heart

The habit of wearing a smile is a good trait for anyone trying to be happy. I was walking down the aisle in church, and I saw someone I didn't know. My face must have had a quizzical look, along with my thought, *Who are you?* I realized that my face must *not* have given a warm, kind message of welcome! I vowed to never let that happen again. I want to have a warm, genuine smile for all I see, to greet them and communicate, "You are okay, and I love you!" Especially at home.

Smiling, I learned, causes lowered stress, lowered blood pressure, a boosted immune system, released endorphins (natural pain relievers) and more serotonin (feel-good properties)![4]

A warm smile is a gift that we truly can give everyone. It is an act of kindness to lift them. Every person we meet is likely carrying some heavy burden, and a smile along with a kind word or a listening ear will help. Even at home.

"In the end," teaches Elder Uchtdorf, "the number of prayers we say may contribute to our happiness, but the number of prayers we answer may be of even greater importance. Let us open our eyes and see the heavy hearts, notice the loneliness and despair; let us feel the silent prayers of others around us, and let us be an instrument in the hands of the Lord to answer those prayers."[5] Let's give others the gift of our genuine smile.

5. A Cheerful Answer like "Yes!"

"I tried never to say 'no' if I could possibly say 'yes,'" is wonderful advice from Marjorie Hinckley. "I think that worked well because it gave my children the feeling that I trusted them and they were responsible to do the best they could."[6]

I discovered that there was a way to say yes and still keep wise limits: "Yes, you can have a cookie, after dinner." "Yes, you can go out to play, as soon as your chores are done." "Yes, I can get that for you, as soon as I get this batch of laundry in." When a child is misbehaving, I could still say yes: "Yes, you can play with this toy (as I put it up high), as soon as you are ready to play nice." And when I had to say no, I could phrase it with a yes: "Yes, I want to see that movie too. We will have to plan to see it when it comes to the dollar theater." Or "I'd like to say yes, but I just can't. I prayed about it, and I don't feel good about you going this time."

6. A Heart Open to Gratitude and Joy

The other day, I was thinking about the previous year. I thought about a death in the family and the severe health challenges Mark and I had faced. I realized that every one of my grown children had been through a major challenge, at work or at school, financial or health, miscarriage or other intense trials. "What a bad year it has been!" I told myself. But my next thought (I'm sure it was a nudge from the Spirit) was "What a good year it has been, you mean!" I came to realize that each challenge, each trial had been overcome! It was a long, hard road, with lots of fasting and prayer, but in just about every case, the problem had been conquered and each young family had been able to move on, stronger than before. My heart filled with gratitude.

Some days I wake up in a grumpy mood. Things just don't look bright, and I know that my foul mood is affecting the whole family. So, I have learned to tell myself, "I am going to have a change of heart!" (see Alma 5:12). I force on a smile and a better attitude and start looking for blessings. They are *always* there for the noticing. I can focus on them if I choose to, or list them, and then my family is so grateful for a cheerful mom again!

7. Forgiveness of Myself and Others

The scriptures tell us how to be filled with joy. "Behold, this is joy which none receiveth save it be the truly penitent and humble seeker of happiness" (Alma 27:18). The formula is to be always repenting and forgiving, as we seek for happiness. Because of the Atonement of Jesus Christ, we can start over, time after time. When we go to our family members and apologize or forgive, and then put the whole incident away, we are teaching them about correcting mistakes and moving forward, letting others do the same.

Often, I find myself replaying over and over the embarrassing or bad thing I did or the mistake I made. Instead, I must fix it as best I can, and then erase it from my mind, focusing instead on the way I would handle it next time. "I'm over that!" is how my friend silences her mind of things she wants to move on from. Just as you wouldn't dig down beneath a beautiful park and find your garbage in the landfill below, you don't need to dig up past mistakes or sins that have been repented of. Instead, you can let the Atonement of Jesus Christ clean and reclaim you.[7] We can simply move forward, improving each day, with minds filled with gratitude for the chance to get better and better.

8. Just One Thing Accomplished

Though many days were filled to the brim with caring for children, I learned there were ways to *feel* like I had accomplished something each day. Oh yes, I knew that raising children was accomplishing something wonderful, but there was also my to-do list, and some days, it was just not getting done. I would sit and nurse a baby, enjoying the chance to rest for a minute, but see something across the room that *still* bothered me! Maybe it was a small thing that needed putting away. Next time I looked there, I could feel happy that it was safely put away at last! Maybe it was a call that

I really needed to make. Maybe it was a note I finally wrote, or an email, or a message tucked in a sack lunch that I'd been meaning to do. If I fit in only that extra thing that day, I would feel so good checking it off my mental list. So much may not get done, but this one did! It was something positive to focus on, and it made for a happier mommy.

9. Uplifting Self-Talk

We talk to ourselves all day long. And what we say makes a huge difference. It is much better to tell ourselves positive, happy things that can become our goals. Remember, we are what we tell ourselves.

Many years ago, my dad taught me that our brains are equipped with a goal-striving device, and that whatever we tell it becomes its goal.[8] I think the gospel equivalent to this would be hope. I began to choose good things to program my brain each day. I even came up with some self-talk to program my brain: **"I am fit and trim, healthy and energetic, neat and comely, cheerful and organized!"** Saying those words to myself still leaves me thinking that I am okay and that I am becoming who I want to be, word by word, goal by goal.

You are what you tell yourself you are!

"Find the donuts today!" I tell my kids as they go out the door. The idea is that rather than focus on the hole, you focus on the donut. Why would you notice the hole, when there is a yummy donut to see? Finding the good is a wonderful go-to place for minds that are turning to negative thoughts. There is always a donut to find. There is so much good to notice, so why focus on anything not so good?

Negative thoughts can weigh heavily on our minds during pregnancy, when there are plenty of discomforts, worries, and complaints. When I was fed up with things during my pregnancies, I would start to think emphatically, *I am SO . . .* Then, I would force myself to finish the sentence with *grateful! Yes, I am grateful,* I would make myself think, and I would find something around me to be grateful for. Maybe my eyes rested on a spoon. *Yes,* I would affirm to myself, *I am grateful for spoons. What handy things.* By then, I would have remembered how grateful I am for this roof over my head, this food to prepare, this family of mine, and even for this healthy pregnancy. Counting blessings in our self-talk is a wonderful pick-me-up.

Sometimes our thoughts linger on a negative conversation or disagreement. It takes effort to kick out bad memories, then turn our thoughts to something happy. When we or someone else says, "I'm no good at this" we can help them add, "Not yet!" When our kids are dreading something hard, we can prompt them to say, "This is going to be an adventure!" Positive self-talk can help us heal and claim blessings, get rid of pride and judgment, and fill us with peace and love. What we tell ourselves is what we become.

10. Perspective

I am at the tail end of my child-rearing days. My youngest two kids left at home are age thirteen and seventeen. They are at the end of my thirty-six-year stint raising our thirteen children. But even with an extra-long season, I still find myself with many years ahead of me to pursue goals, fulfill my mission, and make a difference in the world. Yes, I am still mother to all those children and their families, but they don't need me daily as much as they used to. They take turns needing me, and so I have much more time free to pursue my dreams. If I stay healthy, I have so many productive years left—at least fifty! So, I don't regret in the least the years that I was able to focus almost exclusively on my spouse and my children, giving these kids the best upbringing I possibly could.

My investment in them has paid off, and they are living full and productive lives. They continue to bring me lots of joy. When I had a house full of little kids, even though it was really challenging at times, I knew I had to enjoy this season to the fullest, before they all grew up!

Keeping in mind the long-term perspective, I could better be a happy mommy to my little ones. "Most folks are about as happy as they make up their mind to be."[9] We all have an occasional dragon day. But mostly, regardless of circumstances, we can decide to be the benevolent, happy queen of our castle.

I enlisted my grandchildren to help me illustrate a child's perspective:

Dear Mom,

How I love it when you are happy! Thanks for smiling and laughing with me. Thanks for doing it when you are tired or weary. Thanks for all the extras—I love them, even if I forget to thank you. You make my world amazing when you decide to be calm and cheerful!

Love, Me

A Coach and Leader Daddy

Dads make the best coaches! They can give pointers and perspective on all the current goings-on at home. Dads are also great at encouraging and building up the family! They can hear all the good things that happened when they were gone and make a big deal about them! Dads take so many roles in a family:

1. The Coach

Dads get to help a wobbly youngster learn to ride their first bike. They get to show the best moves at basketball or wrestling, checkers or marbles. Dads can help give extra tips or practice on catching a baseball or hitting a volleyball. Dads do so well at listening to the piano piece before the recital or the talk before church.

Roughhousing with Dad is such a great thing. Kids often have extra energy to spend, especially if cooped up on bad-weather days, so they can use some up that way. What's more, Dad shows how to have fun, but also to use good judgment to not go too far. It is so important for kids to physically play with their dad. It teaches young boys appropriate ways to be masculine and helps both boys and girls feel accepted and loved for who they are. Playing with Dad also helps teach kids proper touch. It keeps their "love bucket" full! In the book *Five Love Languages of Children*, we learn, "Hugs and kisses, wrestling on the floor, riding piggy back, and other playful loving touches are vital to the child's emotional development. Children need many meaningful touches every day . . . even if you are not a 'hugger.'"[10]

2. The Encourager

I often tell my kids to "go ask Dad" when they come to me for counsel. I know Mark is blessed with common sense and will give them sound advice. Once, when the advice he gave was not quite what I would have chosen, I still told them: "You'll be blessed for following his counsel." And it was true.[11]

A great tool and another source of Dad's counsel and encouragement in our family is what we call the Daddy Report. I take a piece of paper and write each child's name along the side. Next to it, I write one good thing that happened to each child that day. I might report a good grade on a test or a great effort at a hard challenge in PE. I might put down who did a good job on their chores or is trying extra hard to learn their new song on the piano. I've even been known to put: "He almost got his room all cleaned up today!" I place the paper next to Dad's dinner plate. During dinner, he reads it aloud and asks for more details.

Each person tells about their day and gets praise and input from him. The Daddy Report lets Daddy hear about details of the day at home and at school that he may have missed otherwise, and lets Dad lead the conversation at the dinner table that is both positive and pertinent.

3. The Leader

A successful company is usually set up with both a CEO and a CFO. Each has great responsibilities and importance. Centuries of experience have shown this to be the easiest and most effective way to lead a company.[12] So it is in our families. A family also thrives with two strong leaders who both work for success. But it certainly is okay for one to take the lead.

For several years, we noticed a trend of how few movies showed a strong father figure in them. Almost none did. The mothers were often strong and capable, but the father figure was often weak or crazy or absent. Though, sadly, many families are not blessed with a father, it is still definitely the ideal to have both strong, capable, and loving parents. Let's champion our dads! Let's build them up, praise them profusely in front of the kids, and help them take their lead roles in our homes!

In "The Family: A Proclamation to the World," we are taught, "By divine design, fathers are to preside over their families in love and righteousness and are responsible to provide the necessities of life and protection for their families. Mothers are primarily responsible for the nurture of their children. In these sacred responsibilities, fathers and mothers are obligated to help one another as equal partners."[13]

My daughter learned something about a father's role during her college summer internship for her family science major. She helped with the Flourishing Families research project in Seattle, a study of five hundred families for over five years. Two interns would knock at each door and administer questionnaires and video communication patterns of each family.

She commented to me about an interesting phenomenon that would happen every time. If the family had a single mom, then this mom immediately would look to the interns, my daughter and her companion, to lead out on what to do. But if there was a father in the home, it was very different. From the first, the father would direct and lead. He would tell them to come in, where to sit, and how to proceed. My daughter was amazed at how universal this response was. These families were a good cross-section of the public—not from one class or religion or economic status. But always, if there was a father present, he would naturally take the lead in his home.

However, my friend showed me that there are times when a mom must step in for dad's responsibilities. After trying to awaken his desire to lead out in family prayer and scriptures, with no success, she realized that if her kids were going to grow up fortified with consistency, she would have to lead out or she would lose them. "So I instituted these practices in our home on my own. Sometimes Daddy joined, sometimes he didn't. When he chose to participate, I would step back and allow him to take lead whenever he would." And today, all her children have "become solid adults in the gospel."[14]

4. The Hard Work

I was blessed to be a stay-at-home mom. Though I taught piano lessons, taught the kids preschool, and wrote at home, Mark provided for us. So, when the kids thank me for a nice dinner or for an item of clothing or toy I have bought them, I have learned to have them thank Dad also. He spends so much time and effort to earn the money for these things. How grateful I am for Mark's years of putting aside his own ways of spending time, and going to work day after day, month after month. Mark often rides his bike to work, freeing up a car for me or the teenagers to use. On a difficult morning out the door, I like to thank him for "keeping the wolf from the door."[15] It tells him I know what he does is tough and that I appreciate the sacrifice in our behalf.

What a gift a father gives his children when he teaches them to work! What a boost to a happy, productive life they will take with them if they have grown up working. Mom can give a child chores and responsibilities, but Dad can too. He can have a child or two there watching when he does a repair on the car or a household appliance, even just to hand him tools and walk with him through the process. Kids learn a ton by weeding and watering and mowing the lawn again week after week. They learn even more when they take care of animals because there is need to take daily, watchful care over living things and the stakes are higher when they are neglected.

Dad can, in many cases, take a son or daughter to his job to see firsthand his daily work for the family. They can then visualize what Dad does all day, and the effort it takes. Gratitude will grow, as will the determination to do likewise for their own family one day. Whatever gifts or talents or abilities each Dad is blessed with, we can build on those by believing in him and backing him up. His is not an easy role, for there is constant pressure to progress. We can help him grow in his confidence with our support.

5. Honoring Dad

My mom was good at saving the biggest piece for my dad, or fixing his favorite food. I'll never forget her over-the-top excitement when she set up a surprise for him. She had saved up to buy him a brand-new bike! She positioned it at the front door, told us to let him answer the doorbell, as she excitedly waited out of sight to see his reaction.

Mark likes new socks! His favorite gift was when each of the kids put their Fathers' Day offering in a sock, and we "socked it to him." Another time, for fun we met him at the front door with water bottles and bandanas around our faces. We forced him to march across the street, and then we all jumped into the neighbor's pool together.

Mark has longed to drive a really nice truck, with air conditioning! (Many summers, Mark has done without.) One time, he sold his beloved truck in order to pay for one of our kids' weddings. He has let his sons drive our used trucks while he drove the much-used family car. I like to remind Mark that instead of nice vehicles, we had a "quiver full" of kids (Psalms 127:5)! We can notice all the sacrifices our fathers make and honor them for it.

6. The Wise Limits

In a game preserve in Africa, there was a sudden problem with the rhinoceroses. Many were found with deep wounds. The culprits were discovered to be teenage elephants who had surprisingly bullied and even killed the rhinos, with no apparent reason why. In this preserve, the father elephants had been separated from the herds for a time, but when they were introduced back, the carnage stopped. The youthful elephants were whipped back into shape and "taught how to be elephants." It was their fathers that modeled proper limits and behavior, and how to deal with hormones of puberty. The fathers were the necessary ingredients to the family.[16]

People too need limits—especially as they grow up—and many of these are best set by a father. He teaches and models how to be a good person and citizen. "Training up a child" is an important service that fathers give their families and society.

7. The Patriarch

I am blessed to have a very wise and prayerful husband. We are so grateful for the priesthood blessings given us. When he gives a father's blessing, we act on it, choosing to fully believe that the words he gave were from God.

In family prayer, it is Dad's duty to call on the one to pray. Then whenever he is not there for a meal, the job falls to Mom. For family home evening or a family council, he presides. Even if Mom has the lesson, she can let him start the meeting, call on someone to pray, and turn the time over to her. This is a visual aid in itself, to show the kids his divine role.

I used to wake up the kids every morning for scripture time by going down the hallways and singing a wake-up song. It was our signal to start the day. Then, there came a time when we decided that Mark should really be the one to call to scriptures. We still sing but do it after they all come to the table. It's a small thing, but it reinforces that Dad is at the head, and I am in no way threatened by it. Occasionally, I have slipped up and led the whole family home evening activity that I had planned myself. I have learned to defer to him to start and end our family meetings and structured activities. In fact, through the years, I have better learned to join with him in planning our family meetings, so that we are both on the same page. On busy Mondays, when we haven't talked over yet what we want to do for family home evening, I often call Mark at his lunchtime at work to talk over what our family needs that night. Often, I am amazed at his insight on what to discuss that week. He has a different view of family dynamics and sees things a little differently than I, who am in the trenches. He teaches us the gospel with his own approach.

8. Mom's Lover

A very important role of Dad is to be Mom's lover. When Dad takes Mom on a date, or tells her she's pretty, the kids smile. When they see him scoop her up in a tender embrace or bring her flowers, they not only feel happy but they also learn to want that kind of affection for themselves one day. If Dad lets the kids hear his compliments to Mom or see him write her a love note, they will see his devotion to her. If he lets them see him do all the dishes or take the baby or rub her feet when she's tired, they know of his concern and care for her. They learn by example to be a great spouse someday as well.

I would submit that the very best thing that a father can do for his kids is to love their mother. Many agree that one of the best deterrents to sexual misbehavior and pornography is an example of parents who love each other. When they see a constant display of tender love and affection, they are more likely to want it too, and not a cheap substitute.

My parents had a happy, successful marriage. Still, on rare occasions, when they would have even a minor disagreement, my worst fears would surface: what if they got a divorce?! Then, when things were patched up, I could breathe easy and feel secure that they loved each other. It is a great source of stability for kids to see their parents' love for each other.

9. The Children Years

There is so much that a man wants to try and to do with his life. If he can just keep healthy, there is so much time after retirement to explore and use talents and try new things. The time given to support a family is consecrated time, and a dad will be blessed for giving it. After the greatest calling, that of leading a family, he will then have many more years to pursue his other callings more fully.

For many years, Mark's only hobby was his kids. Later, he would do things he wanted to try, as long as he could do it with them. In fact, he put aside a favorite hobby when he found himself doing it alone. He knew that the time for that would come, but with kids still at home, he needed to choose things they were interested in. So together they shot off rockets, put together a go-cart, made boomerangs, and went camping. When one son had a goal of running a half marathon, Mark trained with him. Another son was excited to try trading out an engine, so he and Mark figured it out.

With retirement upon us now, Mark is still in good health and is facing many years of pursuing ideas and dreams. During the years of children in our home, he had to simply keep that perspective.

We would do well to let Dad take his rightful place at the head of the family. Nephi was a very capable young man, but he deferred the leadership to his father. When he broke his steel bow and his family was hurting for food, he made a wood one and an arrow. He then turned to his father for direction on where to go for the food the hungry family needed soon! I used to think that Nephi wanted to help his father become humble again by asking the Lord where to send him. But I realize now that Nephi knew that as head of the family, it was Lehi's responsibility to provide, so instead of just asking the Lord himself, he went to his dad. No matter that his father was not perfect and had slipped into murmuring in this extremity, he was still the one in charge, and so Nephi let him lead. Lehi quickly repented and provided sound advice from the Lord for Nephi. When we go to Dad for counsel and direction, he will rise to the occasion and take up the challenge of being the spiritual leader in our homes.

Dear Dad,

I love you. I need you to watch over and protect us, and to provide for our needs. Thanks for coming home to play with me and teach me and love me.

Love, Me

Team Couple

The closer we are as a couple, the more effective we can be in our parenting. We become a team, and together, our synergy helps us accomplish so much good in our family. What's more, children are more stable and better adjusted if they live with an example of a happily married Mommy and Daddy! Of course, a marriage need not be perfect to have a home where there is love and affection, caring and respect. "The best way to love your children is to love their mother [father]. The quality of your marriage greatly affects the way you relate to your children—and the way they receive love. If your marriage is healthy—both partners treating each other with kindness, respect, and integrity—you and your spouse will feel and act as partners in parenting."[17]

If you are walking the road of parenting without a spouse by your side, know that the you are not alone. The Lord is trusting you to carry on, and He is with you. His Spirit is there to guide you. May these principles below help you team up with the Savior in your parenting, as well as those who have a spouse must do.

1. We Must Grow Our Love

"Two little lovers, sitting in a tree." I like to add: "One is Dad, the other Mommy!" We can simply choose to adore our spouse. Love is a choice, and adoring is even better. Training ourselves to find the good, affirm it, and constantly be grateful is so worth the effort. I have found that if I focus on improving myself, he is free to work on himself! To use the Bible language, I have to stop looking for motes (tiny slivers) in my spouse's eye, and focus on finding the beams (2×4s) that are covering my own eye (Luke 6:41–42). Especially the "beam" of being judgmental! C. Terry Warner teaches, "Criticize them, and their conscience will console them. Love them, and their conscience will indict them."[18] It sounds so simple, but is not easy to apply. However, I have found that this attitude is a foundation for a happy, loving marriage. With him taking over the job of "fixing" himself, I am free to adore him!

A friend of mine shared with me her profound discovery: "I used to think that my husband had to meet my needs," she told me. "When he couldn't always do that, I was in despair. I struggled in prayer, then I came to realize: I don't need him to fill my needs. Heavenly Father can do that! When I came to that conclusion, I was free to just love my spouse. I am so much happier, and my marriage is so much better without that expectation."

"Marriage is about fighting the battle between your ears," taught Lindsay Garrison, a wife and mother of four who recently taught about love in marriage. Lindsay used to pray that her husband would change, but now she prays, "Help me love him how he needs it. Help me understand even when he doesn't express it." We can filter what our spouse says to improve the way we receive it, she urged us. Other ways to grow our love are to look into each other's eyes three times daily, to give space when the other has had a bad day without taking it personally, and to let the other be right when it doesn't matter that much to us. And we must pray in detail for our spouse.[19]

2. We Should Treat Each Other like Royalty

How I love it when Mark lets me go first or opens the door for me. Sometimes, if the boys are walking ahead of us, he tells them, "Please open the car door for Mom." He also insists that the first plate of food goes to me. What a training for them and their future spouse! The kids know that he will not allow them to talk disrespectfully to me: "She's my girlfriend!"

We can make our husband feel like the king of the family by treating him like one. We can have him sit at the head of the table and in the great big "daddy bear" chair. Dad can have the best piece of cake. He should be the one to make the final decisions, after listening to the other points of view.

To elevate how we treat each other, we can simply help with one another's duties or pressures. I love it when Mark gives a hand in the kitchen. Sometimes, he makes us pancakes for dinner when I have an extra busy day! Our used cars need fixing a lot, and even though I can't help him with a car repair, he loves it when I come out to check on how it's going and bring a drink of water or a bite of sandwich. And when the repair is extra hard, I have learned to pray for angels to come give him a hand!

Sincerely complimenting each other daily is another way to uplift and build our spouses, which in turn builds our children. "Mom is extra good at that!" or "Dad, you're amazing at that!" When we notice the good things about each other and express thanks for daily service, our kids see it too, and everyone benefits.

Also, we can pray for each other by name in family prayer. That may seem obvious, but it may not be happening. We have a large family, and by the time we pray for everyone in need, the family prayer gets long! In fact, Mark and I discovered that while we were praying for each of our kids and other loved ones, we were neglecting to pray for each other by name. We determined to do this daily: "Bless Dad at work that he will be safe and guided" and "Bless Mom in her projects today that they will go well."

Sometimes we get so caught up in serving our children that our spouse gets moved to second priority! I found that I do a lot *with* Mark, but some days I forget to do things *for* him. I decided to mark off a corner at the bottom of my daily list, as my place where I plan for a daily service for him. Being each other's king and queen sets a high standard in how to treat a spouse, a good goal to work toward.

3. We Must Grow in Unity

When we got married, someone gave me the challenge to never talk bad about my spouse to anyone. I feel blessed to not have fallen into that "bashing" habit that can only bring sorrow. Loyalty is such a great blessing, and when we give it to our spouse, we are more likely to get it back. Once again, we can save our gripes to work out with the Lord. Of course, sometimes there is need for a marriage counselor. But we can reach for the ideal, and when we refuse to belittle our loved ones or make them the brunt of a joke or sarcasm, we are building our family rather than cutting them down, even slightly.

Unity can happen when there is a family issue that we need to discuss in a family council or over the dinner table. Mark and I try to talk it over beforehand, to be on the same page. But even if we have not had that chance, we can still support each other. We learned that even if we disagree, we can hear out and respect the other one's point of view and, rather than shooting it down, wait and bring up our opposing opinion separately. Even if Mark doesn't quite agree with my presentation of my point of view on a topic, he has learned to not contradict me right then, so as to undermine what I said. In private, he can express it to me. Later on, he could give another point of view to the family. Gradually, Mark and I have learned to really support one another, especially in front of the kids.

We can support each other in another way too. I asked my son for a copy of his "I am" poem he had written about himself for English. "No, I don't like that poem! It's too general. I just followed directions—it's not good!" he protested. "But it's about you!" I insisted. When he still resisted, Mark spoke up, prompting him to say, "I'm so glad you love me and are interested in me, Mom! Sure, I'll get you that poem!" We can prompt our kids to respect and defer to our spouse.

4. We Can Show Plenty of Affection

In front of our kids, we should plant a big smooch on our spouse's lips! Or grab them from behind in a great big hug. At one point, I decided to keep a small bottle of mouthwash in the kitchen, so I could kiss Mark good-bye even if I hadn't brushed my teeth yet that morning. I determined to give more hugs, even following him out to his truck if we missed that morning!

Once, when Mark was having a hard time, experiencing exhaustion mixed with low self-esteem, I got the idea to massage his feet. He melted to my tender touch and listened to my loving words. In fact, while I was doing it, I felt like the right words to say were given to me, in answer to my prayers for him. But combining them with a loving touch was the conduit to reach him best.

If we shower our spouse with love, the love spills out to our whole family. Goodness prevails when love abounds. We are putting first our most important relationship, and the kids only benefit from it. We grow together, and the unity and synergy that comes from this will bless our family, worlds without end!

5. We Must Be There for Our Kids

Remember the little boy who took his grandpa's head in both hands (away from his newspaper or phone) and said, "Are you in there?"[20] There are so many distractions in our lives. It takes a conscious effort to tune in to each child's needs. We must engage in our conversations, to tell them they are more important than the diversions and busyness.

We have to look for clues that may tell us about each child, and together, we can be good detectives! If a child does not seem to be himself, there is a reason, whether physical, mental, or emotional. Establishing open communication when there is *not* a current problem will help a child to open up when there *is*. We constantly need to be creating an atmosphere of warmth and acceptance. As a team, we can compare notes and not miss the clues of special need. The answer is more love, along with the promptings of the Spirit to help us figure it out.

6. We Can Use Teamwork

Years ago, our stake president gave us a great idea in stake conference. He said that when one of our children hits a crisis situation, each parent should take a different role. One parent can jump in and tackle the issue, he suggested, while the other one simply shows more love in other areas. How does that look?

For example, when our daughter was falling apart, stressing over a huge assignment that was due, I stepped in. Though I usually leave the kids to do their projects on their own, this time I sat down with her and broke it into pieces. She and I listed all the steps on a paper, with a small box to check when they were done. I brought the paper cutter and scissors, and I checked on her progress periodically, praising her efforts and telling her she could do this! Mark, on the other hand, backed away from the crisis. But he brought a drink of juice to give her some blood sugar, and gave her a pat on the back. He did her chores this time and found other ways to give more love. The crisis passed, and we had solved it together as a team.

7. We Can Live Gratefully

"Happiness in family life is most likely to be achieved when founded upon the teachings of the Lord Jesus Christ. Successful marriages and families are established and maintained on principles of faith, prayer, repentance, forgiveness, respect, love, compassion, work, and wholesome recreational activities."[21]

When irritation with a spouse threatens to invade our thoughts, there is always something to be thankful for instead. Turning to gratitude is turning to happiness. If we both have the same goals, especially family goals, we can focus together on those, as a winning team! President Spencer W. Kimball taught, "Some think of happiness as a glamorous life of ease, luxury, and constant thrills; but true marriage is based on a happiness which is more than that, one which comes from giving, serving, sharing, sacrificing, and selflessness."[22]

Dear Mom and Dad,

I want to be just like you when I grow up, so every day I am watching. I learn the most from who you are, so thanks for all the good you show me. I am so glad that you love each other! Thanks for showing all your affection!

Love, Me

Chapter 2
Create Attachment and Bonding

*N*ew babies require special care. We can provide it better if we understand their brains and their need for bonding or attachment. What a huge gift to our little ones we give them when we attach and bond, along with connecting good feelings to the good things in their lives.

Bonding: The Godly Power of Attachment

It takes love to live. I was shocked and saddened as a young girl to hear that babies in foreign understaffed orphanages actually died from lack of love. In fact, in one of the better orphanages in the former Soviet Union, the mortality rate was fifty percent. These babies had been fed and changed but never held or talked to or loved, so they died for no other physical reason.[1]

Later, I learned about attachment theory, which explains this phenomenon. Attachment is the process of making a connection, especially with one's mother, at a very young age, which makes a profound effect upon one's success in life. "Attachment theory is centered on the emotional bonds between people and suggests that our earliest attachments can leave a lasting mark on our lives."[2] "This theory also suggests that there is a critical period for developing an attachment (about 0–5 years). If an attachment has not developed during this period, then the child will suffer from irreversible developmental consequences, such as reduced intelligence and increased aggression."[3]

The Lord uses attachment. His love is constant and never-ending. "I will receive you. And will be a Father unto you, and ye shall be my sons and daughters, saith the Lord Almighty" (2 Cor. 6:18). "I will own them, and they shall be mine in that day when I shall come" (D&C 101:3). We must take care to not withhold love from our children as a consequence. In all discipline, there needs to still be constant love, and even "afterwards an *increase* of love toward him whom thou hast reproved" (D&C 121:43).

What does attachment look like? Consider these two stories:

Years ago, my brother and sister-in-law adopted three little children from an orphanage in Russia. The youngest, a little boy, had bright, sparkly eyes and a fun-loving personality. But as he grew, he struggled. He had trouble in school and in social situations and began to be aggressive with his brothers and sisters. Violent behaviors began to erupt, bringing chaos and stress to the entire family. They searched to find out what was wrong, and upon checking with his records from the orphanage, they discovered that their son had been taken from his mother with no time to bond and therefore had received little or no attachment at birth and not enough at the orphanage. As a result, his brain and bodily systems had not developed normally.

On the other side of the world, in my own young family, our twin sons were born eight weeks early. They were immediately separated into two isolates in the Newborn ICU and both babies were not thriving. Though Mark and I held them and gave them all the attention we could each day, and I tried to pump breast milk for them, we also had to care for our 16-month and 2½-year-old daughters. As each day went by, our twins continued to lose weight. How I longed to bring them home and hold and love them full-time, but they wouldn't be able to leave until they gained weight. Then, at a nurse's inspired suggestion, we tape-recorded our voices talking to each boy and singing to them. These recordings could be played whenever we weren't able to be there. "Grow, little son!" I would tell them on these tapes. "Get stronger so that we can take you home and all be together as a family. We love you!" That did the trick! Even our voices provided them with extra love and attachment. The boys began to gain weight! And soon after, we brought them home and showered them with much more love and attachment!

From these experiences, I thought I understood attachment theory and the need for bonding at birth, but I was privileged to learn more at the feet of Marlene Hinton, an expert who has devoted years to attachment theory. Dr. Hinton is a mother of eight who received a PhD from ASU in education. She has spent years studying attachment and its essential role in physical, intellectual, spiritual, behavioral, and emotional health. With her permission, I will share her ideas, taken from my notes of her lecture, and reviewed by her for accuracy.

Attachment is one of the earliest systems to wire up in a baby's brain, so it is a foundational element that shapes all other elements of development. Fortunately, God has provided each baby with a mother, and most often, mothers instinctively know to hold, bond, and care for their infants. Here are some important points I learned:

1. Attachment Causes Actual Brain Development

"Mothers have the power to shape the architecture of the brain, and the expression of genetic traits. This is a godly power no one else has," said Dr. Hinton. "At birth, the brain is the only organ that is not fully functional. It is only 25% complete. The structure is there, but only 25% is hard-wired and unchangeable—the part that includes the systems that keep the body alive. The other 75% must wire up and be 'plugged in.' In fact, for the first 8 months of a baby's life, it wires up at a rate of 8 billion connections per second! How exhausting—no wonder a baby must sleep a lot! By the time a baby is one year old, 75% of the brain has been hard-wired."

Inside a baby's brain, there is an organ called the amygdala that is the emotional center. It triggers chemicals in the brain. The only way it can work is through the five senses. When a mother looks into her baby's eyes with that unblinking gaze; touches baby; sings or speaks or gives baby sounds—even her own footsteps; feeds baby; and is near enough for baby to smell her unique smell, the amygdala activates. This sensory input develops the most permanent patterns and connections of the child's life. "This profound connection in response to maternal sensitivity is called attachment or bonding." That is why mothers instinctively coo and cuddle, love and nurture, play baby peekaboo and pat-a-cake, and hold their little one constantly. Our grandmas feared we might "spoil" a baby with too much love, but that is impossible!

When newborns watch Mommy's face, they learn to focus, learn facial recognition, and mimic a smile! They even start to vocalize and work their lips and tongue to produce language. This only happens *if* mommy talks to baby, so she should explain, read, share, show, and talk constantly. If so, Baby starts understanding words and, by nine months old, she can "parse" them (separate the syllables into words). Connections form that lead to good communication. Especially when a voice repeats words over and over, the wires expand faster and more lastingly. These first brain wires are the most permanent and the most powerful.

Dr. Hinton used actual brain photographs to show us that the wires in a newborn's brain are sparse and spread apart. From birth to about fourteen months of age is the optimal window for creating permanent pathways for the brain to use throughout life, such as visual, attention, and communication. Security, identity, trust, behavioral, confidence, and self-worth pathways are being created. Sensitivity to others and the ability to form healthy relationships are established, and attitudes, curiosity, and outlook on life are being established. Physical well-being and spiritual perceptions are also wiring up at this time. All these are rooted in the early sensory responses of the mother (or the primary caregiver). By age six, the brain's wires are crowded and interwoven—in a normal brain. But without attachment, there are large spaces and holes.

When my own first baby was placed in my arms, I looked into her eyes and I remember thinking or saying, "You are my daughter." It was the moment this new attachment began. I understand that a baby's eyes focus the very best the same amount of space that there is between a mother's arms and her eyes! They are hard-wired from the get-go to attach, to make the connections that begin the brain wires to fire up.

My second-to-last baby had to be whisked away for some reason, and there he was across the hospital room, crying, and I could not hold him! It was all I could do to not go over to that station and take him up, but I was still being worked over myself. *What song could I sing him—one that he is already familiar with?* I asked myself. As this was a January birth, I decided to sing some Christmas lullabies I had sung to the other kids before bed. The minute I began, he quieted. He knew that sound. And the brain connections started up for him and boosted to full speed a little later when I finally had him in my arms.

2. Attachment Brings Security

"All attachment is emotional at first. Your baby wants to be with you. You are her source of security, comfort, happiness. She is developing according to the strength of your relationship with her. The brain must feel secure." Dr. Hinton goes on to explain, "Babies turn their heads into a mother's shoulder at the sight of a newcomer, or a child hides behind a mother's skirt or hangs onto her leg. This is a complement to mom. The child is turning back to the secure world she knows. Gradually, she will be able to branch out and not shut out others. Give children time. Our society values independence and seems to rush them. Some need more security than others. Some require a lot of patience."

Dr. Hinton explained that while moms must leave their baby on occasion, when we do, we should reassure that we will come back. Then, it is important that we keep our word about when. Dr. Hinton even suggested setting a timer to help an extra clingy child to know when you will return.

"Cortisol is the alarm chemical produced by the brain. When a baby cries, cortisol levels go up. Then, IF a baby hears a voice in response to her cry, cortisol levels decrease after the initial communication (crying). When the response pattern of prompt and tender attention is established, the infant learns that mother will come, all will be well. She learns to calm herself. Thus, she learns to monitor and begins to control her own emotional and chemical response. It is when there is no attention from a caregiver, that the infant never develops that ability and is on a constant threat alert or develops a non-response (apathy)."

A couple of my babies did life from a position of sitting on my hip. (In fact, I had to be careful to trade hips to not overstrain one of them!) In fact, a friend would comment, "I never see you without that baby on your hip!" That was where those babies were the happiest and so it came to be easiest for me too. And from that vantage point, they sure learned a lot, and grew to be extra bright! Many moms use a sling for extra attachment. Research shows that skin-to-skin contact makes a baby's vital signs go up!

3. Attachment Brings a Sense of Identity

"I was born into this world to be loved and I am important" are the messages we want to give to our developing children, and we do it with our love. Only humans have children in order to love them. For all other creatures, it is just instinct and biology that come into play. Dr. Lawrence Thomas, a psychology professor at Syracuse University, teaches, "Nothing more fully bestows a sense of worth upon a newborn child than parental love . . . the child was brought into being in order to be loved."[4] Mothers are especially blessed to be able to give this love.

Our society often has us in the same room with others, but not necessarily connected to them. Attachment requires face-to-face communication. Children will find a connection, if not at home then with peers. Studies show that beginning about fourth grade, children learn to falsify their behavior—even change their identity—in order to be accepted by peers, according to Dr. Phillip Jackson. The usual pattern now is that kids want to be with friends or on social media rather than be at home playing with a sibling or interacting with parents. We must spend time with our children![5]

Those who have grown up with good attachment become much better at responding to others' distress. "Children whose mothers respond sensitively to their signals and provide comforting bodily contact are those who respond most readily and appropriately to the distress of others."[6]

Further, researchers studying how to prevent terrorism found that the "way our brains are wired can affect how much empathy we feel for others."[7] They also found that people with empathy have a larger amygdala. That tells me that attachment makes the world a safer, kinder place. In fact, negative genetic tendencies can be inhibited by attachment to a loving father and mother.[8]

4. Attachment Profoundly Affects the Ability to Learn

Academic learning and focusing are also very much affected by attachment. On one extreme, if a child has had trauma or chaos that has brought faulty attachment, the result is anxiety and distress that prevent good learning. On the other extreme, if there has not been enough stimulation in the child's life, there is complete apathy. The middle ground of relaxed alertness is the best zone for learning. At the extremes, learning is difficult, but with good attachment that leads to this relaxed alertness, learning is facilitated. Further, without attachment, it is hard to focus on something long enough to process it and it is hard to learn language skills.

By age four, a child has a total exposure of 295 words spoken if raised in a home where the mother does not talk to him. However, by age four, a child has a total exposure of an amazing 13 million words spoken if raised in a home when mother talks, explains, and reads to him. Perhaps he cannot produce many words, but he has been exposed to many more words spoken and is beginning to understand many of them![9]

Research has shown that Finland is top in academic excellence for its children. Typically, children in Finland start school at age seven, which provides them more time for attachment with mother. On the other hand, many Western societies are providing daycares and preschools and all-day kindergartens that push children out of their home earlier. While there are some situations where these are necessary, if there is a choice, decide to keep the home connection for as long as possible. "You can never pay someone enough to love your child," teaches Dr. Hinton.

And when school begins, she insists, the mom and dad, who are the taxpayers, can decide how many hours their child will be attending. Even when only full-day kindergarten is offered, your child can still go half a day. Choose to continue shaping the architecture of your child's brain.

Attachment continues throughout the school years. In fact, the prefrontal cortex of the brain, where one's capacity to plan, understand consequences, make long-range decisions, and think logically and rationally is not fully developed until age twenty-five. There is need even throughout teen years and beyond for more attachment and support from home.

To sum it all up, "Attachment is perhaps the most critical factor in future development. The quality of your child's first relationships has broader and longer-lasting effects than any other factor in your control."[10] "Healthy, happy, and self-reliant adolescents and young adults are the products of stable homes in which both parents give a great deal of time and attention to the children."[11]

> "Hold your little ones close—so close that they see your daily religious behavior and watch you keeping your promises and covenants. 'Children are great imitators, so give them something to imitate.'"
>
> —Joy D. Jones

5. Lack of Attachment

When there is no mother available for attachment, Dr. Hinton explains, one or two things can happen or a combination of both. A baby learns to withdraw, since it does no good to cry. No one has responded to his cry, so his systems begin to shut down. Or, the baby starts to become continually tense, waiting to see if help will come. This can lead to angry outbursts or violent behaviors. The security a baby does or does not feel determines much for the rest of his life. With faulty attachment, brains are physically smaller. All systems are depressed, and a baby may be sickly. It takes love to live.

My friend's third child was very stoic. A son, this child was not like his older sisters. He simply did not respond to touch or stimulation. So, this mom, busy with her others and with life, thought he must not need it. She didn't coo with him or cuddle like she had the others. As this little boy grew, however, he began to struggle with learning, self-control, and other areas. She took him to a specialist, and together, they identified his lack of attachment. "Do it," the therapist told her, "even it if makes him uncomfortable: ooze over him, cuddle him, rock him, and love him." So she did! Slowly, she could see some progress. Now, this mom tries to tell all young moms to "ooze over their babies," even if it seems like they don't respond! Some attachment can still happen later than the ideal, though it is much slower and harder for the connections to form.

At one point, I realized that though I had nursed all my babies, giving them that closeness and nutrition, one of them had missed out a little. This baby had a pattern of waking at five every day, and so we always curled up together on the loveseat and, while feeding, fell back to sleep. The other feedings were during busy times with many other siblings around. I realized that I had not spoken near enough to this baby. This child had not learned to speak until much later than the others, and had been assigned to speech class because, though very bright, he had trouble with "word finding." I decided that even though this child was grown up and living away from home now, I would make up for it as best as I could by calling often for a long talk! I would always mother and would continue to work on attachment!

6. Never Too Late

It's never too late to increase attachment, with God's help. Dr. Hinton gave the analogy that adding attachment later is like going back to fill in the foundation of a house after the walls are already built. It would have been much better to do it earlier in the process. Progress is hard—much patience is required. But though it is slower, it can be done. "Mothers never say never!" she insists, and God helps us to make up for this important process.

After all, the Lord made us flexible. He gave us brains made to love others, such as spouses and children. Scientists may insist that the brain can never fill in the holes left when there is no early attachment, and that the brain prunes away unused connections, but the Lord gave our brains plasticity too, which means that they can keep growing.

For example, a fourteen-year-old girl who had not experienced attachment as a baby had trouble getting the idea of love to stick. She would continually—even hourly—ask her adoptive mother, "Do you love me?" When her mother would answer, "Yes, I love you," there was no "home" in her brain for that response. Attachment takes a long time for repair. Just spending time with someone who struggles, doing many things together, helps repair the brain as much as possible. The book *I Love You Rituals* by Dr. Becky Bailey is a resource for helping connections form. Grandparents can be another connection for those struggling with attachment issues. Singing to them also brings bonds of love and happy memories.

7. Never Withhold Love

Never should our children wonder whether Mom or Dad loves them. We must take care that when we punish, we do not withhold love. We can be disappointed in them, we can administer consequences, but we should always distinguish between the person and the thing they did. "That was a bad thing" must be our message, *not* "you are a bad person." We can still express a constant love regardless of what they do—like the Lord does. Or even express "I love you too much to let you do this." Attachment must be constant if there is to be constant growth.

The Spirit will guide mothers and fathers in this vital work for health and well-being. As we humbly ask for help, specific direction will come to help us love and attach even as we maintain boundaries and expectations.

8. A Mother's Time Is Unequaled in Value

"Spending time with our children is the most important thing Mothers can do in time or eternity," insists Dr. Hinton. Not all agree with this sentiment. A woman running for office actually posted signs that read, "A Stay-at-Home Mom is a Leech on Society." I feel bad for her, but someday she will know the truth, that a Mother truly is the one who shapes the world.

> All true trophies of the ages
> Are from mother-love impearled;
> For the hand that rocks the cradles
> Is the hand that rules the world.[12]

Recently, I had a disagreement with one of my grown children. Sadly, some words were said, and feelings were ruffled, so we parted in a huff. Though I attempted to make a quick apology, things were still unsettled. The next morning, I woke with this "child" on my mind. As I thought about this one's needs, the words came to my mind, *This child suffers from attachment!* I was taken aback. At this age? Still, I wondered, *Could this child oubt my love!?* I decided to go out of my way to show extra love that day, going a long distance to serve that child (which ended up being an answer to their prayers that morning) and initiating conversation to soothe feelings and express love. I learned that attachment is a lifelong need and goal. Like a plant, love needs constant nourishment to assure it will thrive.

"Mothers, take time to always be at the crossroads when your children are either coming or going . . . take time to truly love your children," taught President Ezra Taft Benson.[13] Once a mother, that calling is never over. Our entire lives, we get to watch over, love, and be close to our offspring. Further, we can find others who have perhaps been short-changed in this area, who have no one that is "irrationally crazy about them,"[14] to benefit from our love by mothering them. The Spirit will help us know the best way to apply more love. And wonderfully, the Lord's Atonement helps us make up for any mistakes we may have made.

My neighbor, a young mom, had a baby with croup. It was dark one night, when she walked into his room to check on him. Standing there, when he couldn't see her, she heard this little one-year-old call out, "Mom!" She scooped him up and snuggled him close: he knew where to look for comfort! A couple of hours later, she was still holding him. He looked up at her, right into her eyes and in his scratchy little one-year-old voice, said, "My mom." It was so sweet. God, too, cannot be seen, but He is ready and waiting to scoop us up and give us comfort and love when we call for Him![15] A mother is a metaphor for God.

Dear Mom,

Please accept my eternal thanks for the hours of cuddling and cooing, singing to and playing with me! You were the architect of my little brain! And I still need you and am so grateful for your time and your closeness.

Love, Me

Dad's Role in Bonding

Mark and I had a great relationship with our obstetrician, with our many pregnancies! One time, he told us an observation he saw over and over: For the moments surrounding the birth of a baby, people soften. You can take the hardest individuals, he told us, and for those minutes when a baby is born—and heaven connects with earth—they are different people, gentle, able to be touched. Even tough and masculine men have a soft side when it comes to their newborn children.

After the delivery, dads may be inclined to wait to interact with their baby, since some are at a loss as to how to care for a newborn, but they have an important bonding role for this child. A dad may not be able to nurse a baby, but he can cuddle, coo, talk to and nurture his newborn, and form a wonderful attachment that will truly benefit both of them. Mom can reassure him that he will do fine with his newborn. There are many important seasons for Dad to bond:

1. Newborns and Their Dads

Actually, a new dad can start much earlier prepping himself for his baby. He can interact with the baby inside the womb by talking, starting to build the bond. Each time he goes with Mom to her appointment, takes classes with her, or supports her in any way, it is a precursor to his attachment to the baby. "Become intimately involved with the process because mothers who feel more supported by fathers tend to involve the fathers more with child-rearing later on," says pediatrician David Hill, "and more involved means more likely to bond."[16]

During the hospital stay, there will be movies or suggestions on caring for a newborn. Once home, if Dad is still reluctant, Mom can use Dad for small stretches of time to let him get used to caring for baby: "Please hold him—I just need a minute in the bathroom. You'll be fine!" or "Hold Junior while I get something from the oven really quick." Chances are, Junior will win Dad over, and soon he'll be great at burping or even diapering!

Dads can be such a great support caring for a newborn. My daughter told me how wonderful my son-in-law's part in their nighttime routine with their newborn was. He took the night stretch with the baby, which was the baby's fussy time. He was so good to swaddle her and walk with her and sing to her until she was all burped and settled down. Then later, when it was feeding time, he handed her to my daughter. She had a chance for a good rest, which made such a difference for the next day. That baby's daddy bonded with her nightly! All dads may not be able to do that, but all dads can play an important role in newborn care and bonding.

2. Toddler Time with Dad

A young boy needs his dad to help him grow up well. Around the age of two, the little guy eases up on his strong connection with Mom and turns to Dad. If Daddy takes him along, plays with him, and explains things to him, he blesses the boy immensely. In the process, Dad is showing him how to be masculine. When a father roughhouses with his sons, he is role modeling how to handle aggression and regulate emotions.[17] Dads generally display more risk-taking in their behaviors, and they typically use a higher vocabulary than moms, found Helen Hans, a postnatal leader in UK's National Childcare Trust. "They also use a very *different* vocabulary with their children, often using complicated words where mothers tend to adjust their language down. This helps to broaden the child's vocabulary."[18]

Numerous studies show that a secure attachment with fathers have a profound impact on a child's life. Children with a secure attachment with their fathers are more emotionally secure, have high IQs, higher levels of frustration tolerance, and are better able to handle stressful situations. As they grow, kids with healthy attachment to their dads do better academically. They are less likely to get into trouble and interact with peers better. The conclusion: "A father's role is as important as a mother's."[19]

I observed the toddler's switchover from being totally connected to mom, then to dad too. "That baby is *always* on your hip!" Grandmother told me often about one of my young sons, who especially liked it there. I didn't mind—he was occupied, and I could do all kinds of things with him there! But then, when he was approaching two years old, it was almost time for his baby brother to come. I had been coaxing him off of his place on my hip, but then it became Dad's turn to carry this son for a while. When the new baby did arrive, this little guy had developed a cold. So when Mark brought the kids to the hospital to meet their new little brother, he held this son, having equipped our now almost two-year-old with a mask over his face. And for the next couple weeks, this toddler was Daddy's special pal (to keep him away from the baby while getting over his cold). This turned out to be a good bonding time for him and his dad. Along with being Dad's constant companion, he now had become Daddy's big helper.

A couple of years later, one morning, just as family scriptures was over, I looked over to see this son, now four years old, sitting at Dad's place. He had climbed up, put on Daddy's reading glasses, and was bent over Dad's scriptures in the same pose Mark used! He was a miniature Mark! We all had a good laugh, and I snapped a picture. But when I see that picture, it reminds me just what an influence Mark had on him, how they had bonded through those toddler years. He wanted to be just like his dad.

As a son grows, fatherhood remains paramount. "Find your own best way to connect," taught Elder M. Russell Ballard. "Some fathers like to take their sons fishing or to a sporting event. Others like to go on a quiet drive or work side by side in the yard. Some find their sons enjoy conversations at night just before going to bed. Do whatever works best for you. A one-on-one relationship should be a routine part of your stewardship with your sons. Every father needs at least one focused, quality conversation with his sons every month during which they talk about specific things such as school, friends, feelings, video games, text messaging, worthiness, faith, and testimony. Where or when this happens isn't nearly as important as the fact that it happens.

"And oh, how fathers need to listen," Elder Ballard goes on, "Remember, conversation where you do 90 percent of the talking is not a conversation. Use the word 'feel' as often as you comfortably can in your discussions with your sons. Ask: 'How do you feel about what you're learning in that class?' 'How do you feel about what your friend said?' 'How do you feel about your priesthood and the Church?'"[20] (See "Parent Interviews" in chapter 15.)

3. Daddy and His Preteen and Teenage Daughters

Girls, on the other hand, need their moms as children, but then seem to switch to need an extra connection to fathers as they grow. In fact, preteens and teenage girls need their dads in a special way. They are growing up and learning to start interacting more and more with boys. Daddy's voice is a male voice that tells our daughters that they are okay, and that they are beautiful. In fact, Professor Michael Austin calls a dad's involvement in his daughter's life "a crucial ingredient in the development of a young woman's self-esteem."[21] Not only her self-esteem, but also her self-image, confidence, and opinions about men are affected by her dad's influence. "A positive father-daughter relationship can have a huge impact on a young girl's life and even determine whether or not she develops into a strong, confident woman."[22]

Sometimes, a dad is unsure how to have physical contact with his daughters as they grow and mature. He may tend to hang back and not hug them anymore. However, "it's imperative that, no matter what, dads avoid the temptation to pull away or withdraw during this sometimes challenging stage of growing up."[23] A good solution to this is the side hug! A dad can stand at his daughter's side and gave her a warm hug with one arm. Everyone is comfortable, and he can continue to express his love.

When a dad sees how much preteen and teenage girls are starting to be concerned with how they look, and they need to be told how pretty they are, he can learn to take every opportunity to express that. Dad can watch for chances to comment on his daughter's outfit or hair—or even her shoes!

Just taking interest in all they are doing, driving them somewhere with engaged conversation on the way, and playing tennis or racquetball are wonderful ways to bond with a daughter. There used to be a "Take Your Daughter to Work Day," which my daughters absolutely loved! What a great chance to hang out with dad and see him in action on his turf. We can invent such events to bring connection and bonding.

Dad has the ability to make a girl feel good about herself. One fall, Mark had the prompting that we should take our family to go see the Humanitarian Warehouse and Welfare Square in Salt Lake City to teach our children all about church welfare. It was a very impressive tour and a nice vacation. The only problem was that during this vacation, our eldest daughter was turning eighteen. How could we best celebrate such a milestone? I got to present her our gift of a special necklace, but that didn't seem enough since she was becoming an adult! We decided to have her put on her best dress, and have Dad take her out to a fancy restaurant as a special date, just the two of them. Our family doesn't do fancy restaurants, but this one was extremely so! It was on the top floor of an elaborate building, overlooking the lights and the temple in Salt Lake City. In fact, she called it "over-the-top elegant." Dad was able to make her feel special and have a good talk as well. This daughter was a busy senior, so she was ready for some bonding time. That night, she no longer felt like one of many in the family. "I knew he loved me." Even now, the memory of that night makes her feel special all over again.

Just as our Father above is intimately involved in our lives, through answers to prayer and blessings showered upon us, a father on earth can duplicate that. I picture Joseph, the guardian of the Savior, teaching his son carpentry, reading the stars, and learning the scriptures. The fathers in our family can similarly bless the lives of our children—as can guardians, uncles, and grandfathers. Christ often spoke of His connection with His Father in heaven and referred to earthly fathers' examples as well: "I speak that which I have seen with my Father: and ye do that which ye have seen with your father" (John 8:38).

Elder D. Todd Christofferson emphasized, "Children need the unique style of bonding that fathers can provide. Fathers can build that bond by spending time engaging in physical, intellectual, social, and spiritual activities."[24] Further, once again the *very* best thing a Dad can do for his children is to love their mother. "Loving the mother of his children—and showing that love—are two of the best things a father can do for his children. This reaffirms and strengthens the marriage that is the foundation of their family life and security."[25]

Dear Dad,

I love it when you play with me! I love it when we do fun things together. And I love it when you tell me I'm okay and that you love me! I love you too.

Love, Me

Good Feelings Connected with Good Things

When Mark and I were first married, we went to a college ward where there were a lot of young families. There was this movement going around to teach young babies to be quiet in the chapel. Parents would take their noisy, wiggly toddlers to the foyer and wrap their arms around them to restrain them. The idea was that the child would learn to prefer being in the chapel where he could move a little, and so would learn to be quiet in order to stay there. But I felt sorry for those little ones who surely had grown to dread that foyer. Or possibly even the church building! I bet those little babies cried every time they even saw the church: "This is the place where Daddy is mean to me!"

In contrast, I had a professor in a Family Relations college class who taught us to "bond good feelings with good things." When his little boy got restless, he took him outside to feed the horse who lived over the back fence from the church parking lot. I'll bet this little guy absolutely loved it when he saw the church building: "This is the place where Daddy lets me feed the horsey!" This idea is that we connect happy feelings with happy things, such as:

1. Talk Positively about Good Things

I was trying to set up a carpool in our neighborhood when I ran across a neighbor's refreshing attitude. This neighbor told me that she never joins carpools. She told me, "Driving in the car with my teenager is my time to connect with her. That's when I really talk to her, find out about what's going on in her life, and all about her friends and challenges. That's when we talk things through. While she's sitting there, and not rushing off anywhere or interrupted, we can really have some good conversations."

This all happened before smart phones. So hopefully, today, kids will value these upbeat conversations with mom even more than messages on their phone. That time in the car with a caring mom could generate happy memories and strong bonds of love.

I knew a lady who called her home "a disaster area." It may feel like one at times, but let's be careful what we call our castle. Mark has begun calling our home and yard "our Promised Land." It changes how we feel when we do yardwork and upkeep. The work is more meaningful when we connect such uplifting thoughts to our property. Beautifying our home by painting or planting flowers means more when it is seen as our stewardship over this precious spot of earth, rather than just drudgery, and connects good feelings with good things. In fact, our daughter-in-law told us that her new husband's very best memories are the family work projects!

2. Start Something New

Sometimes, it takes a new idea to bring good feelings. Sunday mornings were starting to get rough at our house. With several teenagers who usually stayed out late with friends the night before, it was getting hard to wake up the next morning. On the Sabbath, Mark and I wanted to have an extra good family devotional, but instead we were having to spend so much time struggling to get the kids to the table at all! Though we moved the time later than usual, the tired teenagers still wanted to sleep in more. What could help them want to get out of bed?

I got it! I decided I would fix their very favorite breakfast only on Sunday mornings. It was a yummy hearty peach crisp. And that did the trick. When we woke them for scriptures and prayer, all we had to say was "come join us for peach crisp!" It helped connect good things with Sunday morning devotionals.

Another time, we also introduced a new idea. Going to visit grandparents on a Sunday evening is a good thing. But I started to notice that on the way home from Grandmother's house, feelings were turning sour. We had had such a great time and a good meal, but usually the last thing that happened was that we tried to convince Grandmother not to send so much food home with us! That food could feed her for a week! We tried to reason with her, but it turned out to be a power struggle. The food issue, coupled with our being tired from the busy day, resulted in negative conversation on the drive home.

I decided it was the perfect time to sing! We began to sing old family favorites like "You Are My Sunshine" and "Horsey, Horsey." We sang rousing ballads, such as "Battle Hymn of the Republic." We tried rounds, such as "Row, Row, Row Your Boat." We sang the designated family song for that extended family: "Because I Have Been Given Much." And we taught the kids the old-time lullabies that Great-grandmother had sung to Grandmother, that she had sung to Mark, and we had learned in order to sing to our babies. Part of our heritage, these songs were being cemented in their minds and hearts to sing them to their own babies some day! This new tradition became the norm that lasted for years, and though both of these wonderful grandparents are gone now, we know their songs to share with a new generation. The singing helped any negative feelings dissipate and connected happy feelings to the happy tradition of going to their grandma's.

3. Add Some Excitement

Positive feelings may require added excitement. One summer the enthusiasm for our weekly trip to the library was waning. While it was still fun to go and get new books, the summer reading program wasn't quite as fun this year. "Just pick up a book or two for me," my kids would say more and more, "I'll just stay home." I didn't want to scold, and I didn't want to beg. So I decided that we would "celebrate going to the library" with something fun on the way home. Sometimes, we stopped at a place that offered quarter ice cream cones. Or, we stopped at the dollar store for a trinket. Once, we drove through an exciting car wash machine! Soon, I didn't have to convince the kids to come along, as they didn't want to miss what was going to happen afterward!

Another time, adding an exciting tradition helped bring more holiday cheer. Christmas Eve was already going well for us. We had in place the tradition of reenacting the nativity while we read the Christmas story from the Bible. We sang carols together. Then one year, after all that was over, out of the blue Mark said, "Let's have a Santa Look-Alike Contest!" We all went in the bathroom and made ourselves "Santa beards" out of shaving cream. Then came a red shirt or hat and a quick picture of our silliness—before the shaving cream started to sting. It was a wonderful addition to our festivities, and it brought fun and laughter and connected more happy feelings with our holiday!

4. Keep Family Time Upbeat

Family home evening is a happy time, so we must connect to it happy feelings. This is not the time for discipline or scolding or withholding a treat for those who misbehave. We don't want our children to leave FHE thinking, "I hate family night!" We must connect happy feelings with happy things.

Family night is a wonderful time to teach principles without singling anyone out, since we are all working on these things! It is a great place to listen carefully and respectfully to each family member's point of view, and to let each of the children bear their testimonies or even do the teaching and be praised for doing so. The message we leave them with should be: "We love you so much that we want to make sure you know this gospel principle, so we can all be happy in heaven someday."

And the family night treat is for everyone, just because he is a member of the family, regardless if he slept through the lesson or rolled on the floor. (Chances are he heard the message, by the way, even if we think he didn't!) The goal is for each to leave FHE thinking, "Family nights are fun!" or at least, "FHE is where my opinions are valued and where my parents tell me how much they love me." (See also "Love for the Scriptures" in chapter 4.)

5. Make Deity the "Good Guys," Not the "Bad Guys"

When we refer to God, we must be careful not to make Him into "The Bad Guy" who is disappointed in or mad at us. Rather, we should wait to bring Him up until we can couple it with praise. Never say "The Lord did not like the way you were noisy in church," but instead wait until you can say, "The Lord must be so proud of you because you tried so hard to be quiet today in His house." We want to show our children a loving, merciful God who suffered to allow us repentance. He wants us to come back to Him so badly, and knows we will only be comfortable there if we have learned to do what's right. We are trying to be more and more like Him, so we will be happy.

6. Keep Special Experiences Special

When I was six years old, I got to have a special experience. My parents decided to take me with them to general conference in Salt Lake City. Just me (and my baby brother)! It was a huge deal to go alone with them, as I had lots of siblings at home and it was rare to do things just me and my parents. It was long, but I was delighted to sit there in the cry room on those smooth benches and suck on lifesavers. (My dad was a dentist and we usually didn't do candy.) Later, there was a box lunch offered on Temple Square between sessions, and it was yummy too! I felt big, and I felt important that I was there to help with baby brother. And from that time, I have always had a great love for general conference. If my parents had expected me to sit still those long hours without anything to do, or if they had scolded me for being wiggly, I may have connected negative feelings with conference. Instead, I grew up absolutely loving general conference, thanks to wise parents.

Much later, Mark and I took our family to experience a special temple open house, in which the public could tour the building before it was dedicated. This was an especially choice experience for our nine-year-old son, who felt the Spirit strongly in that holy place. After recording the experience in his journal, giving a talk about it, and being reminded of those special feelings, he will likely always connect choice feelings with that temple—and with all temples. On the other hand, our five-year-old son was told he had to stick with us the whole way through. So during the entire tour, he struggled with that. He wanted to go ahead and break away from our control. He totally missed the awesome experience and the choice feelings. I wish we had allowed more freedom and had whispered the special things we saw and felt. We had to look for other occasions to provide him a moving experience.

Another year, we took a family trip to visit the Sacred Grove in Palmyra, New York, and were so anxious that it be a great experience. We talked about what happened there and our excitement to be there, where Heavenly Father and Jesus Christ had actually been, in answer to Joseph Smith's first prayer. We anticipated feeling the Spirit there. But we heard that is was the season for mosquitos! That would ruin the little family testimony meeting we hoped to have there in that special place. I heard that garlic repels mosquitoes, so my family had been taking garlic tablets for several days beforehand. So, there we sat, gathered together and ready for a wonderful experience with our kids. And here came the mosquitoes. They were buzzing around us in droves. But we soon realized that no one got bit. Not once! We turned this into own little miracle, which made the whole experience all the better.

There is "opposition in all things" (2 Nephi 2:11), we know, but even still, how our kids perceive the event and how they remember it is partly a result of our outlook and reaction to it.

7. What If Things Go Wrong?

We can laugh: Even the best of plans can go completely wrong, but laughter makes things not so bleak and can even save the day. Laughter will bring back lightness and hope.

We can take them aside to talk to them later: When our kids have a bad experience, we can talk them through it. After the emotion of the moment is over, we can talk over what happened and soothe feelings. The effort to show we care and empathize will help negative feelings to dissipate.

We can learn faith: When bad things happen, it is a great chance to turn to the Lord in faith and prayer. One stormy night our little dog Buddy got out and was hit by a car! We were so sad to see him hurt so bad, with cuts and bruises and his chest caved in. By candlelight, we knelt in prayer for our little dog. "What can we do for him?" I asked Mark as he carefully laid him on a blanket in a box.

"We just have to wait and see how he does through the night," Mark answered.

Everyone dragged to bed, the storm having subsided a little. Mark and I lay there, doubtful that Buddy could survive until morning. Then, our little nine-year-old daughter walked into our room. "I prayed again," she told us, "and I had a good feeling come to me; I know Buddy's going to be okay."

I woke early the next morning, dreading my first look at Buddy. Surely he was dead—such a small dog struck by a car. Still, there was our daughter's faith. . . . When I peeked in the shop, there he was, his head up and looking amazing! It was truly a miracle. How could I have doubted for a second the faith of my child? And how good it was that this trying experience served to build faith.

8. Motivate with Love, Not Fear

When we motivate our children, it is so easy to use fear. "If you don't brush, you will end up with rotten teeth." "If you don't get As, you will not get in to college." President Dieter F. Uchtdorf teaches, "It is true that fear can have a powerful influence over our actions and behavior. But that influence tends to be temporary and shallow. Fear rarely has the power to change our hearts, and it will never transform us into people who love what is right and who want to obey Heavenly Father."[26] Our kids may do the right thing, but since they did not internalize the reasons correctly, it will not likely last.

"There is a better way," he teaches us—the way God does it. "God motivates through persuasion, long-suffering, gentleness, meekness, and love unfeigned [D&C 121:41]. God is on our side. He loves us, and when we stumble, He wants us to rise up, try again, and become stronger. He is our mentor. He is our great and cherished hope. He desires to stimulate us with faith. He trusts us to learn from our missteps and make correct choices."[27]

How can we warn our children and still stay away from fear as our tool? Part of it is simply to rephrase our words: "If you brush every night, you'll always have strong teeth and a beautiful smile." "If you work hard to get As, you have a great chance to earn a scholarship to pay for your college." We can also give them the message: "I love you so much that I couldn't bear for you to get hurt or have this consequence! You are a great person, and I want the best for you."

When Alma the Elder didn't know what to do about unrepentant sinners and worried about doing the wrong thing, he went to the Lord in prayer. In his answer, the Lord told him, "Blessed art thou, Alma" (Mosiah 26:15). He used the word *blessed* five times! He was so pleased with Alma and gave him a wonderful blessing. Then the voice of the Lord told him just how to handle the situation, with mercy and love, while respecting agency. The Lord connected praise and blessing with the good thing that Alma was trying to do, to be a good judge. May we also connect good vibes, good words, and good feelings with the things in our lives that we want our children to feel good about.

Dear Mom and Dad,

Thanks for being patient and happy when we do happy things. Thanks for keeping things upbeat and cheerful. I know that I get tired, hungry, or just upset, but thanks for being nice anyway. I am so grateful for all you do for me!

Love, Me

Chapter 3
Teach Them Who They Are

*E*ven though our kids don't remember where they came from, we know, and we can help them come to know their wonderful past and their great potential ahead. What an amazing responsibility to help them see just who they are. We want them to feel loved and wanted, to love God, and to want to be good and choose to do good.

A Child of God, Loved and Unique

When a sweet new baby is placed in our arms, a great responsibility begins. This little soul needs to know just who he or she is. At first, of course, our baby is practically attached to us parents, relying on us for everything. But gradually, a self-concept forms. By the time they are two, they seem to be shouting: *"I am a person!" "I need to be me!"* This new person needs to have a firm knowledge of just who he or she really is.

Children, youth, young adults, and all of us need to figure out who we really are. We wonder, *"What makes me? What are my gifts and talents? Why am I on this earth and what am I going to accomplish?"* When our children are very young, we can help them start to figure out just who their "real me" is.

We need to teach our children to know that

- I came from a loving Heavenly Father and Heavenly Mother in a heavenly pre-existence.
- I am special, and I have my own unique talents and gifts.
- I have great potential, and I have my own special mission God has given me to perform on earth.
- I have roots and I have a legacy to carry on.

1. Talk to Me about Who I Am

William Wordsworth knew where man comes from:

> Our birth is but a sleep and a forgetting:
> The Soul that rises with us, our life's Star,
> Hath had elsewhere its setting,
> And cometh from afar:
> Not in entire forgetfulness,
> And not in utter nakedness,
> But trailing clouds of glory do we come
> From God, who is our home.[1]

When a child is very young, we can begin to teach them this truth, that we come from "God, who is our home." Children know Mommy and Daddy well, which helps them picture the parents of their spirits, who live in heaven. They form a relationship with their Father in Heaven when they pray to Him. Along with prayers, we can help them know that He is watching over them from heaven. Young babies understand way more than they can express. So we can teach them these truths starting way early using big words—they will understand more than we may think!

When my first little newborn was only days old, I decided I'd better get on with this parenting job and start teaching her the gospel! I think my first "sermon" was on faith. I simply told my "captive audience" everything I could think of about faith. The next day I chose a new topic, and thoroughly "taught" it to her. She sure looked at me like she was listening. It may have been way early and way too much to give a newborn a sermon, but at least talking to my baby from the start was good.

As I found out years later, when I took my five-year-old to meet his kindergarten teacher, talking to our young children is so important. In our conversation together, his teacher told me, "Your son will be fine. I can tell that you talk to him. In so many families," this veteran teacher went on to tell me, "the parents hardly talk to their kids. Those are the kids who struggle." This was not a school where there were many underprivileged families. But apparently, this teacher found that many parents plant their children in front of a screen, and while they take care of their children's needs, they neglect to talk to them. As a result, this teacher had to start from scratch, helping them learn to listen and respond. My eyes were opened to the importance of conversation with our very young children. Of course, we can't totally keep them from screens, but we can turn screen time down a little and turn the conversation up a lot!

Talking to our children validates them as human beings. It shows we respect them as people. When we change their diapers, when we feed them, when we sit together in the family room or roughhouse on the floor, we can talk with these precociously smart kids! In the car, we can talk about what we see and what we are planning to do when we get home. At the dinner table, we can have uplifting conversation—and have each one participate! We can regularly ask them open-ended questions and expect them to respond. With time, they will.

If we start early to teach them where they came from, to talk them through situations they come across, and to teach them the gospel, they will have such a head start on a healthy self-concept and self-esteem. (See also "Bedtime Teaching" in chapter 8.)

We can also awaken feelings of who they really are when we take them to special places where they can feel the Spirit. Then, we talk to them about what they are feeling. "The Spirit itself beareth witness with our spirit, that we are the children of God" (Romans 8:16). The temple grounds are a beautiful place to talk about Jesus Christ and His house. In many visitor centers, there is the special statue of Christ and a recording of His words in scripture. In addition, taking your children to church and Primary gives them numerous experiences, even when it seems like they are getting little or nothing from it. We give them the habit of going to church, we have them participate in the sacrament, and we teach them to be still. As we do this lovingly, it naturally follows that they will come to feel special feelings of connection to God and to begin building their own testimonies. The beautiful hymns and Primary songs are another amazing avenue to their minds and hearts to plant the seeds of truth and testimony of who they are.

2. Help Me Know I Am Special

Reun Singh was a teenage girl from India that Sister Joy D. Jones met. This young girl told Sister Jones, "Before I started investigating the Church, I didn't really feel that I was very special. I was just one of many people, and my society and culture didn't really teach me that I had any value as an individual. When I learned the gospel, and learned that I was a daughter of our Heavenly Father, it changed me. Suddenly I felt so special—God had actually created me and had created my soul and my life with value and purpose."[2]

I too grew up wishing I could be special. "I wish that Heavenly Father really knew me," I told myself. "Maybe if I grow up to be the wife of a general authority then He would notice me." Thankfully, I learned that I could be special just as I was. That I was important to God just as *me*, and that everything I did was noticed by Him. Looking back, I think I learned this best by hearing stories of His miracles in others' lives and gradually developing the faith to receive my own. I grew to learn that our Savior had suffered for my sins too in His amazing Atonement.

> If I were the only person on earth,
> Jesus Christ would still have suffered for me.
> I am that important to Him.

Children need to know they are okay as they are. They need to celebrate their uniqueness. They need to feel wanted and loved.

I discovered that when each of my children was about three years old, each had a need to figure out, in their baby way, just how he or she came to be. My children would start to ask questions about being in Mommy's tummy. They loved hearing that Daddy and Mommy had been anxious for them to be born and to be a part of our family. They longed to be reassured that we wanted them and we love them. If we talked to them about when they were a baby and show them pictures or anything we saved, it solidifies their confidence in our special love for that child.

As he grew, one of my sons was built differently than his brothers. People even commented about that fact. "Where does he come from?" one neighbor asked me. To assure this son that he was one of us and belonged, I showed him pictures of me when I was pregnant with him. And Mark found pictures of ancestors who had a similar build. After that, he seemed to have more self-assurance and confidence to pursue his distinct interests.

Keeping a journal is another way to help build self-concept. Writing down experiences helps us remember them, and it cements in our minds the things that we are learning. Journals became an important part of my life when I was a teenager. I could figure things out as I wrote them down and record tender mercies in my life.

So when I was expecting my first baby, I decided to start her journal for her. I wanted to capture the excitement I felt that she was coming and that I was going to be her mother. I wrote in first person, as if they were her words: "I am coming to earth soon. My parents are so excited to meet me—they can't wait! They love me already . . ." and then more details about her delivery and her first months and years. This way, she had a journal from day one!

As soon as she could, Mark or I let her dictate to us what she wanted in her journal. She would draw a picture about an event, say the words that went with it, and we would write them down. It was fun to watch the transition to her own writing. Some kids take off on writing in a journal, while others need coaxing. For them, we have "journal parties" at the kitchen table with refreshments after we write, or a spoonful of candies and nuts when we visit Grandmother's house if we wrote that day.

3. Help Me Find My Talents and Gifts

It's amazing how different each child is. They each come with a whole package of gifts and talents, ready to be discovered and expressed. One of our little boys slept with screwdrivers in his crib! It was his favorite thing, and he wanted them near him when he slept. And he grew up to be amazing at fixing things. Another played imaginary baseball with me every day—in the house! From the time he could toddle, he would take turns with me pitching (an imaginary ball) and him hitting the home run and running the bases; then we'd switch. This son now excels at athletics. One of our young kids, at the beach for his first time, lay on his tummy to enjoy the sand thoroughly, practically inhaling it! He would also climb *into* our chicken coop often, where he could put his arms around the hens and hug them wholeheartedly! He still possesses great enthusiasm for life.

Still another son asked me to tie his quilt in constellation patterns. Guess what he studies in college? Aerospace engineering. An infant daughter of mine turned everything into a "baby" to care for and wrap in a blanket. Along with all her dollies, once it was a loaf of bread that became her baby and another time it was a squash! She is now studying to be a nurse, so she can do even more nurturing. Interests and talents start to show from very young, and parents can notice and support their development.

Each child is such a unique individual. Each came to this earth with his or her own personality, interests, talents, and spiritual gifts. We parents can help point out our child's good tendencies and unique traits and we can help them develop their gifts.

When I was a timid young teenager, my mother decided that I needed to take voice lessons. "What?" I exclaimed. I was too shy to even sing out loud alone! It was very painful to sing to this teacher. But gradually my voice developed, and my confidence grew. Though it was a long, painful road for me, my mother knew that deep down, I needed to sing. What a huge blessing singing has been to my life—even though I still hesitate to sing solos in public! It is a gift that she gave me; it is part of who I am. I'm so grateful that "she put the music in me."[3]

While we facilitate the development of talents, we must also be careful not to squelch shaky tries at new things, and not to let others' comments or unkindness do it either. We must be vigilant not to let careless words limit exploration and growth.

4. Help Me See My Great Potential to Reach My Mission

"I have a work for thee, Moses, my son," the Lord said (Moses 1:6). He may have not known yet, but the Lord knew his great potential to be a leader of hundreds of thousands. We were each sent to this earth with great potential to accomplish our own special mission. Living in a free land, without bondage, we can discover and work to reach goals that Father plants in our minds and places within our grasp.

I think that both Moses's real mother and his queen mother saw the beginnings of greatness in him. What we tell our children about their potential matters so much. "You have a smart brain!" was told constantly by an illiterate mother to her young boy, who was getting Ds and Fs in school. This led him to push himself to eventually become a renowned brain surgeon.[4] Similarly, high school government teacher Michael Baser in Mesa, Arizona, tells his seniors daily, "You are a miracle! You can do anything!" Those students believe him and proceed to achieve greatness in many fields.

A patriarchal blessing is another wonderful tool for discovering great potential and missions in life. It is a huge help for our youth to find individualized direction from Father in Heaven through the priesthood that leads them toward success and fulfillment. We can show them what a great help our blessing has been to us, thus planting the desire for their own someday. When our youth feel ready, we can encourage them to get theirs. At times of decision and crossroads, our role is also to direct them to reread their blessing, as well as providing other priesthood blessings when needed.

Since each person's patriarchal blessing is different, it reinforces the idea that each of us is a unique individual and that the Lord has need of our own mixture of gifts and talents, in a unique mission of our own, to use in His kingdom.

We read about potential and development in the scriptures. Last time I read about the stripling Ammonites, I could just picture their mothers, back home fasting and praying fervently at the time their precious young sons were facing the strongest of the Lamanite armies. These mothers knew those valiant sons had great potential to each fulfill a special mission—and not just being a soldier! I'm sure those mothers who taught them not to doubt also taught each one to reach for specific and high goals their entire life (Alma 56:44–56).

Obedience also opens doors to reach potential. We can teach our children that as they live the standards of the church, "the Lord will make much more out of your life than you can by yourself. He will increase your opportunities, expand your vision, and strengthen you. He will give you the help you need to meet your trials and challenges. You will find true joy as you come to know your Father in Heaven and His Son, Jesus Christ, and feel their love for you."[5]

5. Give Me the Chance to Know My Grandparents and Other Ancestors

God gave us a wonderful gift when He gave us grandparents. They are a part of who we are. We are so blessed that in many cases they are living longer these days, so we get to know them better. But if not, hopefully there are stories and mementos to help us connect with them.

One of my grandmothers was extra special to me. Since I was born on her birthday, we liked to celebrate our birthdays together! In fact, this grandmother absolutely loved banana splits, but she couldn't get any of the elderly ladies on her block to go with her to get one! So, we decided that on our joint birthday, we would go together and party with a banana split. At times, Grandmother's was the much-needed voice in my life that assured me, "It will be okay. Everything will turn out fine." I knew she loved me dearly, and this was a huge boost.

My other grandmother lived right across the street from the temple. The very first time she met Mark, she went into her room to get me a temple schedule card—an obvious hint of what she thought I should do about him! This grandmother outlived my other one, and for years, whenever I went to the temple and passed her home, even if I didn't have time to stop and say hello, I felt peace. Just knowing she was there was such a stability to my life. "Grandmother will always be there!" I remember thinking to myself often as I drove by. Even though she was frail and practically blind, I knew what Grandmother stood for, that her stalwart testimony never wavered. Though she did finally pass away several years ago, she remains a pillar in my life and I often remember her sweet smile and her love for me.

We wanted our children to grow up knowing their grandparents. So after college, Mark and I were grateful to be able to live close to them. We visited them weekly for many years. Mark's mother got to stay in our home at the end of her life. Caring for her wasn't easy, but the payoff came when my youngest son one day announced to Mark and I, "When I grow up, I'm going to take care of you, just like you take care of Grandmother." The kids' other grandparents shared with us their missions to Indonesia and Nauvoo. Now, Grandmother is a tour guide at the Conference Center, another great missionary example for us.

(*Grandfathers* are just as wonderful and important—it just so happens that in our family, they all passed away much earlier than their wives. We remember our granddads too! Both grandmas and grandpas give us more love. But if that is not the case for you, there are surely some "substitute" grandparents in your neighborhood who would love to fill that role in your family.)

The Lord gave us grandparents to enrich our lives, to show us who we are. He provides a second witness for everything, and grandparents can be the second witness that what parents teach us is true. They reinforce and praise, offering acceptance and love. They are a piece of who we are.

But they also give us continuity with generations past. There is a "chain" that binds generation to generation. Those who lived before us gave us not only our genes, but also our beliefs. They gave us the legacy of all good things we enjoy now. When our hearts turn to our fathers, we better see the continuity of life. We now have the privilege of carrying on this great legacy that we have been given and the responsibility to not break the chain.

As for adopted children, they too can receive reassurance that they are special. Though they have a slightly different past, they still have grandparents and they belong. They still have their traits and talents that are unique and important to the Lord. Though an adopted child may need extra time and reassurance, they can develop a stable self-concept and confident knowledge of who they are, what great potential they have, and how much they are loved.

Moses used his knowledge of who he was to fight Satan: "Who are thou? For behold, I am a Son of God!" he tells him (Moses 1:13). May our children's knowledge of who they really are be a tool for fighting Satan's temptations and for thriving in all areas of their lives.

Dear Mom and Dad,

I need to know who I am—I have forgotten! Will you help me come to know my heavenly parents? Will you look past my immaturity, noticing little sparks of greatness in me and fanning them to grow? Would you also help me get to know my grandmas and grandpas? I need them too. Thanks for helping me feel good about me.

Love, Me

Love for God: The Savior in Their Lives

The Son of God is the light of the world, not just in a figurative sense, but literally the light. To illustrate this, consider this story: George Stephenson was an Englishman who invented the steam locomotive. One day in his later years, he asked his friend, "Just what is the power that is driving yonder train?" The friend answered that it was one of the big engines. Mr. Stephenson responded, "What do you say to—the light of the Sun." He went on to explain how the sun's light is absorbed by the plants and vegetables and, after being buried in the earth, becomes coal. Then, the latent light is released in the coal and made to work for our purposes. It is the power of the light of the sun that affects everything upon this earth.[6] Through modern revelation, we know that the light of the sun is actually the light of the Son, Jesus Christ. "He is in the sun, and the light of the sun, and the power thereof by which it was made" (D&C 88:7). Therefore, Jesus Christ is literally the light for the entire world. He is in and around and through everything.

Prayer is a key to learning love for God. Like our Savior did in The Lord's Prayer (Matthew 6:9), we pray to our Father in Heaven. It is easy for children to visualize a Loving Father in Heaven when they have a loving father in their home. Without that, we must work harder to help them know a loving God who watches over them constantly and hears them always.

As a young girl, I understood about Heavenly Father. I prayed to Him. He was the Father of my Spirit and Heavenly Mother was too, before I was born to my earthly father and mother. But I didn't understand where Jesus fit in. I knew He was a great teacher and He died for me. I even knew that He was my Brother, but I didn't understand my relationship to Him on earth.

Joseph Smith taught that knowing the truth about God is foundational. "It is the first principle of the gospel to know for a certainty the character of God," taught Joseph Smith. "I want you all to know Him," he said, "and to be familiar with Him."[7] We must have "a correct idea of his . . . character, perfections, and attributes,"[8] an admiration for "the excellency of [His] character."[9] We learn that "God is the same yesterday, today, and forever" (Mormon 9:9–10).

As I grew, I learned about the Atonement of Jesus Christ. I made some mistakes that I was ashamed of and then rejoiced when I could try my best to make up for them, repent, and then feel clean and whole again because Jesus died for me. Finally, I learned that my Savior is there for me, through my trials and sicknesses too. His enabling power can help me every step of my life.

How can we teach our children this love for the Savior?

1. Talk about God

In our everyday conversation, we can express how grateful we are to Him for His goodness and give Him credit. There are no coincidences to the Lord. Elder Ronald A. Rasband taught, "Coincidence is not an appropriate word to describe the workings of an omniscient God. He does not do things by 'coincidence' but . . . by 'divine design.' He is in the small details of your life as well as the major milestones."[10] We are our children's example of giving Him credit. The gratitude we can engender in them will bless their lives immeasurably and forever. Christ is "the way, the truth, and the life. No man cometh unto the Father but by [Him]" (John 14:6). Any effort to build a child's relationship with God is without compare.

We can talk about serving Him. After my son-in-law went to help a neighbor move in, his two-year-old son was concerned about where he went. My daughter told him that Daddy went to help someone. He thought about it for a while, then asked, "Daddy go help someone?" They talked about how Jesus said to love and help others. "Daddy is being like Jesus!" they decided. Then after a while, he came up to her and said, "My help someone?" She was touched. He wanted to serve too. She couldn't deny him that, so she decided they would sweep some dirt from the stairs. My daughter made a big deal about it, telling him they were helping their neighbor! He asked her so sweetly: "Neighbor be happy?" Yes, it would make the neighbor feel happy (if they even noticed the little bit of dirt missing). "But I am certain that Father in Heaven was smiling," she wrote, "and it made my heart sing to witness the tender heart of my son, who wanted to 'help someone.'"[11]

2. Teach Our Children to Reverence His Holy Name

If we take care to use the holy name of our Savior with respect, they will too. If we work at not having His sacred names be taken in vain in our home, reverence for it will grow. We also are taught not to have too frequent use of His name (D&C 107:4). "Remember that casualness in spiritual matters never was happiness," said Elder Jorg Klebingat. "Make the Church and the restored gospel your whole life, not just a part of your outward or social life."[12] My neighbor put it like this, "As we treat sacred things with reverence and give proper respect to deity, we invite the Spirit of the Holy Ghost into our hearts."[13]

3. Teach Them to Use Jesus Christ's Atonement

If a child is sorrowing over something they did wrong, it is a perfect time to point them to the Savior. Jesus knew that we would make mistakes. That is why He suffered for our sins and died for us, so that we can repent and change. Without Him, we would be stuck forever, away from God and miserable like Satan. We can help our kids feel grateful for His wonderful Atonement.

One family night, we acted out a great analogy of the Atonement that I got from Linda K. Burton. I had several of my children stand on chairs. These were arranged in a circle in the family room. Everyone put their hands up high as if they were forming a very deep hole. One of the kids lay down on the floor (she had been warned ahead what to do) at the bottom of the "hole," in deep despair because she couldn't get out! Oh no! Then, I got a rope ladder (I learned how to make one from a YouTube video) to throw down to her so she could climb out. Sin is just like a deep hole that we can't get out of alone, Mark and I explained. The Savior comes and not only throws us a ladder—a way to get out—but He also climbs down into the hole to help us climb out! We still need to repent—to do the climbing—but He provides the way and the enabling power and is with us each step if we let Him.[14]

4. Teach Them That He Is Near

"If the Savior Stood Beside Me" includes the verse, "He is always near me, though I do not see Him there, and because He loves me dearly, I am in His tender care." It takes faith to know that He is near. When we feel His Spirit, we can feel our Savior near.

My favorite lullabies I sang to my kids right before bed were those about our Savior. "I'm Trying to Be Like Jesus" was exactly the message I wanted them to have in their minds last thing and throughout the night. Or "I Feel My Savior's Love" or "I Am a Child of God." My daughter likes to sing to her kids "I Know My Father Lives," "Our Savior's Love" (which has a verse about each member of the Godhead), and "My Heavenly Father Loves Me," since she feels these songs teach her young kids important truths about Heavenly Father. "Silent Night" was the all-time favorite quieting down song at our house no matter the season—that song has a special feel to it that calms and soothes and brings the Spirit.

5. Teach Them to Want to Be like Him

By our example, we can show them "I'm Trying to Be Like Jesus." Figuring out what would Jesus do is a great exercise that we want to come naturally to a child's mind. We can use it as a yardstick for how we will treat a neighbor or how much we will share. It will help us decide to forgive when it is hard. Once again, if we share with them our own struggles figuring out how to be Christlike, they will learn the most. If we sincerely strive to have the Savior in our lives, they will naturally do it too.

Again, we must be careful to not turn Deity into a harsh God in their minds. While we talk about wanting to be like our Savior, we don't want to make our kids feel He is mad at them when they make a mistake or even that He expects perfection right now. He must be portrayed as the loving, merciful, forgiving God that He is, so our children will be able to feel His love and want to be close to Him. He expects obedience from us, for our own safety and peace.

6. Teach Them to Have Questions, But Not Doubts

It is good to ask questions! "Ask and ye shall receive" is repeated in the scriptures. But some questions may take years to get answers. In the meantime, on this earth we walk by faith. Even when we don't know everything, we can still believe in God and feel Him close to us through His Spirit. As we try to be like Him, and continue to seek, we will find reassurance and answers. In the meantime, we can trust Him.

While everyone has struggles and questions, we, must "doubt our doubts before we doubt our faith."[16] We, who have such a legacy of generations of faith in these last days, must be strong and true and pass on to the succeeding generations the foundation of the faith of our fathers. Sister Julie Greer taught in stake conference that if we or our family members question the Book of Mormon, we must study the Book of Mormon to learn more, rather than other things that are written about it by those who haven't studied it! If we need a testimony of the temple, we go to the temple more. If we need more faith in Christ, we strive to follow Him better and immerse ourselves in His words. They can learn that faith is action, and turning away will *not* answer their questions.

"Why does God let bad things happen?" is one very hard question that many have to grapple with some time or another. There are many possible answers, such as: He gave us all the agency to choose and many will make wrong choices, so bad things happen. If He didn't let anything bad happen, it would be Satan's plan and we would not grow. Another answer to this question that feels the best to me is: Didn't God our Father let His Son Jesus suffer? He had to allow this sad, hard thing to happen in order to save us all and bring about His plan. Jesus followed the will of His Father by suffering *all* the bad things during His Atonement. He did this so He could know how to help us through hard things and grow to be strong from them. He will help us carry heavy burdens if we let Him.

Testimonies are not just for church. We can bear testimony of God, our Father; His Son, Jesus Christ; the Holy Ghost; and the gospel in our families. Mark and I like to use the first Sunday of the month as a chance for a family testimony sharing. Anyone who wants to may stand and give a simple testimony about what they have been thinking about or studying lately. There in that circle in our family room, we learn to search our hearts and bear testimony to those we love most. In the process, we teach them that there really is absolute truth in this world and that we can come to know things, not just believe. And our testimonies will be another way to help them learn to love God.

Dear Mom and Dad,

Please help me have the Savior in my life. I need a knowledge of Him, that He is near, and that I can have a relationship with Him. Thanks for the pictures of Him in our home and for showing me that He is important in your life.

Love, Me

Desire to Do Good:
Using the Plan of Happiness

"When I was little, I *wanted* to be good," my adult son told me one day, then asked, "How do I help my kids develop that desire?"

That is a good question. A good life starts with the desire for one. We parents have no bigger hope for our kids than their true happiness, the kind of happiness that comes from right choices— which starts with righteous desires. I thought long and hard over how to help him and settled on two special tools to help them want to be good: the plan of happiness and Lehi's dream.

(However, there is an important point to make here, one I learned as a teenager and have not forgotten: it's better not to say "be good," but instead "do good." Every child *is* good already! They must learn to *do* good. We all are children of God and have such great potential, so we are already good. But we choose what we will *do*. So rather than helping them be good, we should focus on helping them want to do good.)

When my son asked me this, I thought back to when I was a little girl. I remember viewing my life as a blank piece of paper, and whenever I did something wrong, I got a "black mark" on it. (In fact, my siblings and I would remind each other, "Don't do that, or you will get a black mark in heaven!") If I wanted to have a nice white-sheet-of-paper life, I knew I had to repent and get it clean again. This concept definitely pointed me to doing right, but I'm coming to realize it wasn't the best way. "People who are fearful may say and do the right things, but they do not feel the right things," taught Dieter F. Uchtdorf.[17] His alternative was love. If we truly love God, it will help us want to do good. (See also "Why We Do Things" in chapter 18.)

1. Lovingly Teach the Plan of Happiness

The plan of salvation is also called the plan of happiness. It is the way to real and lasting happiness. At the center of the plan and what makes the whole thing work is Jesus Christ's Atonement: "I am the way, the truth, and the life," He taught. "No man cometh unto the Father but by me" (John 14:6).

One Sunday, when our children were young, our stake president counseled parents to teach their families the plan of salvation often, and that greater love and righteousness would follow. I latched on to that advice and determined that we would devote one family home evening to that topic periodically, so every other year or so as our kids grew up, we taught it again.

If we're going to teach the same thing periodically, we have to change it up. So, Mark and I taught the plan of salvation several different ways. We first used the cutouts that represent the different parts of life: A circle for **Premortality**, a blue circle that read **Earth Life**, with a sign marked **Veil of Forgetfulness** in between the two. Then came a sign marked **Death**, a circle that read **Spirit World**, in which the half of the circle is marked **Paradise** (see Alma 40:12) and the other half is **Spirit Prison** (see 1 Peter 3:19 and D&C 138:38–40). There's the **Final Judgment** strip (see Romans 14:10 and 1 Nephi 10:20), then the **Three Degrees of Heaven**: the **Telestial** (with the brightness of a star), **Terrestrial** (like a moon), and **Celestial Kingdoms** (like a sun). **Outer Darkness** was a dark circle below (see D&C 131:1–3, 132). We emphasized that we wanted to live with God in His celestial kingdom and that only in the top part of it could we all be together as a family. We discussed that we all must do our best to live to be worthy, so we would be comfortable there. We bore our testimony of God's plan and how much we loved each other, and how badly we wanted to live with Him together forever.

Another time, we had the kids make the cutouts. They cut and labeled the different parts of the plan and then taught us about each other. Whenever children take an active role in the teaching, they learn more!

Still another time, we had fun teaching the plan by taking the "journey" in our home. We set up our family room to be premortality, where we learned about our future testing time and experienced the war in heaven over Heavenly Father's plan. (We were so glad that we chose to follow Jesus. And we talked over how awful it would have been to follow Satan!) The kitchen table became earth life (where the veil covered our minds, making us forget about our lives before so we could walk by faith here). We talked about our physical bodies that need to eat in order to grow, and our spiritual bodies need feeding as well. The bedroom was death—it being a little like sleeping, for our bodies, while our spirits live on. We talked about the spirit world and then final judgment. The bathroom became the telestial kingdom, the pantry the terrestrial, and the living room (the room we tried to keep picked up and ready for home teachers or company) was the celestial kingdom.

As we sat there, we talked about how much we all wanted to be together someday here in the celestial kingdom, and how terribly sad we would be if someone were missing! We talked about how to get here, by doing what is right and repenting quickly whenever we make a wrong choice, thanks to Jesus Christ who atoned for our sins, so we could repent. We talked about Heavenly Father and Mother being there and how much they loved us. We explained how they were doing everything possible to help us come home someday, but they would not force us but let us choose. We ended with a prayer that we would all choose to obey the commandments and receive the ordinances to get us there all together. At the end of this family home evening, we decided to keep calling that room our celestial room.

2. Notice the Results and Reinforce

Something cool started to happen. Through the years, whenever we taught the plan of salvation, I started noticing a wonderful pattern. After that FHE was over, invariably one of the kids would stay around afterward, wanting to talk. A sweet confession would come out, with a desire to make it right. It would end with a big hug and a chance to express lots of gratitude for this son or daughter and his or her effort to repent. "I'm so glad you want to do what's right" was reinforced again sincerely, along with our goal of being together in heaven someday. I marveled at how often this happened. I decided that our kids, upon hearing the truths of eternity, were motivated to change in order to reach the goal of eternal life together. With this perspective, they wanted to repent and do good.

3. Teaching and Perspective

Why is it that in scripture, some generations wanted to do good and others didn't? I submit that the ones who desired goodness did it because their parents were able to reach them with truth, testimony, and love.

There were two contrasting groups of offspring in the Book of Mormon that grew up to be way different. In one set, the "rising generation" had been too young to understand King Benjamin's words. And when they grew up, they became "unbelievers." Their parents had really listened and had felt the Spirit deeply. They had had a profound experience with a "mighty change of heart." But their kids "knew not God" and rejected His gospel (see Mosiah 26:1–6, 4:1–3, 27:1).

The other group of youngsters were also likely too young to experience the same mighty conversion of their parents, but when they grew up, they were firm and steadfast, filled with faith and righteousness. Their parents had been warring, murderous Lamanites but had also had a mighty change and conversion. They felt the Spirit confirm that they should bury up their weapons of war, and some even gave up their lives in so doing. I'm guessing that many of the kids would have grown up without fathers (since they had laid down their lives rather than fight). But their mothers must have championed the sacrifice of those fathers. These mothers took the challenge to raise these kids to want goodness and liberty for all people (Alma 56:47–48, 57:21).

Why did these kids turn out so differently? Both sets of parents had profound spiritual experiences, but only the second group passed on their beliefs to their kids. They surely must have shared their testimonies with their kids and taught the next generation what they knew.

Some kids will rebel despite the best of parenting. Look at Laman and Lemuel, who had the same parents as Nephi and Sam. We shouldn't beat ourselves up over this. But we want to do everything we can to *prevent* it. We want to give them every advantage for a happy life on earth and beyond! So we must give them the teachings and eternal perspective every chance we can.

Eternal perspective is also needed when it comes to dealing with death. When I was a young girl, my baby brother passed away. He was ours for only three months, and how we loved him dearly. Yet, my brothers and sisters and I had been taught clearly the plan of salvation, so we knew that our little brother was in the spirit world and that he was waiting for us there. Though we mourned his loss, this perspective gave each of us motivation to live better so that we too could join him there and be a family forever through Christ.

4. Lehi's Dream: A Second Great Tool

Another way to teach children the desire to do good is to teach them Lehi's dream, found in 1 Nephi 8 and 11. His family is trying to make their way to a wonderful tree with sweet fruit—sweet above all. They stay on the path to this tree by holding to an iron rod. Even when mists of darkness come up, holding tight to the rod gets them safely there. Meanwhile, across the way, there is a large and spacious building filled with people who are mocking and pointing at them, urging them to let go and come join them. Some choose to let go of the rod and make their way there, some fall into forbidden paths and are lost, and some disregard the voices and make it to the tree and taste the fruit there.

The iron rod is the word of God. The mists of darkness are the temptations of the world. The spacious building is the popular worldly vain ambitions. The tree represents God, and the fruit is His love. Some merely cling loosely or occasionally to the rod, while others continuously hold fast. Which group ends up the happiest? Those that held fast, made it to the tree, disregarded the worldly voices, and stayed true, continually partaking of the fruit and holding tight to the rod. We can be truly happy if we choose to constantly read the scriptures and feast on His love.

Still another family home evening, our family tried a different way of teaching our journey through life, similar to Lehi's dream. We asked our new son-in-law to draw it for us on a whiteboard. We had him use the scripture found in Helaman 3:29–30 that has a man of Christ holding tight to the word of God in order to make his way across the gulf of misery. He lands safely in the kingdom of God. So each of us can also reach the kingdom by daily reading the word of God in the scriptures. Satan wants us to let go and land in the gulf of misery, so we can be miserable like he is. This was another way of using the plan to instill in all of us our desire to be good and do what's right, and our goal of where we want to be together someday.

Dear Mom and Dad,

Thanks for teaching me our Father's plan! Then I better know what to do and what will happen because of my choices. Thanks for helping me want to do good.

Love, Me

Chapter 4
Train Up a Child

*I*n Proverbs 22:6, we read, "train up a child in the way he should go, and when he is old, he will not depart from it." The Book of Mormon provides a second testimonial for this approach: "I know that if ye are brought up in the way ye should go ye will not depart from it" (2 Nephi 4:5). What a gift we give our children when we start them way young living the gospel. Set on "the covenant path,"[1] they will have a firm foundation of good habits and traditions that prepare them for a happy life.

Early Teaching: A Great Start

Training is different than forcing. It is expecting certain behaviors and doing them from the start. Starting a good habit before the "terrible twos" set in is ideal—there is less resistance! The child grows up with good actions in place because they are inside his very being. He learns what he already lives.

"He's too young to feel sorry," a mother expressed to me about her little boy, "so why should I have him say it? He really doesn't mean it." This mother felt like it didn't do any good to apologize, so she should wait until this boy could feel the sorrow for his mistakes before teaching him to repent. "By then," I told her, "it will be too late for him to learn the automatic response of apologizing when we do wrong. We have to teach them the actions early, and the feelings of sorrow come later."

Praying can also start young. Some parents may think they should not teach prayer until a child understands what he is doing. But that is way late for starting a foundation of prayer. It is fine for them to not fully know what they are doing, although they do understand a lot more than they can verbalize. Mom and Dad can give them the words to say, to thank and to ask. When they do learn about their Heavenly Father who is listening to those prayers, the habit of praying is already firmly in place, and the child has in place an amazing habit for a happy, successful life. Here are some reasons for early teaching:

1. The Matter of Manners

When I drive a carpool to school or a group of teenagers to an event, it is interesting to observe that some will always say, "Thanks for the ride!" and for others, thanking doesn't even occur to them. I would guess that the "thankers" are those who were prompted to thank others from babyhood. But by now, the feeling of gratitude has caught up with the habit, and they really do feel the gratitude for an adult's effort to drive them places. The habit comes first, and the feelings come later.

So it is with all manners. If we wait to teach our children manners until they feel them, it is so much harder to develop the habit. We have to teach them to say "please" and "thank you" and "excuse me" as soon as they can talk, and they will always have said it. Early on, they can learn to open doors for people, not interrupt people, and apologize when they bump into someone. Later on, they learn that these polite words that they say are about kindness and looking out for others' feelings. Later on, they will feel the godly sorrow and remorse for doing wrong after they have said "I'm sorry" for years. In a family home evening on manners, my daughter taught her family that these courtesies are helping us be like the Savior. They used the scripture "What *manner* of men ought ye to be? Verily I say unto you, even as I am" (3 Nephi 27:27; emphasis added).

2. Healthy Habits

I once saw a pamphlet that read, "Healthy Habits Give Them a Flying Start." I latched on to that. Before my babies even have teeth, I like to give my infants a toothbrush to chew on. That way, the routine of brushing teeth at night has "always" been a part of their lives! Even before it was necessary. Besides, toothbrushes are good for teething!

Along with tooth brushing, I wanted to give my baby a bedtime routine of many good habits, such as telling Daddy good night, singing a Primary song lullaby, reading a bedtime book, and then saying prayers and going to bed. I wrote these items down so we'd do them in the same order every night (and so Daddy and the babysitter would know them too). These things signaled to my baby that it is time for bed—not just a nap.

Likewise, some moms like to set their little ones on the toilet before every bath, way before they were ready to potty train. If you hold them firmly, so they feel secure, for just a few seconds even, while praising them lavishly or telling them they will really be able to go in the big toilet one day, they shouldn't object. (We certainly don't want to make the toilet a bad thing! This might require asking them for a few days, "Do you want to try it?") It should be fun, like a game, something fun to do like the bigger kids do. Not only does this get them into the habit, but also it takes away the fear of the toilet! By the time they are ready to actually go in the toilet, sitting on it is already a habit.

3. Expressing Love

Saying "I love you" is a perfect thing to model and teach early. The feelings of love can catch up later. But love for a sibling or a parent or grandparent becomes easy to express. Of course, we should not insist too strongly. We don't want endearing words to become negative! (See also "Connect Good Feelings with Good Things" in chapter 2.) It can be something that we have always said to each other.

4. Obedience

We all want obedient children. Once again, we can give them the responses that we want them to think. The earlier, the better. Mark and I discovered that we could help each other to give our kids the habit of an obedient response. If Mark said, "Please go get on your pajamas," I would prompt the kids, "Okay, Dad!" If I said, "It's time for lunch" but the kids still wanted to play, he would prompt, "Okay, Mom!" If Daddy wasn't home, and I needed the kids to pick up the toys, I would go ahead and ask, then prompt them myself with "Okay, Mom!" The idea was to train the kids to immediately respond with obedience.

What if the kids didn't obey? Well, sometimes it just took waiting a little, then praising when they did. Or a second reminder. But other times it may take consequences or discipline. But the main thing was to instill the thought process in their minds, so that obedience becomes a natural pattern of response.

Another way to support each other as parents to train up our children is the way we speak. Mark would require the kids to speak to me with respect from the start. "Always talk nice to Mom!" he would remind. And I expected respectful language to Dad too. We like to say, "Try it over," which gives them a chance to think of better words to say. Or we might prompt them, such as "Say, 'Mom, would you please help me . . .'" or "How about, 'Dad, when you have time, will you . . .'" Then we would wait for them to say it, or their own better version, and follow up with "That's much better" or some sort of praise. This way the kids grow up always honoring their parents.

5. Going to Church and Other Nonnegotiables

It's good for parents to decide which pillars in their home are never left undone. Family prayer is a good "nonnegotiable." It's something we always do, and it never has to be re-decided. Going to church is another. It is good to tell the kids, "In our family, we . . ." This phrase not only gives them a foundation for a happy life, but also security that there are some constants in their lives. "If you live in our family, you learn to play the piano," I decided early on. Our kids know that they at least need to stick to it until they learn the basics. (And usually by then, they know enough to enjoy it!)

When we had little kids at home, I was determined to always have family home evening. But some Monday nights, Mark would have a deadline at work and couldn't come home until later. We would keep FHE short and doable. In fact, I learned that almost anything could count as FHE. I just needed to announce, "This is our family home evening this week!" and be determined to have them grow up knowing we *always* have family home evening!

If we ever start to reconsider a constant family practice, we may be inadvertently causing problems, opening doors we don't want to open. Some kids notice an exception and run much farther with it, or remember the exception rather than the rule. One young man recalls the very day when his family started to fall away from the Church. It was a beautiful day, and his mother said to the family, "Do you think we should go to sacrament meeting this afternoon, or should we take the family for a ride in the country?" That comment told everyone that going to church was an option, and that small decision led the family away from the blessings and safety of churchgoing.[2]

We have been counseled to "give highest priority to family prayer, family home evening, gospel study and instruction, and wholesome family activities. However worthy and appropriate other demands or activities may be, they must not be permitted to displace the divinely appointed duties that only parents and families can adequately perform."[3] We must use the early years to start them on our good family traditions and habits for a successful life.

If you grew up with a less-than-ideal family situation, yours is the chance to be chain-breakers. You can start new family traditions and constants that will bless your kids and many generations ahead. Lovingly training up your children has priceless dividends.

Dear Mom and Dad,

Please don't listen to me if I complain about the ways that you are training me or the family things we always do! Deep down, I'm so glad for these constants in my life. Thanks for loving me enough to train me to do good ever since I was little!

Love, Me

A Praying Home

When my husband, Mark, was visiting with his Muslim friend, he complimented this man for praying so often. Mark was referring to their practice of facing Mecca and bowing down to pray five times every day. His friend thanked him, and then commented on *our* prayers: "Think of how many times you guys pray every day! You pray over your food, you have personal and family prayer day and night, you pray at the beginning of meetings and at the end, and you always pray to get home safely!" We do pray a lot! There are so many times to give thanks and ask for divine help.

We are commanded often to "pray always" (see Luke 21:36, 3 Nephi 18:15–19, D&C 10:5). While we can't be on our knees the entire day, we can "leave the phone off the hook." We can try to be constantly on hold for answers and in tune for promptings that we have asked for in prayer. And we can often pray in the moment for help to do the right thing right then! Here are ways ours can become a praying home:

1. Counsel with the Lord

Once, while struggling with a parenting dilemma, I called my sister for advice. Her answer to me was to pray about it. "Heavenly Father answers a mother's prayers for her children!" she insisted adamantly. Her comment was given with such conviction that it struck me—so simple, yet profound. I prayed all the time. But did I pray over this and other daily dilemmas? Of course Heavenly Father wants to help us mothers and fathers, I realized, in all we do to raise children—His children!

We can go to the Lord for any situation we face, no matter how small the issue we are concerned about. "Our Heavenly Father is aware of our needs and will help us as we call upon Him for assistance," said President Thomas S. Monson. "I believe that no concern of ours is too small or insignificant. The Lord is in the details of our lives."[4]

Our five- or six-year-old son began having trouble going to sleep. He was scared at night, and then stressed that he couldn't go to sleep quickly. He would often ask to sleep by me. At first, I was firm: "No, the rule is to sleep in your own bed!" However, after prayer, I felt that I needed to help my young boy get through this. So I spread out a blanket on the floor in our room to let him sleep there. After a few days, all on his own he decided he was ready to go back to sleep in his own room. I was so grateful for the direction from the Spirit after my prayer! Another child would have different needs, and another parent would get different answers, of course. That's the beauty of prayer! God knows our specifics and tailors answers to each of us!

I have thought of my sister's words many times and have gained my own testimony that there is no parenting concern too little to bring to the Lord, and that He will send ideas and help. I have also noticed that the Lord doesn't require me to be perfect before I ask! But it does feel good to acknowledge my weaknesses before Him and to be diligently trying to do better. I know He is willing and waiting to answer and help.

2. Pray for Them

When my husband was a young boy in junior high, he had a bully threaten to beat him up after school. His mother hadn't known about this, but she had felt uneasy all that day, sensing that something was wrong, so she had been praying for him. Remarkably, just as the group gathered to do the damage, a police car drove by, so the crowd dissolved, the fight did not take place, and the incident was forgotten! Later, Mark knew it was because of his mother's prayers for him!

When some of our own kids were teenagers, two of them were T-boned as they drove to high school one morning. I remembered family prayer that morning had included a plea for their safety. Turns out, the oncoming car hit the front side of my teenagers' car, then swung around the car and hit again behind them—missing the area of the front bench where the two kids were seated! The only casualty was a scrape on my daughter's knee! We were so grateful for protection in answer to prayers for the safety of our kids.

> "There are few things more powerful than the faithful prayers of a righteous mother."
>
> —Boyd K. Packer[5]

Fathers too give their families a gift when they pray specifically for each member by name. In fact, those who saw Jesus exclaimed "no one can conceive of the joy which filled our souls at the time we heard Him pray for us unto the Father" (3 Nephi 17:17). It would follow that our kids also feel joy when they hear their father lovingly pray to our Father in Heaven for them! What a great fortification they all feel when Dad invokes the help of the Lord for their precise need that day. He might mention their test or their tryout, their safety or their success. We can all pray to be a light to those around us, and instruments in the hands of the Lord. We like to pray that our kids will discern the truth from the error that may be taught to them at school. We have prayed that we will do nothing to offend the Spirit—and we have subsequently heard our son pray for that too!

3. Pray with Them

I remember as a young child kneeling at my mother's knee to learn to pray, as she sat on the bed. I must have been very young, but I still remember what it felt like. When I became a mom, I liked to hold my tiny ones close to me as I whispered the words of prayer. I loved it when my child finally got a toddler bed, though, so I could teach them to kneel by kneeling beside them. That was my favorite way to teach them, until they took over to do it on their own.

When our little ones are learning to pray, we can start before the prayer by talking over with them what happened that day. We can talk over what we are happy about or thankful for, to give thanks in prayer. We can figure out what we need help with to ask in prayer. This helps a child learn to pray specifically and not just say words. In Alma 31:10, we learn that if we do the daily performance of sincere prayer, it will help shield us from giving in to temptation: "Continue in prayer and supplication to God daily, that they might not enter into temptation." Boy, isn't that exactly what we want!

Even after they were confident about saying their own prayers, my kids would sometimes ask me to pray with them, if the decision they were making was a hard one or if they wanted support: "Would you pray with me, Mom?" When my son was making a tough decision, I suggested he pray about it. "Will you pray too?" he asked me. I was happy to back him up, along with him getting his own answers.

4. The Blessing on the Food

At the dinner table, the short prayer to give thanks and bless the food is a good place for beginning prayers. Little ones love to fold their arms and repeat the short prayer over the food. Soon, they can do it alone, and they are so proud!

But sometimes it goes sour. Maybe the child thinks he should say *every* blessing! We certainly don't want contention about a prayer! Parents have to figure out how to keep helping the new "pray-er" feel good about their efforts and let the other members have a turn too. Taking aside an older sibling to explain that we want little brother to feel good about what he has learned and that we can be patient for a while will make the older one feel grown up and ready to share the limelight.

My daughter's two-year-old boy was fed up with all the prayers. He just wanted to go ahead and eat! Instead of being reverent, he started to be silly or to complain. She was floored that her little boy didn't want to pray! They tried to give him a sticker whenever he was reverent, and he liked that, but it didn't really solve the poor attitude. I suggested that since she had taught him all about reverence and prayer, like bowing your head and closing your eyes, that they not wait for him to do it. Why didn't they try just going ahead with the prayer, with just she and her husband bowing their heads, folding their arms, and closing their eyes. Then, whenever they *did* catch him doing it, they could praise him thoroughly: "You folded your arms! You were being so reverent! Heavenly Father is so happy when we pray to Him reverently! Doesn't it make you feel good inside?" They could also make a big deal when their baby son did any of those, and pretty much ignore everything else at prayer time. This way, their two-year-old got attention for just the good things, so they will likely increase. They were watering what they wanted to grow!

5. Family Prayer

The Savior taught us to "pray in your families unto the Father, always in my name, that your (families) may be blessed" (3 Nephi 18:21). Praying together brings unity and solidarity. "Think of what you teach by having family prayer," taught Elder John H. Groberg, "then think of what you teach by not having family prayer!"[6] The message we want to leave our kids is that we love them enough to pray for them, and we love the Lord and we need His help every day.

We can let even the very young have a turn being voice for family prayer, first by repeating words we give them, and later by saying their own. We parents learn tons about what that child is thinking and about his soul when we hear him express himself in prayer.

Family prayer deeply affected a young elder when he found himself alone on a Pacific island without money, food, or a ticket to his destination island. He had been traveling for months, and there was no one to meet him. When the sun went down, and he tried to lie down on the uneven cement, he struggled to be brave but felt so alone. "Once more, I closed my eyes in prayer," he wrote, "when suddenly I felt almost transported. . . . I saw a family in far-off Idaho kneeling together in prayer; and I heard my mother, acting as mouth, say as clearly as anything can be heard, 'And bless John on his mission.'

"As that faithful family called down the powers of heaven to bless their missionary son in a way they could not physically do, I testify that the powers of heaven did come down, and they lifted me up and, in a spiritual way, allowed me, for a brief moment, to once again join that family circle in prayer. I was one with them."[7] Within half an hour, two elders came up to take care of him. But what a powerful experience was that family prayer.

6. Answers to Prayer

"Does the Lord *always* answer my prayer?" a nine-year-old asked me. "Yes!" was my emphatic reply, glad I had been armed with this answer from a Primary manual. "He sometimes says Yes, he sometimes says No, and He sometimes says Not Now, but He always answers."[8] I have had some prayers take years to be fully answered, but the answer came! The Lord's timing is perfect, and we must trust that.

Different people may receive answers differently, and different prayers may be answered in diverse ways. Some may receive a peaceful or a confused feeling in their heart, some with ideas that come like a voice in their heads, some with a dream or just a feeling as they go forward. I tell my kids to empty their minds like a clean whiteboard, then come before the Lord ready to let Him fill it with answers through the Spirit.

In the end, to have a praying home does not really refer to the number of times each day we pray. Instead, a praying home is where the automatic response to difficulty, be it a lost item, a real dilemma, or a huge crisis, is to turn to the Lord for help in prayer. And the automatic response to receiving a blessing or a tender mercy or a miracle is also to turn to the Lord in gratitude and prayer. My daughter-in-law shared with me this incident. After watching a show, she got in the car to head home—along with her young nephew. They needed to turn around, so they pulled into a driveway and started to reverse when two little kids darted from behind the car. They were so close to hitting them! Yikes! When he realized that these kids were safe, the young nephew quickly suggested that they have a prayer of thanks for not hitting them. He offered a very sincere prayer of thanks for the kids' safety. She was touched by his quick reaction to offer thanks, and felt she truly learned a valuable lesson from him that night.

"Did you think to pray?" goes the hymn, and that's exactly where we want their minds to turn. Plus, we want them to learn to "trust in the Lord with all thine heart, and lean not to thy own understanding. In all thy ways acknowledge Him, and He shall direct thy paths" (Proverbs 3:5–6). When prayer becomes the knee-jerk reaction to all the situations our families find ourselves in, we are equipped to take it all on and partner with the Lord.

Dear Mom and Dad,

I am so grateful to grow up in a home that is full of prayer. Thank you for turning me to the Lord in all my happys and all my sads! It gives me a pattern for a great life.

Love, Me

Love of the Scriptures

One day, my college professor told our class about a father he knew who had a ruler with him when his family read scripture together. If any of the three kids would start to drift off to sleep, he would rap them on the head with it! When those kids grew up, not only did they *not* have a love for the scriptures, but two of the children became atheists, and the other was an agnostic! (See also "Connect Good Feelings with Good Things" in chapter 2.)

Upon hearing this, Mark and I decided that our little kids would grow to love scripture time. So we decided to have refreshments! Our two toddlers were happy to come to the table to read scriptures together because we had graham crackers along with the reading. There may have been some crumbs in the books, but there were happy smiles and tummies while we read! (Later, the refreshments were no longer necessary.)

If we can figure out how to help our kids love the scriptures from the time they are little, what a gift we give them for a fulfilled life. If they build the daily habit of holding tight to the iron rod, they will better make it through the mists of darkness, disregarding those who are mocking from the spacious building. (See "Lehi's Dream" in chapter 3.)

How do we help little kids learn to love the scriptures?

1. Start Early

Research shows that around eighteen months old, babies' ears are especially in tune to language development. This is a perfect time to introduce them to the language of scripture! "Is it surprising that our Father in Heaven fashioned the minds of very young children to be so capable of learning at a time when they need to be taught who they are and what they must do? The years from birth to age 10 are the peak years for acquiring the language that will become the foundation for understanding future knowledge and truth. . . . It is an ideal time for parents to read to their children from the scriptures."[10]

While scripture readers are a great tool, we can also give them a greater gift of scripture language. We should not be afraid of reading directly from the scriptures, even just several verses, and then explain them and talk about how we can apply them. Little children will become used to those beautiful words that we have grown to love, and they will grow to love them too. Think of them as poetry as well as doctrine. All of us can grow to love the beauty and flow of the words even before we totally understand them.

For little ones, before they can read, they simply repeat the words we read, several at a time. As they grow, they can pick out more and more of the words to read on their own. Several of our children loved picking out the word "and" to read all by themselves. (There were lots of *ands*!) What a milestone it is when a child first reads a whole verse on their own! (And the older kids have a great chance to learn patience—after all, they used to read very slowly too.)

2. Small Segments

It is okay to read just a few verses. In fact, "It is better to read and ponder even one verse than none at all. . . . Few things you do will bring you greater dividends."[11] If we read small sections, and then think about them and discuss them, we are teaching kids that every word in the scriptures matters, and each one is there to help us some way. If we apply them to our lives, we give our children an extra gift and a greater love for them.

3. Tell Them the True Stories

While it is good for children to develop their imaginations, they must also learn that many things are true. The stories from the scriptures are true; the miracles really happened. An angel really did come down and shut the mouths of the hungry lions so that Daniel would be safe. The Red Sea really did part and Moses with his huge crowd of people crossed it on dry ground. Then, the Lord protected them from the angry soldiers coming toward them in their chariots. Have kids use their wonderful imaginations to picture such true events!

Use the examples. One time I decided to give each of my children a hero and a label. After much thought, about traits they really had, I gave them a tiny frame that read compliments such as, "Tommy is brave like Nephi" or "Trevor is full of love like John" or "Jane is trusting like Mary." I hoped that planting these great people and their great qualities would help my children see greatness in themselves and develop it too.

4. Their Own Copy

From very little, we can give a child his own scriptures. A paperback copy of the Book of Mormon is a good start. It has pictures in the back! It is small and inexpensive, so it can be well-loved. As kids grow, they can learn to mark their favorite parts, and still later, to write notes in the margins.

Many families give a child a nicer copy of the scriptures when he turns eight. This one he can take care of and cherish. He can learn to treat it with respect. Mark insisted that our kids never put their scriptures on the floor. In this way, he taught them to respect and value the book, because of what is inside.

5. Be Consistent

Scripture time can become part of the daily routine. It takes a while to become a natural part of the day, and as with any good thing, there is always opposition to overcome. But the effort is worth it. A little bit every day is so much better than a lot on some days and none on others. By fitting it in regardless of our busyness, we are showing our children what a great priority scriptures are to us. "Casual, infrequent family prayers, scripture study, and family home evenings will not be enough to fortify our children. Where will children learn the gospel and standards such as chastity, integrity, and honesty if not at home? These values can be reinforced at church, but parents are the most capable and most effective in teaching them to their children."[12]

For years, my sister's family has read at night. It worked well for them. We read early, before the high school kids leave. It takes time for a new routine to stick, but with consistency, it will.

Mark decided years ago that we would begin our scripture time with a prayer for understanding. He calls on someone to lead us in a prayer that the Spirit would be there and that we would understand what we read.

It was me who added a song to our morning devotional. It may be only one verse of a hymn, but the singing is a signal that we are about to start. It helps to bring the Spirit. Sometimes, we sing the same song for a good stretch of days in a row, in order to really learn it. Other times, we just pick a favorite and wake everyone up that way.

6. Be an Example of Reading on Our Own

With time, our family had a good habit of reading scriptures together in the mornings. On extra hectic mornings, we only read a single thought, but most mornings each person got a turn to read several verses. However, we wanted to coax our kids to start reading on their own as well.

I realized that the kids never saw me read, so I decided to periodically say, "I want to share with you something cool I read in the scriptures today!" Mark would do the same.

Then, when a certain child was ready (that is, he was a fairly good reader and the time seemed right), one of us would ask him if he would like to read the scriptures together at night. I would read with one of the children, sitting at the kitchen counter and taking turns reading, making it much of the way through. This child, I learned later, felt loved best by time spent together, so I was glad for the prompting to do so. It was a sweet experience, one that he commented on years later as the beginning of his testimony.

Mark invited several of our children (one at a time) to read through their first time lying next to him before bed each night. It became a cherished memory. From this start, the kids transitioned to reading on their own.

7. Bear Testimony Often

We need to remember to affirm our belief in what we read. As we read a principle in the scriptures, we can often say, "I know this is true." A story about us or someone we know, that goes along with what we just read, will show them how applying these will be a real blessing in their lives.

"Read to your children. Read the story of the Son of God. Read to them from the New Testament. Read to them from the Book of Mormon. It will take time, and you are very busy, but it will prove to be a great blessing in your lives as well as in their lives. And there will grow in their hearts a great love for the Savior of the world, the only perfect man who walked the earth. He will become to them a very real living being, and His great atoning sacrifice as they grow to manhood and womanhood will take on a new and more glorious meaning in their lives."[13] Their testimonies will grow as we read and testify to them.

Dear Mom and Dad,

I know that you love the scriptures, because you teach me that every day. I am growing to love them too! Thanks for the scripture power you give me by reading with me! Little by little, the words of scripture are becoming mine.

Love, Me

Respectful Speech from the Start

We all want our children to speak to us with respect. Is it possible to teach that from the start? Can little children develop the habit of respectful speech? We must insist on only good and kind words, and be vigilant in firmly yet kindly correcting their speech from day one. Here are some things that we tried:

1. Never Allow Garbage Words

What if a child said a bad word that they had picked up from a friend or a TV show? We must not give it too much attention. It would not work to laugh or think it is cute or let it slide, because if we give it that kind of attention, they will say it again for sure! From the start, we can work to never let those kinds of words in our home.

I think it was an old family home evening manual where I found a wonderful idea to help children throw away bad words from their vocabulary. We simply took two paper sacks and labeled one of them "Garbage Words" and the other "Good Words." Mark and I talked with our family about words and how they can help people feel happy, and we all thought of some good words we like to say. We wrote them down on a piece of paper and put them in the "Good Words" sack. Then we talked about words that can make people feel sad, or even take the Spirit from our home. "Let's throw away any garbage words that we know!" Each of us came up with the garbage words, we explained why they are not good, and we decided we didn't want to ever hear them or say them. For example, we wrote down "stupid" and threw it in the garbage. Later, we threw the whole sack away. From then on, whenever a bad or unkind word came up, we reminded the child that that is a garbage word—throw it away!

This approach worked great for some of our kids. Others required a more drastic approach. If I heard a filthy or shocking word that we needed to get rid of immediately, I would resort to washing their mouths with soap, to "wash away" that word for good! I would simply scrape a little bit of soap on the back of their front teeth, not making a huge production of it. While I am doing this, I'd say, "We sure need to wash away that bad word!" I left the child alone to spit and rinse out the soap. Actually, I got so I preferred to tell the child, "Go, take a bite of soap," after talking inappropriately. They preferred it to having me do it. They took a teeny bite, made a face, and spit it out a lot. Then they could "watch" that word go down the drain.

What about swearing that may surface? The Savior himself told His people in two different continents, "Swear not at all" (Matthew 5:34 and 3 Nephi 12:34). By teaching this to our children early, they will be less likely to find any interest in swearing, since Jesus told us not to! If they don't hear it at home, and if we bleep it out of our media whenever possible, they will most likely shun it too.

Of course, we want to focus on and give the most attention to the good words and messages that we want to have happen! We can double our efforts to notice them by saying, "Thanks for talking so nice," or "That was a really good way to talk over that situation!"

2. Give them Respectful and Polite Words

As always, kids learn the most from what we are. We must exemplify the language we want to hear, as well as monitor the kind of language they come across through media. We can use "please," "thank you," and "excuse me"—words that we want the kids to say. If we talk to kids like they are adults, such as "Would you please go get that for me?" or "Excuse me, I didn't hear that," at least in the way we respect them as a person, they will learn to use respectful language too. From very young, they develop the habit of polite language by using it and hearing us use it.

When Dad insists that the children are respectful to Mom, and Mom insists that the kids respect Dad, then children learn to respect both parents! We support one another and insist on respectful speech in our home. Mark is extra good at requiring respect for me, and I work to have them honor him, and both of us are happy with our children's speech!

Along with our example, we can actually *put words in their mouths*. If we give them the kind phrases we want them to say, with patience, these will become their language. When we hear a child say to his sibling, "Give me that toy!" we can simply respond with, "Could I play with that toy as soon as you are done?" The child hears a better response. Often, he thinks he did say it! Even if he doesn't say those words, he hears them, considers them, and learns them. Sometimes I tell a child, "Try it. It works to talk nice." When they see the good results from talking nice, they will learn to do it.

One day, I was dismayed when my six-year-old boomed, "Where is my toast?" "In the toaster," was my answer. "Why didn't you butter it?" he answered back. I did not like this at all, so I responded calmly but firmly with substitute words he should have said, "Thank you for the toast. Would you please butter it for me?" I got him the butter, but then went back to what I was doing. When he did not say those words but still complained, I said, "You need to talk respectfully to your mother." When he chose to speak better words, his tone was still loud and a touch sarcastic. I repeated again, "Thank you for the toast. Would you please butter it for me?" in a straightforward, kind tone of voice. He then asked again, this time with a better tone. I was happy to butter it for him at last!

I didn't insist that he use my same exact words, only that he be respectful. I was not out to initiate any power struggle. I was trying to put better words in his mouth. What would I have taught him by being loud and sarcastic myself? It is hard to stay calm at times, but we have to keep in mind the goal of how we want them to sound.

3. Try It Over

My very favorite way of responding to negative or inappropriate speech is with three little words: "Try it over." Short and quick, this phrase gives little attention to the misdeed. It is a message to the kids, "That is not okay. I know you can do better, and I expect it. Think of a better way to handle this." When Mark or I tell them to "try it over," we wait for the response. If none comes, we might give them better words or actions to try, or we might have them go out and come back when they were ready to try it over. A friend of mind uses the word "rewind!" to help her kids start again. It is a short and quick way to get their wheels turning to search for a better tone of voice or choice of words that would be kinder or more respectful.

My friend's kids had picked up a bad word that they began to use over and over, calling each other "stinky butthead!" Nothing she tried worked! Not ignoring, not restricting the Wii, not even soap. Finally, she decided to use an idea that had helped her two little girls play together nicely: she had set the timer and when they could play nicely for fifteen minutes, they received a reward. She decided to start rewarding with a juicy treat those who went a certain amount of time without saying it. Gradually, they would go longer and longer without saying this, with rewards longer and longer apart. Having the mindset of remembering not to use it, they would over time extinguish the habit. (See also "A Look at Sarcasm" in chapter 7.)

4. Loving Words and Compliments

In college, my parenting class was challenged to turn up our positive words by 10x and turn down our negative words by 10x. It matters so much what we say to each other. We want love to grow, and since words can never be taken back, they have to be chosen carefully. Mark Twain said, "I can live for two months on a good compliment."[14] May we notice and point out the good with our loving words and affirmations. And may we initiate uplifting conversations. If we want our children to talk to us with respect, we must earn their respect. We can make a connection with them by sharing our lives, our struggles, our victories. We can share with them what we read in the scriptures that day! They will admire our valiant efforts, and the words of testimony that we bear to them in a home setting, which are uplifting words of the best kind.

Dear Mom and Dad,

I am so glad you talk to me. And expect me to talk nice. Since you have taught me to respect you from the start, I feel that respect for you.

Love, Me

Modest Princess and Prince

Our young daughters are delightful little dolls! They are truly princesses! Can princesses be modest? Should our princes be taught modesty too? We must teach them that they can and should be modest.

"The most precious thing that a girl has is her modesty and if she preserves this in dress, in speech, in action, it will arm, and protect her as nothing else will. But let her lose her modesty, and she becomes a victim of those who pursue her, as the hare is of the hound; and she will not be able to stand unless she preserves her modesty."[15]

"Be modest." President Benson counsels in a talk to young women. "Modesty in dress and language and deportment is a true mark of refinement and a hallmark of a virtuous Latter-day Saint woman. Shun the low and vulgar and the suggestive."[16] There are many different ways we can teach modesty:

1. Our Bodies Are Sacred

We can teach our kids that Heavenly Father and Jesus Christ created our bodies to be just like theirs. Our bodies are special, with important things to do. In fact, they are sacred like the temple. "The temple of God is holy, which temple ye are" (1 Corinthians 3:17). Satan and his followers didn't get a body, so they are envious. They want us to do anything that will cheapen or even destroy ours.

Anything that is precious should be treated with extra care. That's why we keep it clean and we keep it covered. If we help children learn this principle, they will be more likely to live it later in life. If they grow up dressing modestly, they are preparing for the temple and they won't have to change the way they dress.

2. An Early Start

It is wise to start young. My friend stood up in front of a group of ladies and told them she felt like there was no separate standard for babies and young girls than older girls. "You might say, she's just a baby," she said, "but modesty is important for her too." When, really, do we draw the line? This friend chose dresses with sleeves and tummies covered even for her very young baby and as she grew to be a toddler. She felt that this way her daughter would grow up always knowing that they dress modestly in their family.

Do little boys need to be taught modesty? Another friend thought so. She taught her little boys to wear shirts around the house, and to cover up with a towel in the bathroom. She taught them very young that their private parts were special, since they would help them be a daddy someday. So, they should keep them covered.

3. Our Example

We mothers must set a huge example to our daughters of respect for our bodies. What we wear speaks much more loudly than what we say. Our daughters notice when some cleavage is showing, and conversely, they notice when we pin up our blouse or wear a high enough undershirt beneath. We can let them hear us when we decide not to buy an item of clothing since it is too sheer or too tight, too short or too low. Let them see how we alter our clothing to fit better or be more modest. And even if they roll their eyes when we tell them to take care to sit with their legs together and why, they remember and are careful.

My daughter had trouble with clothes that shrunk and thus became form-fitting. We were in a bind since we couldn't afford to buy all new clothes. It was time to teach her that tight-fitting clothing can give the wrong message to a guy, since it was such a struggle to find clothes that weren't tight. Gradually, we both learned to hang the clothes to dry, rather than let them go through the dryer, to prevent shrinkage.

4. Alter Clothes

I found a great way to teach my little girls modesty. If ever I found a picture of a princess dressed immodestly, I simply took out a marker and "altered" the character's dress. We added sleeves to the sleeveless gowns and we drew in higher necklines. The princesses looked fine, and the principle was taught!

I was reading a children's book to my young son and didn't care for the two-piece swimsuits that some of the characters wore. Since the book belonged to us, I got out markers again and filled in the bare tummies and added straps to the swimsuits without. I let my child help, explaining the need to make these clothes modest. Since our bodies are sacred, we need to cover them. Our very young kids knew what our standard was, and they knew the word "modest" as well.

Another daughter of mine found a swimsuit that she loved, but was simply too low-cut. She purchased an inexpensive camisole that matched the swimsuit and wore it underneath. Once I used the top front of a camisole to sew across the neckline of my swimsuit as a modesty shield. The alterations left us much more comfortable. Along with teaching sewing skills and thriftiness, altering teaches our daughters a sermon without saying anything!

For a Young Women's Personal Progress project, still another daughter decided to purchase some inexpensive clothing at Deseret Industries and remake them to be modest. She added sleeves by connecting a tank top to a T-shirt underneath. She added a panel to the top or a strip to the bottom of a skirt. When she was finished, she asked some younger girls to model her modest clothes in a modesty fashion show put on by the Young Women. They also had modest prom dresses modeled, as well as Sunday dresses and casual dress. Afterward, my daughter donated the clothes back to DI, so more girls could have modest clothes. She and the other young women learned that they could similarly alter their own clothes.

Once, my fellow teacher and I were trying to figure out how to teach the Young Women in our class about dressing modestly without offending them. We didn't want to put them on the spot or make them feel funny about what they were wearing! The Spirit helped us decide to (1) teach specifically from the words of the prophets, and then (2) tell the girls, "We know it is hard to find clothes that fit and still are modest! So we want to offer to help you alter clothes that you are uncomfortable wearing because they are just a bit immodest. Both of us sew," we went on, "so we can help you raise a shoulder seam to make a neckline higher or let out a hem to make a skirt longer." This way we were on the girls' side, rather than the opposition! We could teach specifics, but still remain compassionate rather than judgmental.

Another time, we struggled with one of our Young Women who was a wonderful girl yet dressed a bit immodestly. We were afraid for this young woman, knowing that she would soon be going out in the world. Struggling with how to teach her, we were prompted to give her some materials and ask her to teach it to the others. She did an amazing job teaching the others, and the experience proved to be life-changing for herself.

5. Swimsuit Modesty

Swimsuits can be modest—if we moms insist on it and are willing to search. The cut can be lower on the legs or covered by swim shorts. We can explain the fronts must not be too low or in danger of showing too much when our daughter moves.

A very important part of wearing a swimsuit is simply covering up when you get out of the pool. If we don't allow our kids to lounge around outside or in the house in their swimsuit, we teach them modesty. "In our home, we change out of our swimsuits when we're done swimming," we can insist, "since we want to be modest." And we must lead by example.[17]

6. Modesty at Dance

My sister was perplexed about how to keep her daughters modest at dance class. First, she chose a dance studio that emphasized modesty. She asked about their costumes up front. She looked at some of the pictures of past recitals to see what the dancers wore. She let them know this was important to her. Her daughters were blessed to find a studio director that valued modesty and used good standards in dance clothes as closely as possible.

When girls are well-trained in modesty, then they will lead out when a change is needed. Teach them to speak up: "I feel uncomfortable in this outfit." My son's friend was panicky when her class was about to choose a choir dress that she felt was immodest. Her mother urged her to speak up. "You don't have to say anything more than 'I couldn't wear this! I would feel really uncomfortable on stage in this dress.' The girls can help you figure out a better alternative."

Dance costumes are in some ways like swimsuits. A swimsuit is worn to facilitate swimming. A dance costume also fills a need for freer movement in dance. But just as we insisted that our kids all change out of them as soon as they finished swimming, we can also have them change out of their dancewear as soon as it is no longer necessary, in order to be modest. After dance class is over, our girls can cover up with a jacket and sweatpants or change. Further, we can help our daughters see that at dance practice, skimpiness is not necessary but only clothes that allow movement. When we teach them the principle, our girls will choose leotards that cover them better than other choices. Then, when there is no choice, for example a recital costume chosen for them, they can wear it only during the time necessary and cover up afterward. This shows their commitment to dressing modestly.

Once, I did not care for the skinny straps on my daughter's dance costume. So I offered to alter them for all the dancers in that particular number. All that sewing was quite an effort, but it taught my daughter—and all the girls—about modesty.

7. The Young Man's Point of View

Young women need to understand first for their own self-worth, but also what happens to young men when they view immodesty. We can explain arousal carefully to our daughters, armed with the Spirit to help us. We should help them see that they don't want to be the cause of improper thoughts and stimulation. A young man "shouldn't have to 'hum his favorite hymn' all day to chase out thoughts that he didn't intentionally invite," explained Susan Bednar.[18]

We must help them have a healthy view of the wonderful man-and-woman relationship, which is reserved for marriage. We can help them see the difference between fleeting infatuation and stimulation versus true love, which encourages giving and sacrifice for one another. "Bridle all your passions, that you may be filled with this [true] love," Alma teaches in Alma 38:12.

A panel discussion for Mutual in which the young men tell what they like in the outfits that the girls choose is a good idea. In this setting, straight from the young men's mouths, comes gratitude for modest dress. A young man could tell how he feels relieved to not have to be on guard so much in the presence of a modest girl. It would mean a lot to a girl who is swimming against the current of immodesty, to hear a young man thank the girls for wearing modest prom dresses or even everyday clothes. It is invaluable for a young woman to see a young man's point of view.

Let us protect our precious princess daughters by teaching them to be modest. "The flower by the roadside that catches the dust of every traveler is not the one to be admired" is a timeless analogy taught by David O. McKay. "But the one blooming way up on the hillside, protected by the perpendicular cliff," is the flower that is respected and chosen.[19]

"If we desire the companionship of the Holy Ghost, we must invite it by dressing modestly. If we desire a temple marriage, we must prepare now by dressing modestly. If we truly consider our body to be a temple of God, we must show our appreciation for this precious gift by dressing modestly. If we desire to honor the Priesthood of God and those who hold that priesthood, we must dress modestly. And though we have discussed mostly outward appearance . . . we need to remember that modesty encompasses much, much more. It involves the mind, the body, the heart, thought, language, dress, and behavior. It is an identifying characteristic of who we are. Modesty is truly about reverencing womanhood."[20]

Dear Mom and Dad,

Thank you for helping me respect myself and my body by teaching me to be modest.

Love, Me

Chapter 5
Teach Them to Keep Them

*E*very devout Christian has the ten commandments as part of their beliefs. Do our children know these commandments? Thou shalt not kill/steal/bear false witness/commit adultery/take the name of the Lord in vain, etc. need to be taught from the time they are little (see Exodus 20:3–17). These are "the basics." We should use the great examples of Daniel, David, Jonah, Saul, Alma, the Brother of Jared, and all the rest keeping or not keeping them, and what happened. The idea that if you keep the commandments, you will prosper in the Land, and if you don't, you will be cut off from the presence of the Lord is taught over and over in all the standard works. We must make sure this is in our children's hearts.

Positive Honesty: "I Told the Truth!"

One school day, I somehow stumbled onto the fact that my kindergarten son had been copying answers from another child's paper. It was somewhat vague, and I wanted to shrug it off with a little lecture and go on with my day, but something (I know now it was the Spirit) told me to follow through. So, I got the baby out of the car seat and took my son back to the classroom. First, outside the classroom door, I talked to him about how in school, it is important to do his own work. "It is not telling the truth to copy someone else's work," I emphasized. "In fact, we need to go in and talk to the teacher and make this right by telling her what you did."

This son was a timid child and was totally scared, but I told him I'd be with him. So, we went back into the classroom and found the teacher and he bravely confessed what he had done. The teacher thanked him for being honest, and it was over. I praised him for his courage to do what was right, and assured him that despite his mistake, I knew he was an honest person. And years later, this son commented to me about the incident and how it had taught him an important lesson.

One of the very first tests a child faces in life is honesty. Very young children are incapable of lying, but as they grow, they learn that in order to get what they want, they can alter the truth. "I can have another cookie if I *say* I haven't had one yet," a child discovers. And it follows that choosing whether to tell the truth is a first lesson in choosing the right—and a first step toward the temple.

Creative children have it extra difficult to be truthful—they can think of many creative ways to get out of a punishment! We parents must be sharp! And we must teach our children early to tell what really happened, and that this truth will make them feel good inside.

"If you tell the truth you don't have to remember anything," Mark Twain said.[1] What a happy life we can help our kids develop when their consciences are clear and they don't have to remember any lies. Honesty applies to all areas of life, from respecting another's belongings to doing your own schoolwork. Honesty is a big deal, and if taught well, it will be the cornerstone of a happy life. When we give our children the words to think and the words to say, we are training them up in honesty. Here are some positive thoughts and words:

1. We Want Our Young Child to Think, *"I Always Tell the Truth!"*

Wouldn't it be tragic for a child to label himself a liar? Wouldn't it be sad for a child to tell herself, "I tell lies"? Besides learning to speak the truth, and perhaps more important, the value of honesty is how children view themselves. And even more than teaching our children to be honest, we need to mold their self-concept from the time they are very young to think and know they are an honest person.

Sometimes kids see things differently or reason differently than we do, and they struggle to communicate just right. To them, what they said may have really felt like the truth. In such cases, it takes time to stop and tune in and let the Spirit help us discern what is the best course. When we assume the best about our children—that they really want to do what is right, they just make mistakes sometimes—they will more likely live up to that assumption! While being wise, we must give the benefit of the doubt whenever we can.

Instead of making a child into a liar by focusing on the lie, we can give him words to say to make him honest! The Bible teaches, "Behold, I have put my words in thy mouth" (Jeremiah 1:9). My daughter is good at this: "Are you trying to say that you didn't *mean* to hurt her?" she'll ask her young child, or "You mean that you *almost* made that basket, right?" She resists focusing on a lie, and instead focuses on what the child needs to say to tell the truth. Then the child can feel good about himself.

Family home evening is the best place to teach honesty, since no one is singled out for reproof. All of us want to be honest and need to learn to tell what really happened. I like to use a story to help children see how awful it feels when a person is tempted to tell a lie, and then have to cover it up and live with a bad conscience. The story could also show how good it feels to choose to tell the truth even when it's hard, and how good it feels to repent.

2. We Want Them to Remind Each Other, *"Remember to Tell the Truth!"*

A child runs in to you and announces, "Mandy is a liar!" or "She told a lie!" I prefer to stop them immediately. "We don't say that in our family," I insist. "We don't call people names. Instead, remind your sister to tell the truth." I never want to let anyone label one of ours as a liar! So instead, I remind them to say, "Remember to tell the truth!"

3. We Can Teach Them to Admit, *"I Did It and I'm Sorry!"*

When we *do* catch a child who has said a lie, we should give them the words to say. To make it easy to repent and to help them know how to get out of a tough situation, we could have them say, "I did it, and I'm sorry!" If they grow up using these words, they will learn to confess and come to accept responsibility for what they did. Teaching them to own it and try to make it right is a merciful, more loving way to teach rather than using shame.

Some young parents I know were worried that telling the truth was becoming a negative thing for their daughter. The young dad told me that when he found his toddler son crying, he would ask his three-year-old daughter, "Did you do it?" She didn't always know what to say! She knew that if she admitted hitting him, she would be in trouble. And being a resourceful girl, she could think of lots of ways to deny the action or blame it on someone else. She was stuck! Should she get in trouble or figure out a way not to?

This dad asked my opinion, so I suggested he give her words to say: "I did it, and I'm sorry." Then, when she said them, he could make a big deal about her honesty: "Hurray! You told the truth! Good for you!" This little girl ate that up! Little by little, with lots of practice, she is learning to choose to tell the truth. Giving her the words to say made honesty become positive rather than negative.

In another arena, the child must learn the all-important message that he cannot have things that don't belong to him. We might catch a child taking something from a friend's house or from the store. It takes time and effort to go back to the cashier and pay for the piece of candy a child ate or to help them confess their wrongdoing, but it is so worth it. And if we give them the words to say, such as "**I took this and I didn't pay for it. I'm sorry,**" it can be quick and positive, and we can end the process with praise for doing the right thing. Afterward, we could emphasize to Daddy that "Bobby had the courage to go and make it right!" or "I was proud of Susie for telling the truth and fixing her mistake!"

4. A Child Can Figure Out, *"I Get a Smaller Consequence When I Tell the Truth"*

"When my little daughter finally admits wrong and tells the truth," a young mom asked her friends, "do I still punish her?" One approach is for parents to give a larger (worse) consequence for a wrongdoing when the truth is not told, and a lessened consequence when the truth has been told. "I am sorry that you did that, but I'm glad you chose to tell the truth," is a good message to leave them.

Folding laundry is often the consequence for wrongdoing in our family. There was always plenty of it! I could use it to reinforce honesty, "Since you told me the truth, you don't have to fold as many clothes." That way, the child still had to pay the consequence for doing something wrong, but telling the truth was rewarded.

5. A Child Can Internalize, *"I Feel Good Inside When I Tell the Truth"*

The best thing about telling the truth is how the burden of guilt is lifted. We can emphasize how bad it feels inside when you don't tell the truth and how good it feels to have a clear conscience. We want our kids to realize they are happier when they are honest.

When someone sins, the Lord doesn't stop loving them. We too should not withhold love when we catch a child having told a lie. It is after we sin that we need more love. "You must really feel bad inside for forgetting to tell the truth! How do you think you can repent and fix this, so you'll feel good inside again?" Lovingly helping the child through the process of apologizing and righting the wrong will make repentance a happy thing.

There is a wonderful song from "Joy School" that helps children feel the joy of honesty. It puts into their brains via a second route that they are honest people. If we couple our teachings with song, the concept is better ingrained in their brains and helps them think, "I always tell the truth." This is how I wanted my little children to view themselves, so I sang it with them over and over:

> If you tell the truth, you'll be so glad!
> If you tell a lie, you'll make somebody mad.
> So be just like me, be honest just like me.
> I always tell the truth you see, I tell the truth, you see.[2]

6. How Great to Be Able to Say, *"I Keep My Promises"*

Three of my sons worked for an elderly lady down the street, mowing her lawn. One day, she mistakenly paid them for three hours of work instead of two and a half. The eldest brother arranged for all three to go back to her house for another half hour of work. His example taught his younger brothers volumes about honest work! How we parents love it when they understand what we are trying to teach them from very young and help us teach the younger ones! "I have no greater joy than to hear that my children walk in truth" (3 John 1:4).

One time I promised my young son that he could choose the breakfast for the following Sunday. "Anything?" he asked. "Yes," I promised. Guess what he chose? Lasagna! So, that Sunday, even though I had to work much harder to prepare it, I made lasagna early enough to eat for breakfast, before church. My sixteen-year-old daughter was particularly upset to find out the morning's fare. "That's not a breakfast food!" she exclaimed. But I explained to her that I had promised her brother, and that it was important to me to keep my promise. Later, when I was fixing breakfast food (with the salad) for dinner, this daughter was even more upset! But I held my ground, hopeful that my example of keeping my promise would be worth the bit of trouble now. Besides, most of the kids thought it was an adventure to eat lasagna for breakfast!

My sister learned that being involved in musical theatre helped her kids realize that once you say you're going to be committed to a production, you have to make lots of sacrifices. If something more fun came up (birthday party, school dance, sleepover, etc.), she would teach them to be tough and keep their original commitment.

One time, her family realized late that the show choir's biggest show of the semester fell on the same night as the big student council trip to New York. Another boy in the same predicament felt it was too hard to do both, so he just missed the concert. But my sister and brother-in-law talked with their son about it. They felt he needed to sacrifice, in order to not let down all the youth and directors who had worked so many months to prepare the show. They decided to use frequent flyer miles and pay an extra fee for the late change in flight plans. They helped this son fly home halfway through the New York trip so he could arrive just in time for the show choir concert. They loved him enough to go through the time and expense to make it happen. His director was extremely grateful and pointed out that example to others—even years later—of one who was willing to sacrifice to keep a promise.

7. Another Part of Honesty: *"I Return What I Borrow"*

When Elisha the prophet visited a group of good young men who were building a home for them to live in, one of them was distressed. He had accidently dropped his axe in a stream, and it lay at the bottom. "Alas, Master! For it was borrowed!" he told Elisha. At that point, Elisha didn't hesitate to use his priesthood power to help this man. He cut down a stick from a tree and cast it in the stream, then the axe came up to the surface of the water, floating until the young man could retrieve it (2 Kings 6:1–7). To me this shows that returning what we borrow is not trivial; it is important to God and to prophets. Mark is careful to always return what we borrow, in good condition. Our children see this and will hopefully follow that example.

8. Even in the Small Things, *"I Tell the Whole Truth"*

I have heard great people say that who they respect the most are those who are truthful even in the small things. In Alma 27:26, we read that this group of people were "perfectly honest and upright in all things." What a good standard to work toward!

Our kids hear us talking on the phone, and they note how honestly we tell someone about something. The more careful we are to tell the whole truth, the more we teach them to do the same. Sometimes, our family has to call our neighbors about irrigation issues. It isn't always easy to confess when we have missed our time or accidently took someone else's water. But when we just come out and say, "I messed up. I am sorry, and I will try to make it right for you," we teach our children loads.

We can also teach our kids that one day our lives will be visible to all. "Therefore whatsoever ye have spoken in darkness shall be heard in the light; and that which ye have spoken in the ear in closets shall be proclaimed upon the housetops" (Luke 12:3). (The "housetops" reminds me of a satellite dish or antenna on a roof that allows us to see many hidden things brought to light on the news.) When we all stand before God at the judgment seat, every part of our lives will be visible—except what we have repented of. How glorious to feel joy and confidence at that day, rather than shame and wanting to hide! "Behold, he who has repented of his sins, the same is forgiven, and I, the Lord, remember them no more" (D&C 58:42).

9. We Want our Children to Sense, *"I Feel Safe to Tell My Parents Anything."*

We must develop trust and good conversation with our kids, so they won't be afraid to come tell us what's on their mind. They need to feel safe enough to tell what really happened, even if it is not easy to come and confess.

Once again, family home evening and scripture time are safe times to teach principles to everyone. In addition, we love using a monthly one-on-one interview to really connect with each child. (See also "Fortifications from our Fortress Home" in chapter 16.)

While trying to let the Holy Ghost guide us, we want to believe our children and help them to see themselves as honest people. So after having thoroughly taught honesty in family home evening and around the kitchen table and, of course, with our example, we can give our kids the benefit of the doubt. "I'm so glad I can trust you!" is a wonderful way to build an honest son or daughter.

Dear Mom and Dad,

Please help me to see myself as an honest person. I want to feel good about myself and I want you to be able to trust me. I learn the most when I hear you tell the whole truth. Thank you for that. You give me the lifetime gift of a clear conscience when you teach me honesty!

Love, Me

The Backdoor Approach: Obedience without Force

When my son was still very young, I noticed he had a strong and creative will. Whenever I gave him two choices, he always came up with a third idea as his choice. I joke that this son was born saying, "I already know that!" For example, when he was about three years old, one naptime he came up with an idea he was positive would work: "I am going to build an airplane and fly to Idaho (where his nephew lived). I know how to do it, I'm sure of it!"

When my daughter was very young, I noticed that if I came on too strong, she would crumble! If I were too straight-forward or confrontational with correction, she immediately would go on the defensive and feel like she was being reprimanded.

For both of these kids, and many times with others, I used what I call the backdoor approach. It was a way to require and teach obedience without force or coercion. It saved the relationship. Rather than break the strong wills, or show who is boss, I could calmly insist on obedience, while still allowing agency and creativity in the matter. While learning to obey, the kids still had their choice and creativity. While motivating them to do what I wanted, there was no power struggle.

What do I mean by the backdoor approach? The principle involved here is to allow agency by allowing expression and creative choice. Strong spirits especially have a need to use their strong will, so I submit that there is a way to let them, while still teaching and requiring obedience. They need to have choices, and we want to keep their good self-esteem intact.

1. Use Backdoor Phrases

There are many phrases that will point them to obedience, while backing into it. I like to ask, **"Didn't your mother ever teach you good manners?"** (Or to be kind? Or to be neat? etc.) Rather than put down a child, this response adds a bit of humor and puts the blame on me for not teaching them better! The child gets the message that what they did or said was not appropriate and then lets them refine their own behavior.

"Do I need to find something good for you to do?" is another way of telling my kids that they are horsing around too much and should put their idle time to better use. My kids know there are always clothes to fold or bathrooms to clean! They usually stop roughhousing and quickly find a book to read or a game to play, rather than letting me find an extra job for them! They are prompted out of their behavior without my resorting to scolding or nagging.

2. Give Choices, and Then Really Let Them Pick

We need to let our kids use their agency wherever possible. "Remember that [they] are free to act for [them]selves—to choose the way of everlasting death or the way of eternal life" (2 Nephi 10:23). So we must come up with choices while staying within our set boundaries. With this freedom, they are more likely to be coaxed into making good choices while still very young. However, our boundaries must not be too confining, or a child will fight them—just as anyone who is backed into a corner would fight!

Let the child pick the timing, for example. "You must do the assignment Dad gave you, but you can decide whether to do it now or later this afternoon. But make sure it is done before we go swimming at 5:00." Then you can walk away and leave it to them, but with no swimming if they didn't do it: "That was our deal!" Then, the next time, they will make sure to fit it in!

This is giving the *result* you want and letting the child pick the *path*. Another example was when my pre-kindergarten child was home all day. He had things he wanted to do, but I did too. So every morning we routinely made a list. Then I let him number it. His usual additions to the list were "play" and "eat," and these were most often first and second on the list. So we did those first! I would tell him the time limit, and we would fix a small snack (even though we just had breakfast) and then build a fort or get out a card game, giving him first the time and attention that he craved, and afterwards, doing the items I had to get done that morning. By being a little flexible, I could keep up with this creative, energetic kid who had ideas of his own, and yet accomplish my own list too.

When it was time to grocery shop on a Saturday, I usually took my ten-year-old along, because everyone else was busy. He liked trying free samples or picking out the treat. But sometimes, he really didn't want to go. "I don't like you to be alone," I would explain, and walk away, even get in the car. Usually, he would relent and come. But one Saturday, he had a good book to read and wouldn't budge. "Okay," I relented. "I'll let you stay home, but you have to call me every fifteen minutes. Set the timer and make sure you call me each time it rings, so I can check on you." It worked, but it was a pain to interrupt his reading that many times, so he wouldn't be choosing that option very often. But it was a compromise that fit both needs.

We must be sure to not give a choice when there is no choice. There are simply some things that must happen! "Would you like to wash up for dinner now?" is not really a choice if you mean, "It's time for dinner." But we could allow a child to choose to wash up in the bathroom or the kitchen sink! We used a backdoor approach to address the challenge of getting everyone to the table before the food got cold, without yelling a lot. We installed a doorbell in the kitchen to call everyone to dinner! And when one made their way to the table, I would loudly exclaim, "Charlie came to dinner! Good job, Charlie!"

Another time to be careful with choices is when spiritual things are involved. Keep them positive, by using praise and giving lots of choice. My friend's little girl would not obey when her mother asked her to fold her arms for prayer. "Should I require it?" she asked me. I suggested she say, "When you're ready" and then proceed with the prayer whether or not she did it. When this little girl *did* choose to do it, that is when she could make a big deal: "Good job folding your arms and bowing your head for prayer! That shows Heavenly Father how much we love Him!" Folding arms and bowing heads in prayer should be trained and exemplified but left to the individual to decide. Reverence and submission should not be forced, only taught, modeled, and reinforced. If we were to force it, the child may fight it rather than embrace it. (See "Good Feelings Connected with Good Things" in chapter 2.)

3. Use Hypothetical Situations and Stories

Have you ever had a child have a major meltdown in public? Or make a scene at the grocery store? Tired and done, they express the fact by throwing a tantrum! I learned to calmly say to them, "See that boy over there?" (That in itself distracts them for a minute from the issue they are screaming about!) "He is wondering to himself, 'Why in the world is that child making so much noise? Is she hurt? Does her Mommy need to take her to the hospital?'" Or, "That lady must be asking herself, 'Why is that child being so loud? It hurts my ears!'" Or even, "That worker must wonder, 'He is crying so much, I bet he must have a terrible tummy ache. Is he going to throw up?'" The child is able to realize how it must look to others. Most of the time, they would quiet right down!

When I felt nervous about what my kids might run into at school, I told them stories. Through the characters, we explored both good choices and not-so-good choices, and what happened because of each. The stories were better than a head-on lecture at helping them see outcomes and picking how they wanted to act.

When my sensitive daughter needed correction, I also found that the best way was a story. For example, should she put on dirty socks one day, if I started telling her that wearing dirty socks could bring odor and even sores, she would immediately justify herself and then her feelings would be hurt—majorly. But if I waited until that night, and told a bedtime story about it, the problem was solved with no damage. I would fashion a story, but it couldn't be about a little girl—that hit too close to home. Nor even a little boy. I had to make it an animal, say a porcupine named Patty. One day Patty would get herself dressed so nicely, but then pick up her dirty socks to wear again, since they were her favorite socks! But later that day, Harvey the Hedgehog told her that her feet smelled bad! And when Patty took the socks off, there were some little sores starting to grow between her toes. She quickly put the dirty socks into the hamper and made sure to always wear clean socks. I found that my kids remembered the story about Patty for days, and there were no more dirty socks worn!

> Three little magic words that will produce the behavior you want without scolding, but instead express faith in your child:
> ## Try It Over

4. Avoid Singling Out by Addressing the Group

Some kids crumble when they are confronted and reprimanded, and they get defensive rather than repentant. I found that it is better to address the whole family group, rather than single out one or two to correct. Family home evening is a great time to teach the whole family without pointing out one person's faults. We are all trying to make good choices, based on the gospel.

During a family council, we could announce, "Thanks to all who are remembering to help with the dishes before leaving the kitchen! Even when we are in a hurry, we all can take our dishes to the sink after dinner, and rinse and stack them! It helps our family so much!" This tells the entire family the goal. Or, "It really bothers Dad and I to see shoes left on the family room floor. Please take them to the room, or at least out of sight beside the couch. Any shoes left out will cost you a quarter!" There is not a lone offender singled out, and all are expected to follow the same rule.

When the family room needs a quick pick up, I like to announce, "Everyone needs to pick up seven things in the family room." Then, I wait about a minute and say, "Whoever has not started picking up their seven things yet, now needs to pick up eight." Usually, those who have been slow to start will get up and begin picking up items before I finish the second sentence. They have learned by sad experience that to delay is to do more work! This way, no one is scolded and no one is singled out.

Conversely, "Did you leave your towel on the ground when I asked you not to?!" can be confrontational. Likely, this child was not being belligerent but just forgot. Bright children get busy doing an experiment in the bathtub or coming up with a daydream about sailing! For some children, it is better to use a backdoor approach: "Whoever left the towel on the floor needs to come pick it up." But if we tell them how forgetful and disobedient they are, those labels hurt self-esteem. We want our children to grow up knowing how bright and smart they are, rather than being weighed down with their faults. By using a backdoor approach, we can require obedience but keep a good self-esteem intact.

5. Use Reverse Psychology

Another backdoor approach is reverse psychology. One day, I used it on my two-year-old! I decided to simply let him say "No!" by asking questions that called for a yes or no answer. "Do you want to do a somersault for me?" "No!" "Okay, how about hop on one foot?" "No!" and so forth. It was perfectly fine to answer no. (See also "Talking Out Tantrums" in chapter 6.)

I was worried my children might have trouble starting to fast, and I heard about a mom who also used reverse psychology here. After a session of teaching about fasting, why it is done, who it helps, and its great promises, I would tell my eight-year-old child sincerely, "You know, fasting is really special. You have to be ready for it, old enough to appreciate what you are doing. I'm not sure you are quite ready to fast. Do you think we should wait a couple of months to try it?" My child might agree to wait at first, but soon, they wanted to take it on: "I think I am old enough now!" Our family would talk over who we knew that was sick or hurting and needed our fasting, and then we would begin our fast with a prayer. I would remind them that when they felt hungry, that was when they should kneel and pray, in order to draw closer to Heavenly Father and make their Spirit stronger. Having chosen when they were ready to begin fasting, our kids were much less likely to complain. I let them choose when to break their fast as well. When they were ready, I simply had them go and finish with a prayer, be it one or three in the afternoon. Then, they could quietly fix their own snack. As they grew, of course, fasting became even more meaningful.

Another time, it took a little more reverse psychology. "Grandma, you should see how well he can wash windows!" my daughter said to me, trying to coax her son to go wash the big window like she had asked him. But still, he kept doing what he was doing and did not get up to mind. So then, I stepped in to help by saying, "Are you sure he is old enough to clean that big arcadia door? Isn't it too big for him?" That did the trick! He got up and did his best, in order to show Grandma he could in fact do it!

Forcing simply does not work well, since it takes away all freedom to choose, something we all need. Jenny, a lady I met, told me about a quandary she was in one day! Her daughter Sara simply refused to come to the extended family gathering. The more Jenny explained and pushed, the more adamant she became: "I'm not going!" Jenny really wanted her to come and be with the family and the cousins, but they had gotten nowhere by talking it over! Jenny went to her room and knelt in prayer over this, asking the Lord to help her say the right thing. Finally, she knocked on her daughter's door. "I realize that you have decided not to go to the family get-together with our cousins," Jenny said quietly, "but I just want you to know that you can change your mind." "I love you," she added, and closed the door. A few minutes later, Sara came out of her room, ready to go. She had simply needed to be able to make up her own mind.

Of course, there are some nonnegotiables. Our stake president, Trent Montague, recently taught us, "Don't let kids flex that agency muscle too young!" Some, he cautioned, are too young to pray about whether to go to church or go to the lake! "You're coming to church!" However, as a parent we can instruct them that they still have a choice here: their choice lies in their attitude. They can choose whether they will go to church happy or go to church sad, but we all are going to church.

While they are young, we must still teach and train, especially our little ones. But training is different from forcing. But by using a backdoor approach, we can still require obedience—to the things they have been taught—and yet allow choice while keeping the child's self-esteem positive.

There is definitely a time to be straightforward, but it is wise to sometimes back out. With a backdoor approach, we back out of the power struggle. This is not cowering or giving in but requiring obedience without coercion or contention. The Spirit will prompt us with words to say to help our children feel good about themselves and their choices. Doing what is right is reinforced, since they chose it! We can affirm, "You made a great choice!"

Dear Mom and Dad,

I am glad you teach me to obey. But I am extra glad when you let me choose to obey. Thanks for finding ways to let me use my agency in the process!

Love, Me

Sunday: A Different Day

It used to be that England was "the empire on which the sun never sets." It was such a mighty power that during the nineteenth and early twentieth century, it governed much of the world—more than any other nation at the time. Then, in a very short time, it was reduced to a small island nation. Its downfall? One author feels that this was due to breaking the Sabbath. Keeping the Sabbath day holy is a sign of the Lord's people, and when they turn away from keeping it, they turn away from Him and no longer merit His protection and approval. This author, Herbert Armstrong, quotes the Bible: "If they break my statutes, and keep not my commandments; then will I visit their transgression with the rod, and their iniquity with stripes" (Psalms 89:30). Along with idolatry, "Sabbath-breaking" (Ezek. 20:10–24) was the great national sin which became such a curse to Israel (Leviticus 26:1–2). "My Sabbaths ye shall keep," saith the Lord (Ezekiel 31:12–13), for it is "the identifying sign" of who are His people.[3]

"My behavior on the Sabbath constitutes my sign to the Lord of my regard for him and my covenants with him," taught Elder Russell M. Nelson. "If, on the one hand, my interests are turned to . . . worldly [activities], the sign from me to Him would clearly be that my devotions do not favor Him." So on this day of rest (Genesis 2:2–3, Exodus 20:8–11), we must elevate our activities to be restful, peaceful, even holy. How wonderful to have a day to set aside the chores and worldly pursuits of the week and have a restful day! Mark coined the phrase in our home, "Make Sunday a different day." Here are some ways:

1. Different Prep

In the movie *Fiddler on the Roof,* there is a big push to get ready on time for the Sabbath! For me, there was a time when I realized that my kids weren't seeing me do much to prepare for our Sabbath, since I would clean during the week and then do errands on Saturday. I decided that on Saturdays, I would mop our floor, so they would see me doing something different to get ready for Sundays.

To get her house ready for Sunday, my daughter has a wonderful system for Saturday work. It's called "Job Pleases." Each of her children comes to her and says, "job please" and she tells them their job, to put the Legos away or vacuum the family room. They know there is a set number of jobs, and as soon as they are done, they get free time. This way, they have a great tradition of cleaning the house together, preparing for Sunday.

Different clothes need to be ready for a different day. Saturday is a great day to make sure the Sunday clothes are washed and hung up—and found! I used to have my littlest ones put their Sunday clothes in my hamper right when they took them off after church. I wanted to keep them with my laundry, so they wouldn't get lost in their rooms!

"Look like it's Sunday" is a phrase I like to use as a goal for our house, our rooms, and our clothes! I use it to coax the kids out of their pajamas, or into nicer shirts after they change out of their Sunday clothes. I grew up with the tradition of staying in a dress all Sunday. It reminds me to slow down and soak in peace.

"Does this house look like Sunday yet?" I might ask on Saturday night, to gauge whether we are ready. "Bedroom show at six!" is another way to motivate the kids to have their rooms picked up by Saturday night. Dad and I check out their bedrooms to see how well they are picked up and clean for Sunday.

2. Different Food

Sometimes it's hard to get teenagers up for the Sunday devotional before an early church, especially after a late Saturday night! When I had a house full of teenagers who wanted to sleep in, a friend told me how she used her teen's favorite food as a motivation. So I decided that we'd have a special breakfast on Sunday mornings, one that everyone loves. I only make it on Sunday mornings, and it is a great incentive to get out of bed!

At one point, I decided that I would stop doing a complex meal on Sundays. I would move the fancier meal to Mondays and keep Sunday's meal simpler and easier to fix. I had a friend who fixed waffles on Sunday night for a good, simple dinner. Another friend preferred to make homemade pizza each week—simple for her and loved by all. Her family looked forward to Sundays for the pizza! I have sons who love to cook, and when they all help on Sundays, I thank them for their service to the family on Sunday.

Now that we have married kids and grandkids over on Sundays, things started getting hectic. I was bewildered by having all that company over. In fact, I didn't feel like Sunday was a restful day for me. It wasn't until I changed my attitude that I felt much better. Now, I *choose* to serve my family by feeding them, as our parents did for us. But we do it every other week, and I keep it as simple as possible to not make it seem burdensome. They all are good to help bring food and pick up afterward, and it is so good to get with the family and share our lives.

3. Practicing Reverence at Church

When I was a teenager, I was frustrated with my little sister about how irreverently I felt she took the sacrament. I felt motherly toward this darling little girl and wanted to teach her. So one day I sat her down on the bed in our parents' room to "practice." The two of us pretended to have the bread passed to us and quietly take one, and then the water. I talked to this sister about what the sacrament meant and how quietly and reverently we take it, and to think about Jesus too! I hoped she could feel the awe and respect in my voice and learn that this was more a piece of bread and a tiny drink. I hoped our experience would add to her foundation of warm feelings about the gospel. It was sweet to notice a real change after that.

When Mark and I were raising lots of little kids, we got permission and a key to go down to the church on a weekday in order to practice being reverent. First, we took our young children to the door of the chapel. We talked to them about what a special room this was, a place where Jesus's Spirit was. "When we go inside, we want to be extra quiet, so the Spirit can be there. In fact, we want to think about Jesus." To reinforce our point, a couple of times we entered the chapel practically tiptoeing and immediately began speaking in whispers, emphasizing to the kids that the chapel is for being quiet. Once inside, we sat in a pew and pretended to sing and pray and listen quietly. Then we tiptoed out of the chapel and spoke with a regular voice in the foyer. The children got lots of praise for how well they did! On Sunday, our practice really seemed to have helped.

As follow up, during the Sunday service, when a child grew noisy, one of us would take him out, reminding him that the chapel was only for quiet voices. The child would be brought into a classroom to sit there (with no objects or food) until he decided he was ready to return and be quiet. We tried hard to be matter-of-fact rather than forceful or frustrated—we wanted only good feelings to be associated with Church.

Years later, Mark was called to a leadership calling that required he sit on the stand. We again went down to the chapel on a day it was empty to practice. We talked about where Dad would sit, and how he could see us from the stand and notice how reverent we were being. We talked about how I might have to take the baby out in the foyer if he cried (our youngest was one year old), and that they were expected to sit quietly while I was gone. We emphasized to our kids that this was the very best way they could help Daddy with his new calling, by sitting quietly in church.

Taking kids to church is often hard! But we know it is worth it. The ones who don't seem to get a thing from the effort get more than we think they do. They may feel the Spirit there, or have a question answered. Taking them to church helps keep them "unspotted from the world" (D&C 59:9). And regardless, they are developing the tradition and habit of worshipping the Lord on His day.

4. A Peaceful Day

Our morning devotionals are different on Sundays. Sometimes, we have read through the "Living Christ"[5] or "The Family: A Proclamation to the World,"[6] one sentence each week. We talk about each word and try to memorize it, saying the whole thing up to that point. We have come to love these inspired documents. One season, we read in *Jesus the Christ*[7] each week. It was a great experience to learn about the Savior's life more in depth. Our prayers are different on the Sundays that we fast for those in need. Each of us brings up the name of someone for our family to fast and pray for that day.

Music is an amazing tool for a different Sabbath. I keep a separate playlist of calming music for Sunday, full of peaceful hymns and songs. It brings a different, sweet atmosphere to our home.

5. Different Activities

My neighbors shared that they had been trying to get their kids to do Sunday things for years, such as write in journals, visit the sick, do family history, and write the missionaries. But after the recent emphasis on keeping the Sabbath day holy, they tried a new approach. They gathered their kids one family council and asked them, "What do we want to accomplish on Sunday?" Then they all made a list of the good that could come from keeping Sunday holy, such as finding answers to prayers and solutions to problems, growing closer to the Lord, and storing up peace for the week ahead.[8] "How can we help that to happen?" they then asked the kids and made a second list of what things they could do on Sunday for these good spiritual outcomes. The kids came up with things for their list, which were the very things their parents had been trying to get them to do all this time! But since the kids thought of it, they were on board. They whole family began to have much better Sundays.

Sunday reading could be different. One of my kids especially loves to read adventure fantasy. Occasionally, when he is reading on Sunday, I will ask him if that book is appropriate for Sunday. I don't even wait for a response, really, just trying to help him think about it. Gradually, he has learned to look for biographies and true stories to read on Sundays. I am so pleased that he makes Sunday different in this way.

6. More Time with Family

Sundays are super for connecting with family. Calls, emails, letters, and family chats are amazing. We love that our grandchildren who live across the country know what we look like and visit with us even though we see them in person so infrequently.

As for those still at home, I love when the kids come into our bedroom on Sunday evening. They might come individually for a heart-to-heart, or they might all gather there. We chat and laugh and comment on the day. If the teenagers had a long nap, they aren't tired yet, so they hang out with us! We like to tell them what good kids they are, and how much we love being their parents. We feel peaceful at the end of this different day.

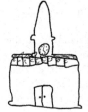

Dear Mom and Dad,

I love it when you study the gospel and do good on the Sabbath. Thank you for always taking me to church. Your example is blessing my life, since I feel so much peace to know that our family is keeping that commandment.

Love, Me

Chapter 6

Live Happily

"We lived after the manner of happiness" (2 Nephi 5:27) is the goal of every family! What can we do to promote a peaceful, happy home? What helps to bring joy and lessen outbursts and contention? Growing up, every time any of us kids asked our dad what he wanted for his birthday, he answered, "A happy family." Because we loved him so much, we tried to put on a smile. It didn't always work, but we really did try to put aside disagreement and contention and decide to be happy! May we trigger that kind of goal in our homes and bring the world a little more happiness and peace!

Help to Be Happy: Gratitude Daily

Gratitude lifts us. It helps us find the good and give God the credit for it. It brings a smile and a contented heart. It brings more love and invites the Spirit into our hearts. God asks us to thank Him, such as in Doctrine and Covenants 59:7: "Thank the Lord in all things." Though our society is filled with entitlement attitudes and lust for more things, how can we teach our children to be grateful?

1. Count Our Blessings

There is a song that goes, "If you're worried and you can't sleep, just count your blessings instead of sheep."[1] I have tried it, and I found it to be a wonderful way to drift off to sleep. In fact, I learned from my son to list them in a little notebook.

When he was a busy teenager, I often saw this son dragging around with a bewildered look on his face. I was worried about him, but I decided that it was just his busy schedule of hard classes and a stressful season of basketball. The holidays came, and then he went back to school. But then, he was a different person. There was actually a skip in his step and a smile on his face! What had brought such a change? I reviewed in my mind that he still had the same hard classes, and he still was playing basketball on the same team. What brought such happiness to his life? I told him I had noticed a huge change in him. "You are a different person these days. What in your life has changed?" He told me that during the Christmas break, he had gone with us to see the lights, and a missionary had come up to him and given him a challenge: "Before you go to bed each night, write down ten things you are grateful for." This son took that challenge and wrote ten things in a notebook every night. What a difference that one little change made to his whole outlook on life.

I wanted the same happiness he had found, so I started the same practice. In a little notebook by my bed, I listed ten things I was especially grateful for that day. What I noticed was that I stopped waking up with a headache! My dreams were better, and my sleep was sounder. I am grateful for gratitude!

There is a wonderful gratitude game called "Aren't We Blessed?"[2] Every time a person finds something new to be thankful for, they follow it with the phrase, "Aren't we blessed?" Driving in the car or sitting at the dinner table are wonderful times to count blessings.

Bible stories teach gratitude, such as the story of the ten lepers (Luke 17:17), which teaches us not to take our blessings for granted but thank God for them. Job teaches, "The Lord gave, and the Lord hath taken away; blessed be the name of the Lord" (Job 1:21).

2. Give Them Words of Gratitude to Say

As we train our children, we can prompt them to thank. Mom can point out how grateful we are to Dad for providing the money we need, and Dad can do likewise for Mom's service. When Dad fixes their bike or helps with their homework, Mom can prompt, "Thanks, Dad!" When Mom fixes a nice meal or does their laundry, Dad can prompt, "Thanks, Mom!" Or we can prompt thanks to siblings who have done something for them. Gradually, it will occur to them to thank without a reminder.

3. Give Them Words of Gratitude in Their Prayers

When we help children with a prayer, we can prompt them to give thanks before asking for something. At bedtime, we can stop to think over our blessings that day to thank our Father for them. Before we have family prayer, we can mention blessings the family wants to remember to give thanks for. Talking over specifics keeps the prayer from being a repetitive list and triggers sincere gratitude for what He has done for us that day. "Be sure to give thanks for helping your sister with her test" or "Let's remember to give thanks that the baby got well."

During the month of Thanksgiving, our family has a tradition of giving thanks for ten things in every prayer. Once, it occurred to me that family members might be just counting them, rather than feeling truly grateful! I challenged the family to repeat in our minds the gratitude expressed. For example, if someone says, "Thank thee for our food," we can think, "Yes, I am thankful for such good food." If one prays, "Thank thee for our nice home" in their prayer, we could think, "Yes, I am sure glad we have this home." I would try to trigger this by saying, "Make the prayer yours!" Repeating in our heads makes the prayer really "ours" and the "Amen" really means that it is our prayer too!

> "Gratitude is a fire extinguisher for pride."
>
> —Mark G. Ellingson

4. Help Them Feel Gratitude for Each Other

We have come up with a game called "I'm thankful for you." It is a game of giving compliments to each other that we like to play for family home evening in November. We pass around a piece of paper for each family member, with each one's name on the top, and list our favorite reason we are thankful for that person on the bottom. Then we fold it up and pass it around, until all have written on all of them. Not only do we realize more what we like about each other, but also everyone's self-confidence is boosted by all the good things listed!

This activity is simple and inexpensive, but the words are priceless. Some of our children keep their sheet for a long time, or even put it up on the bedroom mirror or bulletin board. All enjoy the boost from family!

For a family Valentine's Day activity, we like to do something similar. Our high school student council used to tape one construction paper heart for each person in the school on the hallway walls on Valentine's Day, so messages could be written to each person. (The student council would make sure that each heart had many nice things on it.) So, I cut out a large valentine for each member of my family, with the person's name at the top. We pass around the valentines and each person writes a message on it. Some years we write a compliment about that person. Or we might each put "I like it when you _____" or some other message. We tape them up on the door. Our kids have become good at coming up with nice things about and thus being more grateful for each other.

5. Grow More Gratitude

We can do our families a wonderful service by pointing out the beautiful sky or the good-smelling flowers or the cool breeze. God is good to us; just look around and see!

If it is hard to be grateful for a certain member of the family for a season, we can look in on them when they are asleep and remember feelings of love for that person. They are easy to love then! Even better, we can pray to be filled with love and gratitude when we need a boost in that area. When we are trying to follow the Savior, He will give us charity, His pure love.

After our families have learned to be grateful for the good things, we can take it one step farther. Elder Dieter F. Uchtdorf teaches,

> We sometimes think that being grateful is what we do after our problems are solved, but how terribly shortsighted that is. How much of life do we miss by waiting to see the rainbow before thanking God that there is rain? . . . Could I suggest that we see gratitude as a disposition, a way of life that stands independent of our current situation? In other words, I'm suggesting that instead of being thankful for things, we focus on being thankful in our circumstances—whatever they may be.
>
> When we are grateful to God in our circumstances, we can experience gentle peace in the midst of tribulation. True gratitude is an expression of hope and testimony. It comes from acknowledging that we do not always understand the trials of life but trusting that one day we will.[3]

Corrie Ten Boom lived in horrific circumstances. She couldn't understand why her sister Betsie insisted they give thanks for the fleas that infested their barracks in the concentration camp. It wasn't until later they realized that thanks to the fleas, they were left alone by the guards, who would have stopped their nightly Bible study that got them through each day.[4] Like a loving father watches his child struggle to learn to walk or to figure out how to ride a bike, our loving Father above also lets us struggle, knowing we will learn and grow because of it—like the struggles we have to raise a difficult child—and be better for going through it. May God grant us eternal perspective to see past the daily struggles, and may we better thank Him for the ride!

Dear Mom and Dad,

Thanks for reminding me to thank you, and for reminding me to thank God for everything. Please forgive me when I forget! I am so much happier when I think to thank.

Love, Me

Talking Out Tantrums
(Toddler or Teenage)

My mother was extra good at ignoring. I would guess that she had no idea what was really going on, then found out later she knew exactly what was going on but chose to ignore it. We do not want to feed a tantrum by giving it a lot of attention. So ignoring is a good approach. Still, figuring out what is going on will help us understand them. And sometimes, we need to talk them out.

Throwing tantrums seems to be a constant for most toddlers, a part of their difficult season around the age of two. Some start closer to eighteen months, and some wait to hit this stage until age three or even four. Understanding "terrible twos" can help. And in fact, many of these principals apply to later stages of growth challenges, such as teenage years!

1. Factors That Affect Tantrums: Two-Year-Olds

Communication: A large part of a tantrum seems to be related to a struggle to communicate. Babies understand language way before they can use it. The child knows what everyone is saying, but he lacks the words to tell what is on his mind. Or he desperately wants something—not sure just what—and needs to be heard! A mother recently told me about her little boy, "He talks pretty well now, so he has no more need for tantrums."

Identity: Another part of the issue is the need to assert themselves. The baby is becoming their own person. "I am me!" they are telling us. "I am no longer just an extension of my mother! I have my own definite ideas, and I can disagree with yours. (Even if I don't quite understand them.) I desperately need to try my agency." In his intense need to get these points across, a tantrum erupts.

Knowing this helps us see that our little ones are not necessarily being belligerent when they want things a certain way. Though there are some times when parents must say no, most of the time it will not hurt to go ahead and comply with their wishes.

Physical: Of course, if a child is hungry, tired, in pain, or getting sick, there is more chance of a meltdown. Parents have to constantly be detectives to figure out just what is going on. My daughter's young son developed migraines. She learned to listen to his complaints, and not dismiss them or ignore them as she would a tantrum. Instead, she would watch for them with plenty of understanding when a headache was coming on. The Spirit will help us discern physical reasons for outbursts.

Stress: Too much pressure on a child or too much bottled up energy may erupt in a tantrum. There may be a huge need to get outside and use large body muscles on a playground or by running. Again, discerning such cases is tricky, but if we pray for it, the Spirit will help us see the realities we need to see.

1. Factors: Teenagers

Communication: Most teenagers also desperately want to be heard. They have new ideas and opinions they are exploring and they want a listening ear from someone: "Please understand and consider my ideas—even if I'm still figuring them out!" It may be tricky to verbalize why they feel upset.

Identity: Teenagers are also in a becoming stage. They are leaving behind childhood and facing adulthood. They also may feel the need to assert their independence. "I am an independent person with my own ideas!" they may be screaming. Yet, really, they still need our guidance and especially our limits. The struggle between becoming an adult and holding on to childhood may burst into an eruption or a meltdown.

Physical: Puberty is such a huge change. Hormones can bring on emotion. Acne is hard to deal with. It is also tricky to deal with this fast-changing body (and voice), which can be embarrassing at times.

Stress: Teenagers have so many stresses! "Do I look right?" "Are my clothes okay?" "Do I fit in?" There are issues with friends—choosing them, keeping them, getting their approval. There are hard high school classes, and pressure to do well in order to get into college or get a scholarship. There are all the extracurricular activities that take a chunk of their time as well, with the pressure to do them well. There are money issues. Then there's an unknown future: "What will I major in and what will I do with my life?" No wonder there is an occasional meltdown!

Mark and I noticed a trend in our family. Partway through their junior year, our teenager would have a crisis of some sort. All the various pressures would come to a head and the teen would erupt. We came to realize we should be extra careful to be there, to listen, and to reassure during this time. We even warned the younger ones how hard the junior year might be, and to pace themselves accordingly. We would offer sincere prayers for the teenager at this time and Mark would offer a priesthood blessing. Together we could all get through it.

2. Preventing a Tantrum: Toddlers

There are also certain times that tantrums are more likely for toddlers. A nap, a meal, and a change of atmosphere can all help prevent one.

Talk It Through: The grocery store is a particularly volatile place for tantrums. I learned that if I would spell out clearly that the child could pick one thing, I would save some difficulty later. There was much less struggle (since he was holding his one choice!). As they grew, I could start to reason with them about us not spending too much money. A tantrum was avoided by talking it out.

Distract: A wonderful tool for parents is distraction. We can redirect attention away from a tense situation and point our child to something interesting or new. A different toy pulled out at just the right moment does its magic. A snack at the right moment does too. A new thing to look at or a song or story may be the ticket to prevent a tantrum.

Helping with Communication: Many parents have learned to use sign language to help young pre-talkers express themselves. What an amazing help that can be! Now a baby can "tell" you he is hungry or he wants more—before he has learned to verbalize it.

Choices: Giving choices starts to be an important thing at this age. Let them choose what to wear or what toy to play with. Let them decide what kind of sandwich they like or what color ball to pick. Let them decide whether to eat lunch first or read a book first. Giving them choices lets them feel like they are directing an outcome, that they have some control. For most, the more times they use agency, the happier they will be.

Special Time: A special time set aside to talk is another great idea. Set up a certain time—one on one is best—to talk about that day or to explain upcoming stresses in the family. We can listen and reason, encouraging the growth of conversation. Helping them verbalize is invaluable: "Are you feeling tired?" we may ask, or "Are you angry?" "Did she hurt your feelings?" or "Did that make you sad?" We can talk about how to express those feelings appropriately.

2. Prevention for Teenagers

Meltdowns became fewer when my teenage daughter started running regularly. The running helped lessen the tensions when they built up. She felt calmer and more ready for a busy day after a morning run. Joining a sports team or dance group may help also.

At one point, to use up extra stress or excess energy, Mark would send the kids outside to jump on the trampoline fifty times. Or we would find some hard work for them to do, helping them expend energy in acceptable ways. I even told my kids that they could hit their pillows all they wanted (but not their brothers or sisters)! My friend had a houseful of boys, who were wrestling constantly. They might wrestle Dad or each other. Their grandma, who had raised mostly girls, asked, "Do they do this often?" "Yes!" my friend replied, knowing that by expending all that energy, her boys were better adjusted and had less need for explosive tantrums!

Teenagers benefit from some physical work too. Saturdays spent working in the yard, or even doing housework, can relieve some built-up stress. Playing piano and singing is another positive way to prevent outbursts of frustration! When I was in my first year of college, I learned that when studying started swirling around in my head, I went to a practice room and played and sang! I didn't pay attention to the mistakes—I just sang even louder! Pent up frustrations would melt away and I could return fresh to my studies.

One of my sons remembers when he was a teen that his favorite stress reliever was simply being with the family, doing projects, working, playing together. He observed that since teenage tantrums usually involve distancing themselves from parents, parents need to be around their teenage kids as much as possible. If we are around them a lot, they will open up when they are ready.

This son's favorite solution to stress and meltdowns in high school was when Mark would come and sit in his room on Sundays. Mark never called it an interview—he would just ask about the things that were important to this son. He could then open up as little or as much as he felt like. Mark expressed his love for this son by caring about what he cared about.

3. The Need to Say "No!": Toddlers

One day I discovered a wonderful way to help dissipate a tantrum! If my child seemed to have an intense need to exert their independence by saying "no!" I would let them get it out of their system by letting them say their "nos" in a positive way! I asked them, "Are you a lion today?" They answered with a resounding, "No!!!" "Well, are you an elephant today?" "No!" "Are you a hippopotamus today?" "No!" It was perfectly fine to give an emphatic no, and even laugh when it got silly ("Are you a turkey today?"). Gradually, their answer became less forceful, until the need petered out altogether.

3. Emphatically Disagreeing: Teenagers

In another arena, my high school–aged daughter came home from school worn out and grumpy! She was terribly out of sorts and exclaimed to me, "I just want to say 'no!'" "Well," I replied, thinking of my success with two-year-olds, "Do you have any mosquito bites today?" "No!!!" "Do you have any ingrown toenails?" "No!!" "Do you have any boils?" "No!!" "Do you have leprosy today?" "No!" By that time both she and I were laughing heartily, and all was better. This technique that I had used on my two-year-olds brought great results on my sixteen-year-old too!

Extra acceptance and love are needed at this volatile time in a young person's life. They long to feel loved exactly as they are. Don't stop giving hugs or kisses! Maybe give extra!! "I love you just the way you are" cannot be expressed enough. I remember feeling so upset on my twelfth birthday. I ranted and raved to my Dad and couldn't figure out what was really going on. Inside, I was desperately needing him to just tell me he loved me. Bless him, he did! My tears dried up and, with that assurance, I was so much better.

4. Search for the Real Reason: Toddlers and Teenagers

Perhaps what your child says during a meltdown is not the real reason behind it. It would be good to search for the real reason. Pray to figure it out, and the Spirit will help with this process. "What is this child really trying to tell me?" When needs are met, the need for a tantrum is minimized or even eliminated.

My friend's young son was not himself. He would tease and misbehave and yell! He couldn't tell her what was wrong—he didn't quite know himself. So, one day, she sat down with him and had a heart-to-heart. Knowing her son was extra bright, she asked him, "How is school really?" "Fine," he answered slowly. As she probed deeper and asked more questions, a light went on in his head. "That's it!" he realized. "I am totally frustrated with school." Together they uncovered the real problem, that there was too much busy work and not enough challenge. She moved her son to a school that was less structured and more geared to one's own pace. "I have my son back!" this friend rejoiced, for once these needs had been met, her son was content and pleasant again.

In another situation, a fifteen-year-old girl I know burst into tears one day in PE class. She had not made the varsity team she so desperately wanted to be on, but the real reason was not sports at all, she realized much later. Her tears were shed over her suffering relationship with one of her parents. How she longed to connect with that parent! But even she did not figure out the real reason for her outburst until much later. It takes help from the Spirit to discern these things.

In the story of Lehi and Sariah, at one point Sariah is extremely upset. "You are a visionary man!" she accuses Lehi. At this point, Lehi could have gone on the defensive. He could have pridefully exclaimed, "I didn't ask for this revelation to leave Jerusalem! Do you think I like living in a tent? Don't you think I also miss our family and friends and all our riches?!"

But no, Lehi must have known the real reason she was lashing out. His poor wife was desperately worried about her sons, gone back to the city for days on a dangerous errand to confront an evil man. "I know I am a visionary man," Lehi answered calmly, agreeing with her and dissipating the tension. Then, he addresses the real problem. "I know that the Lord will deliver my sons out of the hands of Laban." Sariah is comforted, and the conflict is settled. May we fill our hearts with extra love. It will bring much more happiness and peace in our home.

Dear Mom and Dad,

Sometimes, I feel I just want to explode! Thanks for loving me enough to help me through and helping me figure out what's going on. You're the best!

Love, Me

Peace: A Formula for No Contention

Our family was having a big problem with contention! There was too much bickering and arguing! "He took my piece!" "No, I didn't!" "Yes, you did! Mom!" Mark and I longed for peace and harmony, for love to grow in our home rather than be stifled by contention. We decided to have a family home evening all about contention. We covered the topic thoroughly, but that week, we actually noticed an increase in the fighting and arguing! How could that be?

Then we remembered a quote from Boyd K. Packer: "True doctrine, understood, changes attitudes and behavior. The study of the doctrines of the gospel will improve behavior quicker than a study of behavior will improve behavior. Preoccupation with unworthy behavior can lead to unworthy behavior. That is why we stress so forcefully the study of the doctrines of the gospel."[5] We had studied the unworthy behavior! And sure enough, it had led to more! Rather than study contention, the next week we decided to study peace.

I turned to the Book of Mormon, and discovered in the chapter Words of Mormon, that "this King Benjamin—he had somewhat of contentions among his own people." (Words of Mormon 1:12) Mormon spells out, step by step, how the king rid the kingdom of all contention! There it was, a formula for ridding our "kingdom" of contention as well, replacing it with love and loyalty:

1. Gather the Family Together

When the armies of the Lamanites were coming to battle against them, the first thing King Benjamin did was "gather together his armies" (Words of Mormon 1:13). We too have daily battles we must gather against, the bad guys being Satan and his forces. We must become a team: at prayer time, at meals, and on Sunday. We gather together for family home evening, and we gather together for wholesome activities. Many times, members of our families are pulled in many different directions, so we must make a real effort—even a priority—to gather:

> We counsel parents and children to give highest priority to family prayer, family home evening, gospel study and instruction, and wholesome family activities.[6]

We must not be afraid to claim our family times and our Monday nights together.

There was a point when our family had a hard time getting everyone together. Our senior in high school seemed to spend every free minute with friends, and was rarely available to do things with the family. Mark and I decided that we had to plan ahead better. For example, if a school holiday was coming up, we planned a family bicycle ride or a cookout and game night. We gave our child the message that we wanted time with him especially since he would soon be leaving home! This way, he could tell his friends, "Sorry, our family has something planned that day. But you can join us!"

2. Fight Evil

King Benjamin took a definite stand against the evil that was infiltrating his kingdom (Words of Mormon 1:13). The king's people were sure of their king's stand. Our families must also be sure of where we stand: "No child in this Church should be left with uncertainty about his or her parents' devotion to the Lord Jesus Christ, the Restoration of His Church, and the reality of living prophets and apostles."[7]

Contention is an evil in homes, because it is the pride of seeing only *my* needs, *my* wants, *my* comfort rather than seeing yours too. We taught our kids that when our voices are raised in angry contention, the Holy Ghost leaves. To have strength and discernment to fight evil and keep our home peaceful, we must be peacemakers by talking things out quietly and calmly. "Lower our voices a few decibels," Gordon B. Hinckley counseled.[8]

It may seem strange that a formula for stopping contention in the family would talk so much about fighting. But there is, today, a constant battle raging for our souls. We must fight evil! King Benjamin and his people fought "in the strength of the Lord." Throughout the Book of Mormon and the Bible, the Lord provides strength for battle. In our homes, family prayer and the promptings of the Spirit give us strength to fight the evils of deception.

3. Drive Out All Enemies

"Sisters, fight!" warned Julie B. Beck to mothers, "We cannot sit and act like victims. This is the work of a determined adversary, and we have to take responsibility for defending our homes."[9]

Do we have enemies? King's Benjamin's enemies were the Lamanites, but he also mentions the enemies of false Christs, false prophets, and false preachers and teachers. He didn't rest until "their mouths had been shut" (Words of Mormon 1:15–16). What are these in our day? Perhaps they are deceptive ideas taught on the media or at school.

Just as King Benjamin drove his enemies "out of all the lands of their inheritance," we must also drive out all the tools of the enemy from our home. One powerful tool of the adversary may be media and electronics. Some media "assaults the senses and batters the soul with messages and images that are neither virtuous, nor lovely, nor of good report, nor praiseworthy." M. Russell Ballard taught that our family councils must "limit the amount of time our children watch TV or play video games or use the Internet. . . . Virtual reality must not become their reality."[10] We tried to make sure all electronics were out in the well-trafficked area for better monitoring. We started limiting more carefully TV, movies, and internet usage.

We battled the notion in video and computer games that there are several "lives" for each participant. (Do they subtly learn that death is no big deal, since there is "another life"?) How sinister is Satan in so deceptively captivating one of his main opponents—the future missionary force—in games that make killing more and more literal and great fun! It is a dangerous notion, since we have but one life only and we cannot throw it away or lessen its value.

We tried to talk over what the kids learned at school, so we could correct false ideas. We have taught the kids to "trust no man to be your teacher . . . except he be a man of God, walking in his ways and keeping his commandments" (Mosiah 23:4). We explain that they can listen and learn but must be careful not to internalize something that is not taught by a godly person. Further, in our prayers we ask that our children shun the evil and embrace the good that is taught them and discern the difference.

4. Find Truth in the Scriptures

King Benjamin and his prophets "did speak the word of God" (Words of Mormon 1:17). Words of truth such as "let us love one another, for love is of God" (1 John 4:7) taught to our kids will change them from the inside. It will take time and patience, until they internalize and apply what we teach and try to live. When our children see how much we value the words of scripture, they eventually will too.

In a parable, the Savior teaches that the empty house, if not filled with goodness, will attract more evil than before (Matthew 12:43–45). When we remove something, we must replace it with something better. King Benjamin took care to teach his people "to keep the commandments of God, that they might rejoice and be filled with love towards God and all men" (Mosiah 2:4). He also urged parents to teach their children to "love one another and to serve one another" (Mosiah 4:15). Family history work is a great way to serve others! Computer lovers could replace the time doing questionable, mind-numbing, or less-than-productive things on the computer with writing letters, doing mind challenges, or indexing.

> "Learn of me, and listen to my words; walk in the meekness of my Spirit, and you shall have peace in me."
>
> (D&C 19:23)

5. Get Help from Prophets

King Benjamin was not too proud to get help with ridding his kingdom of contention. He used "the assistance of the holy prophets who were among his people" (Words of Mormon 1:16). He surely used both current and past prophets.

Mark likes to think of prophets using the analogy of the watchman on the tower. He can see "afar off" and warn us of danger approaching. If we listen, we will be prepared and watched over. If we teach our families to revere prophets, then it will follow that they will value their words. We must teach them about ancient prophets, such as Noah, Moses, and Abraham, and the prophets of the Restoration, such as Joseph Smith, Brigham Young, Gordon B. Hinckley, Thomas S. Monson, and Russell M. Nelson.

If we read their words, and the kids see us try to apply them, we will plant seeds of humbly following counsel from God through prophets. The Spirit we feel will bring personalized direction. During one general conference, Mark and I were listening to a message, when we turned knowingly to each other. We had both received a similar prompting about the needs of our child at the same time.

King Benjamin is called "a holy man" (Words of Mormon 1:17). We too can look over our lives and keep trying to make them more holy. We will earn the respect of our kids—even teenagers—if they see us sincerely trying to be just and holy, apologizing when necessary, and holding ourselves to a high standard. It was not easy for him: "With the help of these [holy prophets], king Benjamin, by laboring with all the might of his body and the faculty of his whole soul, and also the prophets, did once more establish peace in the land" (Words of Mormon 1:18).

6. Peace from the Savior

"Peace I leave with you," promises our Savior Jesus Christ. "My peace I give unto you. Not as the world giveth give I unto you. Let not your heart be troubled, neither let it be afraid" (John 14:27). "In the world ye shall have tribulation," He tells us, "but be of good cheer. I have overcome the world" (John 16:23).

If we seek the Lord, trying to be His true followers, we can be blessed to feel His peace. In a busy family, there can still be times of real peace. We can plan for these times, work toward them with all our hearts, and be blessed to see the fruits of our laboring for peace.

Dear Mom and Dad,

Even though I can be rowdy, I like times of peace too. Thanks for helping me work out problems and avoid contention. Thank you, especially for teaching me true doctrine to help me become a peacemaker.

Love, Me

Loving and Serving
Each Other = Getting Along!

One of the most challenging of commandments for me is "Ye will not suffer your children that they . . . fight and quarrel one with another, and serve the devil, who is the master of sin." The answer is in the very next verse, but it is a tall order: "But . . . ye will teach them to love one another and to serve one another" (Mosiah 4:14–15). Don't we long to have them get along? Just how do we get our kids to love and serve each other?

1. Talk It Through

It happened to be Mother's Day, and my sister and brother-in-law were fed up with how their kids were acting. All seven of them were picking on each other and quarreling! My brother-in-law sat them all down, and with some emotion, leveled with them. "My biggest fear," he said, "is that you won't like each other as adults. We want you to be friends when you are adults and want to be together. Not like some families, who hardly have anything to do with one another." For a long time, he and my sister talked with their kids trying to paint for them the bigger picture of when they would grow up and leave home and current friends. The kids gradually began to see that through thick and thin, it would be family who was going to be there. It was amazing how a step back to realize how important these family ties were really changed the way they treated one another.

The whole issue here is helping them learn to love one another. If parents can get their children to serve one another, love will grow. This is an "active love. It is not manifested through large and heroic deeds but rather through simple acts of kindness and service," taught M. Russell Ballard. "Charity begins at home. . . . By our example, let us teach our family members to have love one for another."[11]

When two of my sons were twelve and six years old, the older brother was constantly telling his younger brother, "Get out of my room!" I was frustrated with this, and I had told him to treat his brother like one of his best friends. During monthly interviews, I would ask every time about relationships with his siblings. "Do they know that you love them?" In the last interview, our twelve-year-old had resolved to work harder at getting along with our six-year-old. One evening, as the family was settling down for the night, this older brother came into the bathroom where I was and said, "Mom, he is in my room. What should I do?" My reply was, "Go and talk to him like he was your very best friend, then see what happens." When I returned to the kitchen, I found both boys there. Younger brother was flying his older brother's prized hover plane around the house. He didn't even seem to mind when his younger brother would crash it to the floor. I was so pleased! "One more time, and then you need to go to bed," was my input (so as to avoid injury to the plane). But I was high-fiving inside! And I gave my twelve-year-old a quick hug, to compliment him for being such a good big brother.

2. Find Ways to Serve

We found that when our kids shared a bedroom for a while, it helped their relationships. We tried to make it clear not to allow contention in our home, but to find peaceful ways to work out their differences. We learned at a church Sunday School course that conflict is not wrong; it is just part of being different from each other. It's when conflict is raised to contention that there are problems.

However, if I figured out that two children were together a lot, such as going to and from school together every day or being on the same sports team or club, I would arrange that at home these two roomed with different siblings. This helped peace prevail, for they had a rest from each other.

I wanted to encourage more service in my home, so I tried to watch for times when one of my children was having a bad day or didn't feel good. I would then pull a different child aside and whisper, "Your sister is having a hard time today. Let's do her chores for her and surprise her!" I didn't force the issue if the child was reluctant, but often, enthusiasm was engendered by the element of surprise. (Although I did, on occasion, tip big sister off to notice what had been done for her!)

I also tried to help love to grow among my kids by helping them remember each other's birthdays. At one point, I would provide little gifts for my kids to give each other. I would set up a little "store" on my bed, where each child could go chose something for the birthday child and "buy" it with what they could afford at the time. But gradually I realized that I was providing too much. Tuning into what that sibling might like and sacrificing their own time and money or energy or service for the birthday person helps love grow. I backed off and let the kids do birthday gifts more on their own.

3. When You Serve Someone, You Grow to Love Them

When I was about twelve, I got to go visit my cousin at BYU. In her apartment, I met her roommate, who was busy baking brownies. "Yes, I am baking these for my cousin, since I am so mad at her," she told me. *Huh?* I wondered. She went on, "My grandmother had always promised me her piano, but my cousin got it. I'm mad at her but I don't want to be, so I am baking her these brownies." It really struck me that when you are mad at someone, you serve them, so you won't feel that way anymore! I have told my kids this story and urged them to serve a sibling they are mad at.

4. Serve Together

Sometimes, there has to be a designated place to talk things out. I was trying to come up with a place, because my mother-in-law insisted that bedrooms were not a good place for kids to go when upset—they needed to stay peaceful places for sleeping. The front of the house had too little privacy and the bathroom certainly wouldn't work! I chose the laundry room. And since there was always plenty of laundry that needed folding, my kids would fold clothes together while they talked it out. It would be service for the family. Folding clothes was not their favorite thing to do, so it was extra incentive to work out the situation. Consequently, whenever someone hits or fights, I insist that the two involved "Go to the laundry room and fold clothes until you're friends."

Most of the time, I just let the consequence do the trick without intervention. They work things out quickly and soon are back reporting, "We're friends now!" But occasionally, if things are too heated, I may listen in from behind the door. Usually, they want to stop working and go out, and they know they can stop folding as soon as they work it out! But if there are any put downs or contention, I intervene briefly and urge them to see the other one's point of view. If they are slow at working it out, I call in, "Okay, fold the entire basket of clothes," which helps them both want to get this figured out! On a couple of occasions through the years, I've had to bring out another basket of clothes as well! But overall it has worked quickly and well. My kids are removed from the family area. They learn to talk things out. They learn to avoid contention. The problem is theirs to fix, not Mom's or Dad's, and they learn that choosing to be friends is much more fun than fighting!

Another time, I had to do something about unkind words. I decided my kids would sing together when they quarrel. I typed up the song, "Let Us Oft Speak Kind Words,"[12] and then posted it up at the entrance to the hallway. Here, the two could be away from the family yet close enough for me to monitor. The kids were required to stand together and sing the song. Usually, they were done with the argument before the song was half finished! Similarly, a friend of mine told her kids, "If you are going to have an argument, sing it!" It was impossible for the two at odds to stay angry if they were doing it opera style! Invariably, they ended up in giggles!

5. Surround Our Kids with Peace

What do our children see each day? I once heard a story about a mother, who, having lost her husband at sea, longed that her son not go to sea also. When he left in spite of her pleadings, she went into his bedroom, grieving, and there on the wall for him to look at each day was a picture of a sailor on a boat at sea. She realized that having that picture up had inadvertently made going to sea this boy's goal!

I then looked around to see what was posted on the walls of our hallways and bedrooms. What was being implanted in my children's minds? Along with pictures of the Savior and the temple, I started taking pictures of two or three of them with their arms around each other or having fun together. I would frame these and place them in strategic places, such as in bedrooms, bathrooms, and halls. When two of my children were having a particularly hard time getting along, I would search through old pictures to find those two having a good time and hang it where it was very visible. With time, the animosity would dissipate, and these two kids would be pals again!

What do they hear? Music is a powerful tool to dissipate tenseness and calm words and feelings. Soothing lullabies, soft religious or classical music, or happy upbeat music help the mood of the family. We must be careful to turn off the sounds we don't want to go through our kid's heads, such as music with a negative beat or lyrics.

My sister-in-law chose a theme for her family that her kids hear often: "Treat the Best Those You Love the Best!" Her kids hear the theme often and see it up on the wall as well. They talk about who are their very best friends forever! She frequently reminds her kids, "Treat each other better than your best friend at school!" Our family theme is similar: "Stick Together Family."

What do they do? Could service be a part of our kid's week routinely? One summer we made Fridays service days, and so we looked for ways to serve someone each week. One friend asked us to help their family scrape mud balls off their back fence. We wrote letters or weeded for others and picked up trash. Whenever we helped a neighbor, we let them help too.

6. Take Over as Boss

I was frustrated when one of my children would begin bossing a younger sibling, reminding the younger one to follow a family rule or even dishing out consequences themselves! I began to say, "Let me be the mom!" If a younger child seemed bombarded with scolding and preaching from older siblings, I would explain, "She only needs one mom! Except when you are babysitting, I will worry about this."

At times, I would have chosen to ignore a certain behavior and to wait to praise the positive ones. I would let them know I needed to "be the mom" and deal with this. "But you're not dealing with it, Mom!" an older sibling exclaimed, so I took that child aside and explained my plan to extinguish that particular behavior by ignoring it! It was a good chance to teach her that principle.

7. More Love and Attention

One time, Mark and I were worried about our ten-year-old son. He was usually such a happy, energetic boy who took most change in stride. But in the last five days, I realized and told Mark that he had actually cried three times over his chores or over an unusual assignment at school. He was having trouble with fighting as well. Were his chores too challenging for him? Was he not getting enough sleep at night? "You know," said Mark, "it's hard when your brother gets so much attention on his birthday."

"You're right!" I realized. "He's had two brothers have birthdays in the last week. His little brother's new bike goes faster than his now, and he'd spent both of his hard-earned dollars on their gifts." We both agreed, "It's time to shower this son with extra attention!" We decided we would play catch with him, and board games, and chat with him about his interests more often. I was really grateful for Mark's insights. If we are watchful, we can regulate sibling dynamics so that everyone feels loved.

One year in early December, our family read together "A Christmas without Presents" by James E. Faust.[13] We were struck by the simplicity of that family's Christmas and decided we too would have a homemade Christmas that year. Everyone drew the name of one family member they would give to and took the challenge of finding something they could make for that person. Mark and I helped brainstorm ideas and provide materials to use. (We helped the little ones a whole lot!) Each child put lots of effort into serving that sibling. It was sweet to avoid so much commercialism and to really focus on a gift we could create for each other. We enjoyed our experience so much, love grew, and a homemade Christmas became a tradition for every other year. May we grow the love and service in our homes.

Dear Mom and Dad,

Thanks for helping me see my brother or sister's point of view and for helping me find ways to serve them so I can love them more. I really do want to be best friends with my brothers and sisters!

Love, Me

Chapter 7
Water What We Want to Grow

*I*n our flower gardens, we wouldn't dream of deliberately watering the weeds! Just the beautiful flowers that bloom and bring joy. In our families too, we should work hard to water only that which we want to grow. If a child gets lots of attention for his misbehavior, most likely it will continue and even increase. But if we ignore the naughtiness as much as we can (though we teach the good behavior and the doctrine in other settings), it will likely wither and die. If we water profusely the good things we catch our kids doing, they will grow and grow! Kids and flowers thrive on water and attention!

In our home, when one child snatched away a toy, often I would go to the one who got it snatched away and say, "I'm so sorry that she took your toy! I'll help you find another one." In the process, I would give no attention to the offender, who would usually drop that toy pretty soon. No, she shouldn't get away with it, so yes, a few minutes later I would talk to her about sharing and give her the words, "Could I play with it when you're done?" To extinguish a behavior, ignoring it whenever possible is key. (And help from the Spirit to know when to ignore and when to step in!)

The Power of Words: They Live On

"Words, when you say them out loud, those words, they never go away. They live on, even when we're gone."[1] Have you ever noticed how one criticism can undo many compliments? And how one compliment can stick for days? Words can build or tear down.

It matters what we say! We have to be careful how we word things and what we focus on. The power of words is that they can form what we believe about ourselves; even careless words can affect a lifetime. A lovely lady I know of is a good example of this. When she was a teenager, her older brother was just teasing when he told her she had a funny nose and she believed him wholeheartedly. She started covering her nose every time someone took her picture and even now that she is a grandma, she still does that. Every family picture shows grandma covering her nose! Even though that brother told her many times that he was just teasing, the words stuck and she has believed them to this day. What makes this even sadder is that she has a very normal-looking nose! Words profoundly affect our families:

1. Words Can Encourage and Build

Jessi hated athletics! She especially hated running, since she usually came in near the last. She longed to be like Kathy, who was so confident and loved to run!

On the day of the big one-mile running test in PE, Jessi found herself walking out to the track with Kathy, so she confided in her how much she dreaded this run. "You can do it!" Kathy insisted. Not only that, when Jessi's heat lined up, Kathy started running alongside her, telling her what a great job she was doing! Kathy ran the entire four laps with her, encouraging her the whole time, and Jessi could not believe what a great time she got on her mile! She could actually get a good time on a run! What a sacrifice Kathy had made for her, since her own lap was the very next heat.

But what a difference that gesture made in Jessi's life. With a new confidence that maybe she could do athletics, Jessi tried out for the dance team and started to enjoy basketball and volleyball with the Young Women. She even earned toe shoes in ballet. Those words of encouragement changed her life.[2]

Kind words are what we always want to use and to teach our kids to use. "Do you like my dress?" someone might ask our child. What if they really don't like it? A favorite Primary song goes, "Would my words be true and kind if He were never far away?"[3] I like to help them search for things to say that are *true and still kind*, such as that you like the pockets or the sleeves on that dress. There is always something to like, so truthfully and kindly, their answer could be, "Yes, I love that color on you!" This way the words will not injure but build. Besides, we can teach our kids that if we always say *only* kind things, our friends will know that we will not talk about *them* unkindly behind their back.

Compliments are gifts. Years ago, I was selling concessions to raise money for choir tour at an ASU football game. A stranger bought the popcorn or peanuts I was selling and then said to me, "You have a million-dollar smile!" and disappeared into the crowd. Wow! Was that a gift to me! Out of the blue, from someone I will never see again. Yet I have thought of that compliment many, many times through the years. It still remains an uplift!

2. Words Can Tear Down

Compare this story with Jessi's: When my father, Jay, was a young man, growing up in a very small town, basketball was a huge deal. His older brothers had led their tiny high school team—that barely had any substitute players—all the way to win state! Well, several years later, when it was Jay's turn to play high school basketball, he and his twin brother were so excited to be on the team. They practiced constantly. Then one day, a man in the town came up to my dad and said, "Jay, you'll never be an athlete like your brother Jorth, but you're doing pretty good anyway." My dad was totally shocked. "I'm not an athlete?" The thought had never occurred to him. What was meant to be a compliment was a slam, and my dad believed it was true.

When I was growing up, I was afraid of athletics. When I expressed my frustration at home, my dad would always say, "It's my fault that you aren't that good at sports," or "I'm sorry, it's in your genes to not be very good." The one remark made in passing way back in high school had stuck and affected me too. I never thought I was any good, and I wasn't. In fact, in Young Women's basketball, when I finally made a basket after so many tries, the other team cheered!! I avoided the softball games at the reunions, because I knew I was no good at it. I had nightmares over the presidential fitness tests we were required to take at gym class. The only C grade I ever got was in junior high PE!

Well, I grew up and married, and my husband would not hear of this talk! He simply wouldn't allow me to talk about not being good at sports. "You are fine at sports," he insisted. In fact, he told everyone about the time I had said I wasn't very good, but then beat him at bowling. He simply told me I was a good athlete, and before long, with some tips, I could hit a few baseballs with the kids and actually serve a volleyball over the net!

> "I can live for two months on a good compliment."
>
> —Mark Twain

3. The Silent Treatment

What we choose to say to our kids brings such lasting growth, for good or for bad. The same thing is true of what we do not say. I learned that we should never punish our children by using the silent treatment, or saying nothing for an extended length of time, as this is actually a form of bullying. We must also be so careful about using sarcasm, especially with children. (See "A Look at Sarcasm" in chapter 7.) Correcting our children is so much more effective when we use our words to teach and encourage rather than ignore or put down.

4. The Goal

We parents can do much to help our children see themselves as competent, successful individuals. We can start from babyhood telling them how wonderful they are. We can work to protect them from those who put them down or cripple them with misplaced words. I know a book called *I Love You the Purplest*, in which a mother tells each of her competitive sons about their differing talents—both of which are good! Without comparing her two boys, she compliments them both differently but equally, reinforcing their unique gifts and talents.[4]

Our children's patriarchal blessings and father's blessings tell us what great possibilities for good they have. The scriptures affirm that each person has gifts given to him (D&C 46:11), and we can help our kids figure out what theirs are by watching carefully and pointing them out. The Spirit will help us have the words to say that convey our love and build. We must be careful what we tell our kids, because they will believe it!

Dear Mom and Dad,

Thank you for choosing carefully the words you use when you talk to me. I feel so good when you tell me my talents are great. I'm glad you believe in me!

Love, Me

Validation and Reassurance

My friend Cara was frustrated with her little boy's obsession with airplanes! All he could talk about was airplanes! But then, the Spirit helped her see that she should embrace this and validate him. Little children long for approval. Actually, everyone needs validation. All need reassurance that "I am okay," that what I think has value, that I am worth listening to and loving. Of course, parents are the source of most validation of young kids. But if they don't find it from us, they will have to look for it elsewhere, from teachers, from friends, or even from negative behaviors. As they grow, we must grow in our ability to provide this needed reassurance of their worth and their value to us.

What does validation look like? My daughter helped me realize that there are two types of validation, the one being a message of acceptance and approval, such as "You're okay. You have worth," and the other a message that what you are feeling is real, both your negative and positive feelings, which tells someone, "You're okay for feeling this way." Children need both kinds. Here are some ways to validate:

1. Truly Listening

Cara's little boy who loved airplanes talked about them constantly, colored pictures of them, and watched for them in the sky. All he wanted to do was fly in an airplane! She found herself getting annoyed and exhausted with this obsession with airplanes! Then one day, she decided to change her interactions with her son. She started talking with him about how he would become a pilot someday. Now, whenever she drops off her husband at the airport, she takes him afterward to the cell phone lot to watch planes for a while—even letting him sit on her car's roof! Every couple of months, she takes him to ride the Sky Train, watching the planes as they ride it back and forth. It is absolutely the happiest time for this boy—his face lights up like she can't believe! Extended family members have joined her by taking him along when they go to the airport. Grandpa even showed him and let him climb in a small plane he flies! All of this tells him that they really hear him and his great love for planes.

Another little boy loved to explain things. He jabbered and jabbered to anyone in his large family about his little boy dreams, his big plans, his questions, his ideas. When my friend told me about this little boy—her little brother—she told me that he talked so much that soon his family members began to tune him out. They might look at him when he began to chatter, and maybe nod their heads, but with barely a comment back. Gradually, they hardly gave him even that much attention! It wasn't long until he started to withdraw. Sadly, she told me, he stopped talking altogether. This former chatterbox never spoke anymore. All those ideas were stuck in his own head, and he had given up on receiving any validation for any of them at all.

It takes a conscious effort to truly listen to our kids, to engage, to internalize what they are trying to tell us, and to respond with approval and reassurance that what they think is valuable. They are worth our time and effort to truly understand and validate. We are busy parents. There is a lot on our minds, with many lives to manage. I often slip into forming what I want to say next, instead of really listening for understanding and empathy. I wish I would form kind, clarifying questions the show I care instead. "Tell me more" is a gift of a response, and really listening is a validation that carries with it the reward of a strong bond of love.

I once overheard a mom say, "Yes, I'm fortunate to be a stay-at-home mom. But how much of the time am I engaged?" She realized one of the many distractions that keep us from validating our children and families was cell phones. One solution might be to set certain times for no cell phones, such as the dinner table, so as to encourage good conversation. We try to talk about a favorite thing that happened that day, a funny thing to share, or a service we did that day. The goal is to open up and really engage in each others' lives.

2. Acknowledging Feelings and Efforts

Children need to hear that it is okay to feel the feelings they are having. We can help them acknowledge them, with words such as "I can tell that really upset you!" or "That is so exciting!" We can teach them to express their feelings appropriately. If a child is feeling angry, for example, we can tell them, "I understand you are feeling angry. Why don't you go jump on the trampoline to help you cool down, and then we'll talk about it." A few minutes later, we could talk it over and help them see the other person's point of view. My daughter is really good at expressing to her kids how she understands their feelings: "Is it hard to share that toy? I understand," she'll say. "But he'll give it right back—I'll make sure." Her child feels validated and reassured.

In another arena, we parents can take care to notice what our children *tried* to do. Effort counts. Diligence matters. What a boost we give when we acknowledge effort, even when things didn't turn out as we hoped. Mark always goes to the "effort" grade on our kids' report cards first. He notices their effort in school and validates what they worked hard at, no matter the other grades. We can build our kids up by recognizing good motives and validating them, even if things went wrong.

If a child were to break a picture frame while trying to help dust, for example, we can spend more time talking about the helping they did, rather than the annoyance of the broken glass. A frame can be replaced, but unkind words cannot be unsaid.

Many times, a granddaughter has picked a flower to give to me, so pleased with her own thoughtfulness. I have had to bite back the words of disapproval for picking my newly planted petunia and replace it with praise for their kindness in bringing me a flower. (I leave it to their mother to remind them to be careful with the new flowers and ask first before picking them.)

I remind myself that my flower will grow back, but my scolding would mask my chance to acknowledge and praise a grandchild's thoughtfulness.

3. Agreeing

Whenever possible, let's agree. Even agreeing with part of what that family member says is validating to them. Many times, I realize that rather than making the effort to tell a family member that I agree with them, I often assume they know that and just move on to the part that I think needs fixing or adjusting. Later, I realize that I really should have reassured that I do like that part of the idea and will support it. "You're right" is a super validating thing to say.

For example, Lehi set the example for us, by answering Sariah's fears about her sons with: "You're right. I am a visionary man." (See 1 Nephi 5:2–6.) He then went on to bear testimony of God's plan for their family and His protecting care of their sons. He validated her feelings, then reassured and met her needs.

My daughters are really good at validating their children by supporting their interests. One of my grandsons had a particular interest in puffin birds last fall. So, my daughter put together a puffin costume for him that Halloween. It wasn't easy, but it sure validated him! He loved it! My sister-in-law has a young son who absolutely loves maps. So, in his bedroom, she took the time to recreate, on his wall, a map of the NYC subway system map! The different routes are represented with different colors of electrical tape. It is marvelous, and her son knows that it fits his interests perfectly! He feels truly validated every day!

4. Reassuring

So many people that we run into each day are going through hard things. No matter what someone is going through, we can always respond with reassurance that we will be pulling for them in prayer. Even when we can't reach out to someone—like a person on the street—we can pray for them. Sweet words of reassurance to anyone would be, "I'll be praying for you."

Children too have worries and fears, disappointments and concerns. They need oodles of reassurance: that this will be over soon, that we are really almost there, that their "owie" will get better, that we will find the lost toy/doggie/tooth they wanted to put under their pillow! Reassuring is very validating. And it brings security and peace.

5. Empathy

Some people have the gift of feeling what another is feeling. A close friend of mine shows it in her face that she is feeling just what I am feeling—that she truly empathizes. I feel validated when I open up to her. Taking time to empathize with our family members will be such a loving gift.

The Savior exemplified this validation when He cried with Mary and Martha. Even when He knew they would be seeing their brother shortly, He still stopped to feel their pain with them (John 11:32–44). May we feel what those in our family or friendship circles feel, like the Savior did. Trust in each other will grow, love will be nurtured, and family bonds will be tight. Sweet and long-lasting friendships with our kids will form.

Here is an extra good example of validating feelings. My daughter's young boy—I'll call him Tyson—was playing at the community park near his home when he was four years old. Another little boy, who was known for being the tyrant of the playground, came up to him and pushed him. This was not just a small push—it made Tyson fall all the way down a small hill! He ran to his mom and slumped down next to her, so mad and sad! He just couldn't believe what happened! It was not fair—he truly felt the injustice of the whole thing! He sat there, angry for a long time, his feelings hurt! My daughter listened to him, and then answered, first trying to help him justify his emotions. "Are you really mad? I can tell you are really frustrated—I would be frustrated too! I want you to know that it's not okay what he did to you! But we can forgive . . ."

She next came up with scenarios for him of why this could have happened. "Maybe this boy has a terrible ear infection. Maybe just before we came out here, someone threw a rock at him! Maybe he actually wants to be your friend, but his mom is still teaching him *how* to be friends with someone! I bet he needs friends!! What do you think?" She just kept listening and talking, helping him work through his intense young feelings.

My daughter did such a good job of validating both him and his emotions, that the next thing this little boy did all on his own was to go inside and get a couple of his favorite cars. He asked his mom to go with him to this boy's house, where he handed him the cars. He told him how it was his favorite thing to push the cars down the slide, and that maybe they could be friends. If she had not helped him work through that, he could have been scared of this boy, and afraid to go back to the playground. Now, he had not only gotten over it, but had also gained a friend!

God gives us a gift of validation when He lets us feel His Spirit in our hearts, to confirm what we are doing. There is no sweeter experience in my view. May we share the wonderful gift of validation to our children.

Dear Mom and Dad,

How I love you for validating me, that I am okay and that my feelings and interests matter. Thanks for noticing my efforts, and for giving me the reassurances I need. It shows me you really love me.

Love, Me

A Look at Sarcasm

What is the problem with sarcasm? Isn't it just humor?

Gordon B. Hinckley taught, "I am asking that we stop seeking out the storms and enjoy more fully the sunlight. I am suggesting that as we go through life we 'accentuate the positive.' I am asking that we look a little deeper for the good, that we *still voices of insult and sarcasm,* that we more generously compliment virtue and effort."[5]

A while back, I had a vivid dream. I was sitting in a large room, and way across the room, far from me, I saw a coiled rattlesnake. In a split second, even before I had time to exclaim, the rattlesnake bolted forward the entire length of that room and bit me! I immediately woke up in a panic. While it was good to realize this was a dream, I felt like it was so vivid that it must mean something. For days afterward, I wondered just what the snake biting me so swiftly and alarmingly could possibly mean?

I came to realize that the culprit was sarcasm. Our family had begun watching a show that was filled with sarcasm. I asked myself, *While humor is good, could sarcasm be like venom?* In James 3:8, it says the tongue can be "an unruly evil, full of deadly poison." We are reminded in D&C 63:64 that words "must be spoken with care, and by constraint of the Spirit," especially when speaking to children. Consider the following:

1. Isn't Humor Good?

Yes! Humor can be "an escape valve for the pressures of life," taught Richard G. Scott.[6] One of Mark's and my favorite memories are of a good laugh together that wouldn't stop!

"Sharing witty remarks or humorous experiences can ease tense, uncomfortable situations and can create a subtle bond of fellowship between strangers. . . . Puns, exaggeration, understatement, irony, and clever twists on common situations teach profound lessons on life, stimulate the imagination, school the emotions, and reveal hidden relationships."[7]

However, "a most damaging form of humor is sarcasm, or cutting, hostile, or contemptuous remarks. . . . When humor is such a powerful tool in building subtle bonds of brotherhood, in cheering those who suffer, and in teaching profound and memorable lessons, why should it be used to belittle and discourage? Those who profess belief in Christ should shape their humor in the light of Christ's teachings."[8]

2. The Problem with Sarcasm

"The Greek root for sarcasm is *sarkazein* and means 'to tear flesh like dogs.' Sarcasm can convey aggression and insult, it can be used to dominate others, and it can communicate contempt and anger," teaches Jennifer Grace Jones in her article "No Corrupt Communication." "Not all sarcasm is intentionally sinister, but it has a hypocritical edge because it requires us to say the opposite of what we mean. Some use it for humor, but it often damages our relationships because it leaves our friends and family doubting our sincerity and confused by what we say."[9]

Jennifer used this personal example:

I moved away from my college town immediately after graduation and was eager to make friends in my new area. I quickly acclimated to a good group of people, and I enjoyed getting to know them. But some of my new friends relied on sarcasm to be funny, sometimes exploiting others' weaknesses for humor. At first I ignored it. However, months of interactions in which humor came at the expense of someone's feelings—including mine—left my heart heavy. I yearned for friends who would encourage me instead of make fun of my shortcomings.

I returned to my college town for a short visit and reunited with women whom I admire for their faith, vigor, and optimism. We spent the day playing sports and talking. They were eager to hear about my life, and they listened without belittling me. We laughed hard and often—but never at someone else.

As I sat with these women in the afternoon sunlight, I looked into their cheerful faces, and my heart lifted. Their kindness soothed like a balm, and I resolved to become a better friend, especially when it came to uplifting others with my conversation.[10]

"Though often meant to be harmless, sarcasm denotes insensitivity to the feelings of others, stemming either from thoughtlessness or maliciousness. . . . Recall the perverted brand of humor of the soldiers who mocked our Savior by putting a crown of thorns on his head, clothing him in a purple robe, and saying, 'Hail, King of the Jews!'" (John 19:2–3)[11]

In short, sarcasm gives people the "dishonest opportunity to wound without looking like they're wounding."[12]

3. Harmful to Children and Teenagers

Sarcasm is particularly harmful to children, since they recognize it but don't understand it. "Parents and siblings who use sarcasm against young children often cause more damage than they ever intend. Studies show that children as young as five years old can detect sarcasm immediately. . . . Parents are 'much more proficient at using [sarcasm] than children,' and it can become a veil for 'undisclosed anger, annoyance, even jealousy.' This unequal power changes parental sarcasm from a joke into a form of bullying."[13] We would never intentionally bully our children! So let's remove sarcasm from our conversations with them.

Teenagers also suffer from sarcasm. Consider this example of teens and sarcasm:

"Nice pants," a girl giggled as she walked past me into class. I stood in the hallway of my new junior high school, confused by her sarcasm.

"What's wrong with my clothes?" I whispered to myself.

It didn't take me long to figure it out. In this school, designer clothes were the standard, and my jeans didn't have the right label. I just didn't fit in.

As the unkind comments grew, so did my feelings of inferiority. Along with my schoolwork, I started studying the other students' styles. Time and new clothes helped end the teasing. Yet I still spent hours worrying that I didn't measure up.[14]

Sarcasm can cause great damage to another's self-esteem. Let us steer our families away from using it!

4. Replacing It, So There's No Sting

"To avoid using humor as a dangerous weapon, we must be compassionately considerate of all that is frail, and humbly mindful of all that is sublime. Would it not be better to 'lift up the hands which hang down, and strengthen the feeble knees' (D&C 81:5) than to humiliate and disgrace one of our neighbors?"[15]

What do we replace it with? In a word, sincerity. I have tried to teach my kids that whatever they say to someone should never leave a *sting* afterward. Words cannot be taken back, nor can the tones of our voices, so we must plan carefully what we say and how we say it. Particularly, when we talk to children, let us give them the example of speaking kindly and saying things directly. Let us take on the goal to be sincere and take care with our humor.

Since my dream, I have discovered that I slip into sarcasm easily. I have had to make a real conscious effort to resist that tendency. May we all strive to speak, to everyone and especially to children, directly and sincerely.

5. Put-Downs

President Hinckley went on to caution against put-downs, "What I am suggesting is that each of us turn from the negativism that so permeates our society and look for the remarkable good among those with whom we associate, that we speak of one another's virtues more than we speak of one another's faults."[16]

Put-downs in any form can leave more than just a sting. Even in jest, a put-down can leave scars behind. Children believe what they are told, so their self-esteem can sustain permanent injury. May we evaluate carefully the media we watch, and even more so, what our kids hear from us. They will learn to speak uplifting, kind words if we teach them and they hear us say those instead.

Dear Mom and Dad,

Thanks for giving me a gentle, loving atmosphere at home. It's not that way out in the world! You help me feel safe by your words to me.

Love, Me

Chapter 8

Fill Their Minds with Goodness

Our children's minds are like empty vessels waiting to be filled, and we have the blessing and the responsibility to choose—or at least monitor—what goes in: pure water or spoiled garbage! Just as we would never let our kids pick up something off the ground that has been stepped on and put it in their mouths, we must watch carefully for what goes in their minds. Attitudes are forming, and foundations are being built. Let's make sure they are strong and true.

Creativity is also growing in these fertile minds. We do our kids such a service to let them develop their imaginations, but we must take care to protect their pure, innocent minds.

Teaching Them First

I noticed a long time ago that when given two opposing ideas, my children tended to believe the first thing they were taught. Their first exposure to something was totally true, in their minds, and anything to the contrary was therefore questionable. For example, if we had talked about an event in history or a current event, what they were told first stuck. If Mark and I could have open conversation and present ideas to our children first, before they got a conflicting idea from the world, they would much more likely hold fast to what we had taught them.

Of course, it is important for children to have many and varied experiences. The more they have, the more places in the network of their minds to put new concepts they learn! We would never want to shut them up in our narrow environment exclusively, in order to prevent them from putting something harmful in their minds. Instead, we must try our hardest to teach them first. We can watch for new movements in society and teach our view of them before they get a possibly distorted view in school or out in the world. *We can't always choose their teacher at school, but we can be their first teacher at home!*

1. Teach Early—Five Years Early

Teaching our kids what they will need in five years is a good goal: "The world will teach our children if we do not, and children are capable of learning all the world will teach them at a very young age. What we want them to know five years from now needs to be part of our conversation with them today. Teach them in every circumstance; let every dilemma, every consequence, every trial that they may face provide an opportunity to teach them how to hold on to gospel truths."[1]

Upon hearing this, I took the advice and carefully figured out what each of my kids would need in five years. Then, during their interviews, in bedtime stories, and around the kitchen table, Mark and I would try to arm our children with what was ahead. We would use older children's examples, both in and out of the family, as well as our own past. We would explore together the long- and short-term consequences of, for example, quickly getting a job after high school versus going to college. We would even teach marriage principles, knowing our teenagers would have these challenges and opportunities in a few years.

Even the littlest kids need to be taught ahead. When you stop and count up, that means starting to teach children about high school issues at age nine or ten, about baptism at age three, and prepping them for what they may find at school starting at birth! Of course, we have to keep it simple and teach in a way they can understand, but teach the concepts early.

For example, society's current trend is to humanize our heroes, so we need to teach about them first. I have always held Christopher Columbus in high esteem. He had to have so much courage and perseverance to carry out the mission the Lord had for him, to discover the new world. I have read well-researched books that affirm his greatness and his concern for the native peoples they encountered.[2] That's why I have trouble with the accusations against him these days. In fact, one of my kids brought home a grade school worksheet that called Columbus a "pirate" more than once! It did not list any of his great accomplishments. So I have tried to teach my kids first about the greatness of this good man. If I had taught my child ahead of time that Christopher Columbus was a great man, and even referred to in the Book of Mormon, when they encountered this kind of thing at school, they would think, "I already know about this man, that he was a good man called of God." But if I let the school teach him first, then when I try to correct it, they may cling to first impressions of him being like a pirate in *Peter Pan*!

2. Be Prepared to Express

We mothers must be ready to counter worldly untruths. Our youngsters are encountering difficult questions every day. President Russell M. Nelson taught us that we must become "women who have a bedrock understanding of the doctrine of Christ and who will use that understanding to teach and help raise a sin-resistant generation. We need women who can detect deception in all of its forms. We need women who . . . express their beliefs with confidence and charity."[3]

For example, I once had a hard time when a government program was made mandatory at our neighborhood school. Mark and I spoke with the principal, who actually agreed with us but also needed the government money that went along with the program. We shared our opinion with our children at the breakfast table, before the program was instigated, and tried to explain carefully how we felt. After this, our sixth grader bravely chose to opt out of it, since he knew how we felt. It was tough on him at times, but we supported him at home and applauded his decision to leave it alone.

3. Open Conversation

It can be difficult to provide a safe place where our children can ask questions and explore ideas. I can recall family conversations at our kitchen table where various distorted ideas were brought up. I am afraid that I tended to jump on the ideas too forcefully, to "set them straight!" It would have been so much better if I had listened more calmly, and then reasoned with them about what they had brought up (which they are more likely to bring up *if* I remain calm). I can draw from conference talks and scripture to compare this new idea to the truths of the gospel. But it would be even better to teach them first—*before* they encounter these strange ideas of the world.

Of course, we are always working to teach our children the pure principles of the gospel. In fact, one mother of young children "decided to take a proactive approach to inoculating her children against the many negative influences they were being exposed to online and at school. She chooses a topic each week, often one that has generated a lot of discussion online, and she initiates meaningful discussions during the week, when her children can ask questions and she can make sure they're getting a balanced and fair perspective on the often-difficult issues. She is making her home a safe place to raise questions and have meaningful gospel instruction."[4] (See also "Bedtime Teaching" in chapter 8 and "Parent Interviews" in chapter 15.)

4. Truths

We must teach truth, so that our kids will recognize and react appropriately to untruths. One time, I visited a small country school with my cousin. In math class, the teacher taught the kids that a fraction has a denominator on the top and a numerator on the bottom. I sat there in my seat, knowing that this was wrong, since I had been taught otherwise first. *Should I speak up?* I debated in my mind. Finally, I decided that all these children in that class needed to learn it right! So I raised my hand and said, "I was taught that the numerator is on the top." The teacher laughed and switched the two, thanking me. I was so relieved to get that off my shoulders!

This math "truth" is very insignificant compared to other untruths our kids could learn at school or from playground conversation. At home, we must not only teach the truth early, but we must also encourage our kids to bring home any questions that come up in their minds. One of our prayers that our children hear from us is that they will discern the truth from the error that is taught them.

5. Attitudes

What attitudes do our kids pick up from TV or movies, commercials or political views? I once ran into an article in a magazine that ranked the happiest countries in the world. The ones they chose were those that had a government that provided everything for them. I talked about it with my kids: is that what brings happiness? Is it really best for the government to take total control of all the aspects of our lives? I had them remember Satan's plan, to force us all to choose the right, and thus take away agency and growth. It was a chance to make them aware of slants that are out there.

What slant do our kids' schoolteachers have? What attitudes do their friends teach them? We try to teach our kids to "trust no one to be your teacher nor your minister, except he be a man of God, walking in his ways and keeping his commandments" (Mosiah 23:14). It is also important for children to choose close friends who have high standards and good attitudes. Yes, they can and should reach out to all, but they should also be aware and not assimilate philosophies and attitudes that don't agree with the truths of the gospel.

6. Sexuality

Our kids could possibly pick up "the birds and the bees" information from other sources, but it's very unlikely that they would pick up a gospel perspective on the subject. That's for us to give them! If we teach them that intimacy is from God, that procreation is sacred and saved for marriage, what a gift we give them! When the world tries to cheapen and even desecrate procreation, they will know differently, having been taught first, at home. (See "The Special Talks" in chapter 8.)

7. Yes, We Teach Tolerance and Love, but Also Truth

"I worry that we live in such an atmosphere of avoiding offense that we sometimes altogether avoid teaching correct principles," Sister Bonnie Oscarson taught. "We fail to teach our young women that preparing to be a mother is of utmost importance because we don't want to offend those who aren't married or those who can't have children, or to be seen as stifling future choices. On the other hand, we may also fail to emphasize the importance of education because we don't want to send the message that it is more important than marriage. We avoid declaring that our Heavenly Father defines marriage as being between a man and woman because we don't want to offend those who experience same-sex attraction. And we may find it uncomfortable to discuss gender issues or healthy sexuality."[5]

The world will teach our children falsehoods, so let's get there first with truths. Let's make sure they learn the plan of salvation and the gospel of Jesus Christ early and first, years before they will need it. And when they learn a confusing, contrary idea, may they feel safe to bring it up and talk it over. May we stay calm and have the Spirit help us explain and lovingly correct, so that our children will be "brought up in truth" and free from deception and lies.

Dear Mom and Dad,

Thank you for talking openly with me, and for listening when I talk things out with you. I love feeling safe in our home where I first learn from you what is true.

Love, Me

Bedtime Teaching:
Books and Stories

When our kids are in bed waiting to go to sleep, we have a captive audience for some bedtime teaching! What children hear right before bed is repeated over and over in their minds while they sleep. I believe that, because my kids remembered the details of bedtime stories amazingly well—much better than I did. Let's take advantage of this and use this precious time to teach them. On nights when nobody would cooperate and get ready for bed, I learned that I could start on the story and then when everyone was into it, I'd stop and close the book. I then could insist that everyone brush their teeth or get into their pajamas before we continued. It was great motivation for getting ready for bed—they wanted to get back to the story!

Who doesn't love a story? I asked a group of kids in Sunday School class one day what they remembered from the sacrament meeting talks that day. It was the stories they heard in those talks that they remembered. Jesus taught with stories as well, with His many memorable parables. We love learning something from other people's true-life experiences and we remember their stories!

When Mark and I were drawing plans for our home, we wanted a spot for bedtime reading. So, in the hallway at the spot where three different bedrooms open up, we designated a "Book Nook." There was room for a bookcase and a rocking chair! The children could hear me sing a lullaby and then read while they were lying in bed. This way, they would calm down and be ready to go to sleep as soon as I finished reading.

I chose as my lullabies songs that not only settled the kids down, but also reinforced beliefs I wanted them to form, such as "I'm Trying to Be Like Jesus" and "I Feel My Savior's Love." One season, I decided that three songs was my signal. The kids had that much time to get ready for bed and settle things down for the story. My youngest would remind me, "Mommy, your three songs!" He was anxious for the story afterward!

There are many ways to teach at bedtime:

1. Books

I would be tired by bedtime, but if we had a fun book we were "into," my excitement would almost match my kids'! "Is our character going to be okay?" "What will happen next?"

Books are so much preferred to movies, as in a book their imaginations form just what they are old enough to conceive and mature enough to conjure up. In a movie, all the details are given them, but in a book, they make the pictures in their minds—picturing just what they can handle. Their imaginations are being developed. Besides, if a book got intense, I could shield them from too much evil or violence by skipping a little bit. Reading aloud books also does so much to help children learn to focus and thus curb attention difficulties.

We can read to our *very* little ones. Babies love the sound of Mama's or Daddy's voice. They learn so much from being read to, way before they ever understand the story! When my son was twenty-one months old, I found a sturdy board book all about trucks that he absolutely loved! I would read it to him before bed. If I asked him if he was ready for bed, he would say "No!" But if I asked if he wanted to go read his truck book, he said, "Yeah!" and would follow me into the bedroom. He sat next to me on big brother's bed while I read; then we had a song and a prayer and hopped him in his crib. As the book got very familiar, I pointed out the dog sometimes, or we pretended to eat the ice cream from the ice cream truck. Or, I had him point to the red pickup truck on each page. Sometimes I pointed at the words as I read them (to teach left to right reading). I had learned that reading the same book over and over develops vocabulary and rhythm of words. After a couple weeks of that book, I located another board book all about toys. He liked the change and loved this book too—although sometimes he wanted to read the truck book again. Then came a book about animals. Gradually, I added new books one at a time from the library or from a thrift shop. My baby got to pick which book, an old favorite or a new one. He loved to keep his stack of books at the foot of his crib.

Back at the book nook with the older kids, I could choose books that we all enjoyed together. I thought the "Little House on the Prairie" books would not really appeal to our boys, but I was wrong! They are full of adventure, so boys absolutely love them as well as girls (and grandsons as well as granddaughters)! I learned to not be afraid of reading long books, but to just try to be as consistent as possible, even if it meant only one chapter or even ten minutes a night. The children so looked forward to it and learned so much!

My toddlers usually loved it when I read them a favorite book before bed. But when I started to read a chapter book to the older kids afterward, one young son complained! It was too hard to concentrate on those long chapters. And there were no pictures! This one, *The Yearling* by Marjorie Kinnan Rawlings, was extra long! What should I do? Pick an easier book? The Spirit seemed to urge me to stick it out. It took a while, but gradually, as days went by, this son quit complaining. I would still read him the baby book first. But little by little this child could concentrate on the chapter book too! Long before the end of that book, he could understand and follow the story! I could tell by his comments that he knew what was happening, and even looked forward to what was going to happen next.

Sometimes, I had a stealthy plan! If there was a book I wanted the kids to read, I would simply start reading that book to the kids before bed, as was our usual practice. Using my most expressive voice, I got through the introduction parts and into the good stuff. Invariably, the kids would ask for more and since I left the book there in the hallway next to their bedroom doors, one or another would pick the book up and finish it off! Success!

2. Fun Stories

Stories that we tell, as well as books, can build young imaginations and bring delightful memories. I made up an interactive story about a boy and his escapades with bubble gum! The kids get to insert the people—real or imaginary—that this boy shares his bubble gum with. Mark used to lie down on the floor and tell an ongoing story about a magic Frisbee. Each one was a different adventure that Frisbee had, whether he turned into a hub cap, a garbage can lid, or even a pizza! Our kids asked for them again and again! In fact, one of our sons started telling these stories to his nieces and nephews when he babysat them, to use up the minutes and hours it took to get them to settle down! In his version, the magic Frisbee decides he doesn't like being all those things, after all. He just wants to be himself, a Frisbee, even if it means spending time sitting on the roof!

3. Situational Stories

How sad it would be if our kids had to learn everything by their own experience! We can save them lots of grief by letting them learn much through stories of others' experiences!

To illustrate, I had twin sons who had been entirely homeschooled and were about to enter the public-school system for second grade. They didn't know many of the conventions and expectations the other kids had been learning for two years. I wanted to prepare them for a good experience, so I was prompted to use bedtime stories. For weeks before school was to begin, I told a story each night that taught about raising your hand, being on time, or not cutting in line. I told about someone being asked to give their answers and how to respond to cheating. Within a story about another child, I taught them "stranger danger," bike safety, or what to do if either got into a bind.

Usually every story had a student who chose the wrong approach, and one who chose a better way and felt so much better. Or the story would have a child who tried a negative way, then tried a better one the next day. I was amazed at how many details the kids remembered later on—way after I had forgotten them! Through stories, I could help them see what they would be facing soon without lecturing head on.

Sometimes rather than make up characters, I would search my experiences to remember a situation I had heard about and turn it into a true story. I remembered one about a friend who chose to disobey and her consequences, or about a tender mercy when someone made a right choice. I love the stories in the Church magazines, which make great bedtime stories too!

4. True Stories

As my children have grown, they often ask, "Is this story true?" I love to answer, "Yes, this really happened!" I tell them true stories from my life or those I know, and we love seeing the Lord's hand in a real character's life. Since my children usually choose fantasy to read on their own, I like to bring perspective and faith by recommending or choosing biographies or true stories to read them. While fiction is good for their imaginations, true stories promote unshifting foundations of faith.

We can tell stories from the scriptures. Children love to hear about Noah and the ark, David and Goliath, or Daniel in the lions' den. There's Ammon and the king's flocks, or Samuel on the city walls. Don't leave the telling of such stories only to film, picture books, or Primary. Let our children hear them from us, along with a simple testimony. They can use their great imaginations to picture these true stories.

I like to tell my kids and grandkids some of the perhaps lesser-known Bible stories, along with the old favorites. There is the one about the boy king Josiah, Gideon and his Army who were helped by the Lord. There is Elijah and the Priests of Baal, and young Samuel who hears the Lord's Voice, and Joseph who stays true despite set-backs. All Christians have these Bible stories like we do.[6]

These things *really took place*, I emphasize. In fact, the Book of Mormon is another witness of the miracles of brazen serpent (Helaman 8:14), the parting of the Red Sea (1 Nephi 4:2), and the reality of Noah's ark (Ether 6:7). In the Pearl of Great Price, Enoch sees the ark his great-grandson Noah built, another witness (Moses 7:43). The Lord provides us a second or even third witness that something is true.

5. Family Stories

If we are blessed to have stories that our ancestors recorded, they make excellent bedtime or anytime teaching. This is our heritage, and the stories need to be told over and over, embedded in our children's hearts. Family home evenings, talks our children give, even casual conversations can include our family stories from the past.

We also have our own family stories that we are living out daily. The trick is to write them down, so that we will remember the details and can cement the concepts in our children's minds. Ours are called "The Small Plates of Ellingson," which is growing larger every year, a collection of stories that are a powerful way to teach truths.

One family story we tell and retell is when our little family all went down to the high school to shoot off a rocket. Unfortunately, we had chosen one that was too powerful for our little set up, and it shot up too high too fast, and got lost. We prayed to find it and searched and searched until it got dark. Sadly, we went home. The next day was Sunday, and though we were tempted to go look for it, we decided it was not a Sunday thing to do. That night, a big storm arose. Then, after family night on Monday, we went to look again. There it was, under a big tree. The wind from the storm the night before must have blown it down, and because of this, we wouldn't have been able to find it the day before. We counted it a great blessing for keeping the Sabbath Day holy.

President Thomas S. Monson liked to quote:

> You may have tangible wealth untold;
> Caskets of jewels and coffers of gold.
> Richer than I you can never be—
> I had a Mother who read to me.[7]

Our children may be truly rich if we fill their minds with goodness, from uplifting, thought-provoking stories and books we share with them at bedtime. But not only at bedtime! Other times we can let them see us read—even the newspaper or the novel we are reading. We can provide books from the library or purchase new or secondhand books for gifts. We can listen to audio-books on road trips to cut down the miles. We can keep good reading material in the bathrooms! Bedtime is a precious time to express love, when we give of our time to teach them as they lay down to sleep.

Dear Mom and Dad,

I love it when you read to me or tell me stories! Thanks for giving me that special time, to learn all kinds of things from you! It's not hard to go to sleep when I hear your voice reading to me.

Love, Me

Reaching Out to Others

Children are naturally selfish. "Me" this and "me" that. As they grow, how can we coax our children to think outside themselves? Parents have a chance to lift them to a higher plane of unselfishness, by helping them reach out to others. This process of loving others starts in the home, and from there to neighbors and friends, to the community and to the world. What a challenge! Once again, they learn the most from what we are, so if we show them kindly service and love for others, they will learn to live it. Consider these principles:

1. Horizontal World View

Some children seem to be born competitive. "There's one in every family!" Grandmother used to say, referring to the child who keeps score. This one knows exactly how many cookies each member of the family ate—and makes sure it's even! They are constantly comparing, and simply *have* to win whatever game the family plays.

Growing up, Mark was a very competitive young man. He told me that he played every sport and pushed himself hard to be the best. Then, after struggling with injuries and burning out some, he was simply through being so competitive. He lost that drive and started to be content with let-ting those kinds of attitudes go. Now, I catch him applauding the other team for a good pass or good skill!

Every person could evaluate their view of the people around them. One of my professors taught our class that we can either have a vertical or horizontal view of mankind. A vertical view sees every person figuratively standing on top of each other's shoulders. We are all struggling to climb higher in the upward chain, and our climbing up leaves someone else moving down beneath us. The vertical daily struggle is a competition and comparison between us and others. A horizontal view, on the other hand, puts all people side by side, holding hands and equal in posi-tion. In fact, when one person goes higher, they bring the others along with, since all are holding hands! I love this view!

The Spirit could help us teach a horizontal-type view to our children. In any confrontation, the goal should be "win-win," that both sides end up happy. Such as, "I'll play with the blocks while you play cars, then we'll switch!"

2. Helping and Sharing at Home

Daily interactions at home are a chance to start planting seeds of unselfishness and service to others. Parents have such a huge opportunity to gradually coax kids, such as suggesting, "What if we helped Sam do his chores? He would be so happy!" or "Let's surprise Daddy by picking up all the toys before he gets back. He will love seeing a nice clean family room!"

Another early lesson is learning to share, which can be tricky. Some kids are particularly apt to grab a toy and yell, "Mine!" I love it when a child chooses to share, all on their own, and I reinforce it with praise galore. "You were being so nice to share that with her! Doesn't it make you feel good inside?"

Keeping it positive will only help a child's world view. If we make them feel shame for not sharing, we have not accomplished our design—that they change their *hearts* to be more giving and outreaching. Instead of shaming, we must patiently coax and then reinforce.

I have found that it works well to let a child have their most precious belongings set aside, and these are the ones they're not required to share. For example, if a child got a new truck for his birthday that he loves dearly, he could keep that in his room and, when friends come over, not be required to share it. But if he leaves it out, then it needs to be fair game for all to play with. This way it's his choice when to share those items, and when he does, we can be so proud of him! "Wow, you shared your special truck! I'm so proud of you!" Or even better is telling others, such as, "I was so proud of Bryn for sharing her birthday doll today! She was amazing!"

3. Reaching Out Nearby

Children stay inside for much of their early years. But gradually, they venture out and meet the neighbors and make little friends. They go to church and play among the others at nursery. They notice others in the grocery store or post office. We can help our kids learn to understand about other people, and even help them. Service can start early, the younger the better.

They could start by doing service along with us. A "Relief Society baby" (whose mom has a service-related calling) could have lots of chances to observe and even take part in giving service. "Could you carry this bag of rolls?" we can ask a toddler (if it's not too big) or "I need you to hold this bowl for me" in the car (even if you could have managed it all on your own). Take kids along, and they are doing it too!

We can all watch out for our neighbor's needs. "Why don't you take that flyer off of the Johnsons' door, since they are out of town and they don't want their house to look like no one is there." Or, "I bet the garbage dumpster is hard for Mrs. Carrillo to move. Let's move hers when we do ours." Holidays are a great time to bring goodies to the neighbors. And my big boys absolutely love to doorbell ditch surprises!

4. Kind and Generous to All

In the Book of Mormon, Amulek tells us to let our hearts be "drawn out in prayer unto [the Lord] continually for your welfare, and also for the welfare of those who are around you." He goes on to counsel us to not turn away the needy and the naked, to visit the sick and afflicted and to give to those in need. And he warns that if we "do not remember to be charitable, [we] are as dross," which is the impurities thrown out by the metal refiners (Alma 34:27–29). It is important to reach out to others in charity, the pure love of Christ. It should be a priority in our teaching.

What does reaching out to a bigger circle look like? A great place to start is to visit grandparents and to serve them when they are sick. Kids can draw pictures and sing for them, send cards and letters, and help bring food. Kids can give that extra penny to the humanitarian effort—or to the bell ringers at Christmastime. They are more apt to want to share their precious coins when we explain about the people in Florida whose homes are flooded or the people in the Philippines, who had an earthquake that broke down lots of their homes and buildings. Or when we tell them about the people in our town who are going to bed without eating any dinner, and how we can help.

When we serve, we should include them whenever possible. Kids can help. Even just having them in the way is worth it, to let them be a part of service and get this kind of outreach planted in their hearts. Kids can help collect books for an Eagle project. They can help scrape gum off the high school cement with the community. There is a wonderful organization in our community that allows children to help package food for the hungry. The workers tell us to which country our food is going. They show pictures of those getting the help and give statistics. And they let the volunteers pray over the food they are sending across the world. What a life-changing experience for our kids to help this way!

5. Sharing the Gospel

Teenagers develop an outreaching attitude when they have caught the desire to share the wonderful blessing of the gospel with others. They live differently when they are motivated to teach the gospel by the way they live. A young person who is trying to be an example will take care that all his actions are doing that.

We can talk in our families about what our lives would be without the gospel and what we would not have daily. When they have internalized this, our teens will more likely want to share what we have. Gratitude moves us outside ourselves to thank God and then to want to share. For example, if a teen brings her friend to church, she is much more likely to sit still and listen, even listen from her friends' point of view. And if we have emphasized to the whole family about how important this friend's first exposure to the gospel is, they will more likely do the same.

6. Living the Golden Rule

There was a time when I was struggling to figure out how to handle a tough situation with another person. It came to me: the Golden Rule! Of course! I had been taught this as a child, and it truly was the answer to just about every dilemma. It was a yardstick, a go-to concept to cover almost any situation in figuring out the right thing to do: What should I do? Well, what I would want done to me, if the tables were turned!

However, as a mom, I quickly observed that my kids' natural response was "do to others what *they did* to you!" It took a whole lot of effort to switch that thinking to "do to others what you would *want* them to do to you." Or the Savior's way of putting it: "Therefore all things whatsoever ye would that men should do to you, do ye even so to them" (Matthew 7:12). His phrase may be a little more complex, but it involves first stopping to see another's point of view and to put yourself in their shoes—or to love them—and second following through and doing the thing that way.

"See that little boy over there?" we can point out to a young child to help him see another's point of view. "He has been waiting for a turn on the swing for a very long time. He must be tired of waiting. Remember how it feels to have to wait so long? Why don't you let him have a turn now? We'll come back later." However, even before they are able to empathize and visualize what another may think, kids can learn to apply the Golden Rule. We can help this growing process of learning to empathize. It is a chance to teach more love.

I once got to attend an interfaith banquet, where I was amazed to find out that just about *every religion* has a version of the Golden Rule! At the opening ceremony, there were six different people from six different faiths who came to the podium to give the Golden Rule as it is found in their religions. It was inspiring to learn that all these religions had their own variety of the Golden Rule, such as Buddhism, "Hurt not others in ways that you yourself would find hurtful" (Udana-Varga 5:18) and Hinduism, "This is the sum of duty: do naught unto others which would cause you pain if done to you" (Mahabharata 5:1517).[8] The Golden Rule is truly universal. Our goal is to have it come to mind whenever our children are choosing how to treat other people.

Dear Mom and Dad,

Thanks for helping me see my world as full of people like me that I can reach out to and help. When you do service with me, you help me want to be someone who does the work of the Savior.

Love, Me

The Special Talks: Correct Information and Good Attitudes about Sex

My friend did not get notice ahead of time about the growth and development presentation her daughter would be viewing at school. She found out when a secretary called her, requesting permission for her fifth grade daughter to attend that very afternoon. This mother had wanted to teach her daughter about puberty first, but she and her husband had been hesitant about how to approach this tender subject. This was their eldest child. They had studied "A Parent's Guide" and were preparing to introduce the subject at their first special talk with their daughter. Then came this call. Quickly, this mom got a babysitter for her younger kids and hurried to the school to be with her daughter for the big talk. As the class got underway, my friend noted the presenter's negative attitude about body changes. In fact, she said she would be talking about "the dreaded period." This was not the first attitude she wanted her daughter to pick up! So, this mom and her daughter quietly slipped out the back.

She took her daughter to get a smoothie and they sat down together in a private place and had their own talk. She started by telling this young girl about Heavenly Father's wonderful plan for our bodies to get ready to have babies. The attitude that she wanted to give her daughter was that our bodies are amazing! They talked over what to watch for and how her body would change, and she emphasized to her daughter to be sure to come to her with questions. She was excited for her daughter to go through this wonderful change, and her daughter was excited too. It was a sweet time together, and an important special talk.

Parents are often hesitant to talk about maturation and sex. I was wondering why it was so hard for me to talk about sex, but then I realized that in my home all of growing up, I am pretty sure I never heard or said the word *sex*. Fortunately, I had a wonderful example of loving parents to save me when my cousin gave me *misinformation* at a young age.

Many of us parents probably grew up without a lot of talk on the subject. We learned eventually and grew up okay, but the world is a different place now! "Children and youth receive so many toxic and distorted messages about sexual intimacy. The home is the ideal place to teach them. It's up to parents to teach them plainly and boldly. . . . The world emphasizes sex as just a physical experience. The gospel teaches, if in within the proper bounds of marriage, it's a unifying of the body and the spirit."[9]

So that is the attitude we want to convey! We parents need to be plain and bold. We need to set up timely and effective special talks with our kids to give them correct information and good attitudes.

1. When to Have Special Talks

"A Parent's Guide" is a fabulous tool to help us with these things. It suggests "letting the child set the pace," when they are ready. Some kids ask us questions. Others use a shocking bad word to tell us they need to know more. Still others are embarrassed and shy. We can deal matter-of-factly and sensitively in each of these cases, ideally *before* our kids find other sources.

The ideal for special talks is that we understand four different stages of growth and development and give our kids (at least) four different talks: Infants/Toddlers age 0–3 years; Children aged 4–11; Adolescents aged 12–18; and Courtship and Marriage. Of course, while arranging these special times, we also want to be open for informal conversation on these important subjects at any time.

We start with the very basics and then add more as the child is ready, "in a layered fashion."[10] Like layered clothing, teachings can be added on top of each other when the child is ready. "Parents should never drive their children, but lead them along, giving them knowledge as their minds are prepared to receive it," taught Brigham Young.[11]

Mark and I had already had a special talk with several of our children as they became ready. But one son was different. As he approached the beginning of maturation, he just didn't seem ready for the burden of these things. I watched him carefully, knowing that we wanted to be his first source of information, but I felt restrained. When it came time for the health and development presentation at school, I had always prayed about them and felt to have our children go ahead and attend them, and then come to me with any questions. In fact, most of my kids would have felt really embarrassed to be kept behind from the presentations. Not so with this son! He asked if he could please do the alternative activity. This time when I prayed, I felt good about letting him wait. I questioned this son to see if he ever was exposed to any confusing information about sex, and he quickly said, "No!" So we let a year go by before the Spirit helped Mark and I feel like he was at last ready.

2. A Good Climate for a Special Talk

"Love can free our youth to listen to those whom they know they can trust!"[12] A peaceful, secure climate where they feel love is the best. They will be more likely to respond better and develop a wholesome attitude if we come across confidently, despite any jitters we may feel.

Having open communication already set in place is a huge benefit. Kids need to report to us regularly. (See "Parent Interviews" in chapter 15). Just as the Savior constantly checked in with His Father in prayer, our kids need to talk to us about their successes, get comfort about their failures, and talk over their lives. "It is impossible to overestimate the blessings a child receives who is able to report in some manner to interested, patient, and accepting parents."[13]

Mark and I establish open communication by having monthly interviews with each of the kids at home. Each child knows he will have a monthly talk with one of us, and he even knows what questions he will be asked, as we have a typed-up sheet. In addition to asking about their behavior and obedience, we also open it up to "What's on your mind?" as well as expressing our love. With this interview time set in place, there are already talks going on, and each child is more comfortable when it is time for a special talk.

While our regular interviews are best with just one parent, ideally two unified parents are present at a special talk. For us, Mark is typically the one who is more open and comfortable explaining. My job is to reassure and watch the child's expression. I might even signal to Mark when it's time to stop for now and tell more at the next one. We make sure to tell our children that if they ever have questions, to please come to us, as others may not give them correct or moral information.

Another approach works best for our friend's family, who chooses to divide up the responsibilities for the more detailed special talks. Mom talks to the girls, who are less embarrassed talking with her about menstruation, for example, rather than Dad. He talks to the boys, who are less embarrassed talking about private parts to him than they would be if Mom were there. Their early special talks about our bodies being special and modest were comfortable with both parents there, but later, more specific talks were with one parent in their home. The Spirit helps us to know what is best for our kids.

3. The Goal

What is it we want from these talks? We want well-adjusted, secure children who are taught the truth, and therefore can enter into happy relationships. We want them to develop healthy attitudes and to be able to learn self-control and self-restraint.

Special Talk #1: Infants & Toddlers, Birth to Age 3

- Gender security comes from acceptance from both parents.
- Loving correction is needed. Do not withhold affection to correct, or they might not learn to give affection to others.
- Discovery of his or her body is natural. This requires a neutral reaction. Neither worry about it, nor encourage exploration. Remaining neutral helps a child accept these body parts as good, just like other body parts.
- Consistency is important, both in meeting the need to be clean and fed, and giving approval.

This age group's "special talk" is simply about being thankful for the wonderful body that Heavenly Father gave to us. Whichever gender they are is just right, and they should feel good about being male or female. We can teach the value of loving and being loved. Healthy habits can begin.

Special Talk #2: Children, Age 4–11

- Now is a crucial time for open parent-child communication.
- This is an interim time without massive growth or change.
- Character refinement is needed. Teach them to be clean and considerate of others. If they learn kindness now, it will help them have better intimate relations later.
- Social interaction is learned, which establishes a good foundation for later intimacy.
- Delayed gratification is important to teach.
- Acceptance from fathers is needed by boys. Identifying with mothers is important for girls. Both begin to learn roles.
- Healthy habits are a great preparation for puberty. Hygiene, self-respect, and attention to their bodies are important. Teach modesty.
- Care is needed, so they won't view the world as an ugly place! There are many good people with happy, healthy family relationships!

My girlfriend told me that she went overboard trying to teach her little boy what to watch out for when he was going to start kindergarten, which left him scared to go! Upon hearing that, I decided to couch my warnings within stories. As I told stories about what my child would face, they could then examine the issues and resolve how to handle each. I also found a wonderful, fun resource for teaching personal safety called "Safety Kids."[14]

The Special Talk for this age group is teaching sexuality "as they become ready to learn."[15] As our children grew and began to ask where babies come from, Mark and I would tell them about the "special tunnel" a mother has, where one part from the mother and one part from the father come together in a wonderful way, so a new baby can start to grow in Mommy's tummy! For us, this was a good way to describe what happens before they are ready for more accurate terms.

Later, as they were ready, we taught them more. For a concise summary of the processes of human sexuality and development of a baby in the womb, including accurate terms, see page 30 of "A Parent's Guide."

It is important for parents to teach about sexuality. Our kids cannot avoid hearing about it in today's world, and what they likely hear most often describes those in this world's abuse of the power of procreation. Accurate and morally correct information falls to us parents to teach.

Kids generally believe the first thing they are told. In fact, I have observed that by about age eleven, our kids stop believing what we teach at face value—they question it or rethink it. So now, age 4–11 is the best time to teach the truth, when the Spirit helps us know when each child is ready.

One of our sons was so grateful that we took him aside a few days before the sex education video was to be presented at school. "Dad told me how special and sacred it is to be able to conceive a new life," he told me. Then, at school, when all the other boys started laughing, he knew that that was not appropriate. "If this was so sacred to Dad, I didn't want to laugh," he said. His special talk helped him have the right attitude.

A caution: We do not need to refer to our *own* relationship as an example. It is best when you "draw a veil between the children regarding private, intimate life. This is not a veil of fear or disgust, but one by which the body and its functions are robed in modesty and honor."[16]

Special Talk #3: Adolescents, Age 12–18

- A profound change happens to their bodies.
- They have an adult appearance, but not adult experience.
- There is a great need for clear family rules, set together.
- Acceptance from moms is needed by boys, while approval from dads is needed by girls.

- Now is a great time for teenagers to learn and teach the standards from "For the Strength of Youth" to their families for family home evening.[16]
- There is enticement "to be materialist, haughty, fad conscious, and sexually self-focused." "They will be assaulted directly from all sides." So we must teach them and fortify them.[17]
- Wholesome social experiences are needed. Trust your teen whenever you can. "Do not make the mistake of distrusting them. Many adults fall into this trap because they tend to be more eager than wise."[18] Expect the best from them.
- Modesty is important. Help girls learn to help boys to have clean thoughts. Good boys who are trying hard appreciate a girl dressed modestly.

The special talk at this age is about puberty. It is an exciting time, knowing that they will be able to be a mom or dad someday! Help your teen deal with all the changes and feel like he or she is okay. We must teach that our bodies are good, not to be abused in any way. They are temples for our spirits (1 Cor. 3:16–17).

Mark would ask our kids, "Why did Heavenly Father make it so our bodies can have a baby at this time of our life, but are not supposed to yet?" He then helps them see one answer: This is the time of life for both boys and girls to learn to *control* their bodies' sexual abilities.

"Masturbation is considered by many in the world to be the harmless expression of an instinctive sex drive. Teach your children that the prophets have condemned it as a sin throughout the ages and that they can choose not to do it. . . . Masturbation is not physically necessary. There is already a way the body takes care of excess fluid.[19]

Teach total morality. Virtuous behavior leads to self-esteem, peaceful feelings, and a knowledge of what's right; carnal behavior leads to misery, unhappiness, and loss of the desire to do right.

Adolescence can actually be a time for growth of spiritual power. Teens can learn to rely on the Spirit to help guide them into a pure and happy life, filled with peace and understanding.

"Parents often give far too much negative counsel to their teenagers. While it is true that you must solemnly warn your teenagers against all types of sin, you should place more emphasis upon the goodness of growing up. Teach your children that it is good to mature, and that adolescence can be filled with beauty and power. Praise them for their spiritual development and maturity. Teach them also of Jesus, Joseph who was sold into Egypt, Moroni, Joseph Smith, and others who were teenagers when they began their ministries. These great leaders developed the foundations of their spiritual strength during their teenage years, and your teenagers can do the same."[20]

"Help us to keep the Spirit in our homes and with us, and to do nothing to offend it" is a phrase I like to use in family prayer. It is a good reminder to give our teens as we send them off into the world and all they are exposed to. "Our body is a temple" (1 Corinthians 6:19) is another foundational teaching.

Keep them busy serving others and being missionary-minded. Consider this powerful statement: "When youthful boys and girls are given family, church, and civic service opportunities, they readily develop a sense of responsibility. This vital process has far more to do with developing sexual virtue than does sex education."[21]

Special Talk #4: Mature, Courtship & Marriage

- The journey is theirs. We can provide tools to help the couple, while not being too invasive.
- A premarital exam may help facilitate a choice experience.
- A book that spells out details may help the couple, such as *Between Husband and Wife* by Lamb & Brinley or *And They Were Not Ashamed* by Brotherson.

While my daughter was excited to be engaged, she and her fiancé wisely decided that their focus during the engagement would be on the temple. She was soon to be going through the temple for the first time, so she and he read together the temple preparation manual and attended the class. It wasn't until after that experience, just days before the wedding, that they finally allowed themselves to read and talk about their upcoming wedding night experience, and about each other's expectations. They felt that any earlier would just increase their curiosity too early and take away from the temple experience. They knew that their experience would be a journey for the two of them to work out together. Mark and I were watchful and grateful that they set their own wise time line.

This special talk can be full of reassurance and practical advice. Accountability is often a help to the engaged couple. Mark asked our daughter and fiancé, "How can I help you at this important time?" Their reply was, "Have us check in with you once a week. Every Monday night, we'll report on being appropriate in our relationship all week." Knowing they were going to report helped keep them from danger and temptation.

Have the courage to talk to your kids about important special things and growing up. Provide the first information they receive on sex, information that is accurate and moral, as soon as they are ready. Help them prepare for a happy, fulfilled life ahead!

Tools to Use

- "Family Conversations": www.mormonchannel.org/watch/collection/family-conversations -talking-about-healthy-sexuality
- *A Parent's Guide*: www.lds.org/manual/a-parents-guide
- Family home evening lessons to help parents teach about sacred and sensitive topics. Includes "My body is from God," "The Spirit can help me choose good media," "What should I do if I see pornography?" and "The Savior desires to forgive and heal the wounds of pornography?": overcomingpornography.org
- *For the Strength of Youth*: www.lds.org/youth/for-the-strength-of-youth

Dear Mom and Dad,

I feel so big when you take me aside for my own special talk! Thanks for walking me through such important messages to help me have a wholesome view of all the stages of my growth!

Love, Me

Chapter 9
Set Boundaries Confidently

*I*t's not usually the popular thing to set limits. But parents can do so confidently, knowing that kids really do need them, and even want them. "You can blame me for it!" I tell my kids, after counseling with them, for example, about what time would be best to come home that night. "Tell me I have to do my homework now!" a daughter would ask, knowing that it's hard to just do what needed to be done by self-motivation alone. Sometimes, a parent's direction or even commandment is needed and wanted. Limits and boundaries let them know we care, and we want them safe and happy.

Wise Limits: A Turtle Adventure

I had an experience that taught me all about setting protective yet loving boundaries for our children. Interestingly, it involved our pet turtles!

One Christmas, two of our sons received small desert turtles they named "Crush" and "Speed." Originally, both turtles lived in an aquarium on top of our bookshelf. They had plenty of lettuce and each other for company, so they should have been fine. But after some time went by, my high school son told me he was worried since the turtles didn't seem to be growing. Surely, they needed more sunlight. So we decided turn them loose in the planter outside, to see if more sun helped them to thrive.

We set them free below a large tree in a planter to the west of our house and watched what they would do. Crush stayed put! He would burrow down in the leaves, but he kept to that spot! Speed, on the other hand, immediately took off! In fact, we lost track of him! The row of spiky aloe vera next to the tree had been no setback for his taking off! Crush could always be located somewhere near his spot, but we didn't ever know where Speed was!

Then one day, as I was headed over the berm and past the curb to the next-door neighbor's, I happened to look down. There at our feet was a turtle! Speed was found! We both marveled at how little Speed could have come that far over or around the brick wall barriers. When I put Speed back under the tree with Crush, he didn't pause for a second, but took off again immediately.

Several days later, Mark found Speed in the driveway. Fearful of running over the little turtle, he took our pet to the backyard. Once again, he got lost. A couple of days later, however, we realized that irrigation would prove a possibly deadly consequence for this new location. We offered the grandchildren a surprise if they could find Speed. Several days went by, and irrigation would be coming before long, so I offered a prayer, asking that we find Speed to save her from drowning. Shortly thereafter, our dog was barking intensely and clawing at something. Mark went to check it out and found Speed! When Mark picked up the turtle, we were both horrified at its appearance! Speed looked mauled. He was so tucked in his shell we wondered if he was even alive.

I then got the notion to block off the brick planter in the front yard west of our home where we had left them before, with a long piece of wood, right where the bricks step down. Big rocks held the wood in place. It was here under a rosebush that we placed Speed. For the next several days, I searched, hoping to see the little turtle. I heard a rustling sound once, but there was no sign of the turtle. I guessed that if he were alive, he was so unusually sedentary due to recuperating from the bad shock. Days went by with no sign of Speed.

Worried, I turned again to prayer. "Please let me just see this turtle again," I asked. "I just want to see if Speed is okay after the dog incident." That very day, I walked up to the bush and there was Speed in full view, with all appendages complete and working fine! There was his full head and eyes peering at me. The next time I went out, Speed was in full view again, only from under a different bush! I was so grateful. The encounter assured me that Speed was alive and could move. I guessed that he would be more cautious than before but was grateful that there was still some room outdoors to roam a bit! What a loving Father in Heaven we have, who not only cares for creatures but also allows those of us who care about them to have reassurances when we need them!

Our other turtle, Crush, has started to roam a little from his spot under the tree where he had stayed before. He has left the tree to explore the bushes. He started growing—in fact, now he is quite a bit bigger than Speed. Both turtles are happy in their yard, secure in their boundaries.

I learned quite a bit from this adventure, not just about turtles, but about parenting too:

1. Too tight of boundaries, such as the turtles' aquarium, may provide for needs to be met, but does not allow for growth. Our children need a little room to explore and to discover things. When we take the toddler out to experience the grass or sand or an airplane in the sky, we are allowing new networks to grow in their brains and new vocabulary to develop. They are getting a taste of nature, and may even meet other children who may be at the park that day too.

2. Not having any boundaries brings danger, severe consequences, and trauma. We do not do our children any service by having no boundaries. Toddlers, children, and teenagers need limits set to protect their safety and to communicate our love.

3. Boundaries with just the right amount of room provide security and safety along with adventure and growth. We cannot keep our children by our sides forever, and they must gradually learn to navigate the world around them. Wise boundaries and limits allow for this gradual growth, while still bringing security and protection. Wise curfews, for example, can allow our kids to get with friends but return at a set time. When we counsel together about the limits, we hear their input but also let them know we want to lovingly protect them.

One of our older daughters had a curfew that was a little earlier than most of her friends, we found out. We were adamant that she be home by that time. But since she didn't drive yet, parents took the kids home, and the driver often became put out with her for insisting she be dropped off first—even if it was out of the way. We should have listened carefully to her dilemma and done better at relaxing our curfew a little to accommodate this problem!

4. Heavenly Father always knows just where His creations are, even the sparrows and the turtles! If His creatures are that important to Him, how infinitely more are His children worth. We can teach our children that He is always watching over them, and He expects us to obey so that we will be safe.

To illustrate, I used to tell my young kids the story of a caterpillar who lived underground. When his mommy left to go to the store, she told him to be sure to stay in the hole where they lived, so he would be safe. The family rule was that he could only come up from the hole with his mom or dad when it was dark, so no birds could see them. But he was curious about what was above ground, so he climbed out of the hole. But a bird hovered nearby. Suddenly, the bird flew down and bit off his tail! (I would yank off the last two puff balls that were Velcroed to the puff ball caterpillar!) Oh no! The caterpillar quickly climbed back in his hole and wished he had obeyed his mother! His tail grew back, but he learned to obey so he would be safe.

There is a promise of safety that goes with the commandment to "honor thy father and thy mother that they days may be long upon the land" (Exodus 20:6). God blesses children with parents, so we will live long, safe lives if we obey them.

5. He will answer prayers about how to connect with our loved ones. I was amazed at how Father in Heaven allowed me to see my recovering pet! I grew in my love for Him because He cared about my concerns. If we pray for it and obey the promptings He sends, I feel certain that we will be blessed to be able to connect with those we love.

6. Each child has his or her own timing. Given the right amount of freedom, each will blossom and be ready to explore at the right time for him or her. Some children are cautious like Crush and need to get used to their surroundings before they are ready to venture out. Others have an intense need like Speed to take off and explore. We should study each of our children's needs. God will send promptings from the Holy Ghost that will help us figure out how to provide optimal growth for each child, while keeping them safe with wise boundaries.

Dear Mom and Dad,

I am glad that you love me enough to protect me from danger, while still letting me venture out into the world to experience it. Thanks for figuring out just the right balance when you set my boundaries.

Love, Me

Managing Cell Phones;
Limiting TV and Electronics

I was really frustrated with cell phones at one point! "Let's throw them all out!" I determined. They are so dangerous! In fact, they can lead to pornography, and Sister Linda Reeves taught, "Pornography is more vile, evil, and graphic than ever before. . . . Parents, are we aware that mobile devices with Internet capacity, not computers, are the biggest culprit?" But then she went on, "As we counsel with our children, together we can create a family plan with standards and boundaries, being proactive to protect our homes with filters on electronic devices."[1]

As I cooled down, I started to realize, here is a great opportunity for our kids to learn self-discipline! If Mark and I set careful limits and boundaries, our kids will be protected. We needed to be wise and confident in helping them manage these tools. And someday, in heaven, we all will have far more important things to manage. So now we can learn to discipline ourselves, in preparation for then! We all need to learn to manage cell phones, TV, and the internet.

Cell Phones and Mobile Devices

One day my friend came over and told me that she was getting her thirteen-year-son, her oldest son, a cell phone as a gift. "I wasn't going to get him a cell phone yet," she said, "but it's all he wants! How can I keep him safe and wisely monitor his cell phone use?"

1. Limits

Her family already had a policy of only using the internet in the family room where others were around, and I urged her to keep that policy with phones too. She said that they planned to disable the cell phone's internet completely. That is wise for one so young. Stake President Montague warned parents, "Why would we give something to a child that adults struggle so much with!" referring to the pornography that is so accessible there.

I told her about our family's charging station in the hallway, where everyone is expected to plug in their phones by 9:30 p.m. on a school night, later on weekends. I told her about our monthly interviews with our kids where we ask them "How do you feel about your electronic usage?" "When is the last time you saw something inappropriate on it and what did you immediately do?" and "Are you trying to live a transparent life?" (See "Parent Interviews" in chapter 15.)

2. Conversation Instead

My friend and her husband might consider talking to him about when to put the phone away and choose face-to-face communication instead. Certainly, during church would be one of those times, or when company comes to visit. Our tongue-in-cheek rule is that cell phones at the dinner table have to go in the oven! It's a humorous way to ensure we have conversation without cell phone usage when we eat. Thankfully, our kids do not bring their phones to the table now!

We have taught them that they would need to be good at face-to-face interaction with people throughout their lives and especially on their missions. We know that too much screen time will isolate them, dull their minds, and ruin their concentration.[2] Putting away phones makes good conversation much more possible. When we teach them the whys, our kids are much more apt to listen and follow good counsel.

3. Leverage

This friend told me that she felt this phone would give her husband and her something to take away from her son, if ever he misbehaved. I would urge her to set parameters together with her son and to be careful about random or angrily snatching it away. Taking away a phone for an infraction totally unconnected to phone usage may not make sense and bring resentment or a power struggle.

My daughter pointed out that having a cell phone is a privilege. Just like driving the family car is a privilege. A child isn't entitled to a phone; the privilege is earned. If they don't comply with family rules or expectations, then a natural consequence would be not having that privilege. A good approach might be letting the child choose the privilege earned. Do that ahead of time and then taking the phone away isn't ever random. The child understands why the phone was taken away for not doing their chores, because they chose that as a privilege they would earn if they did do their chores. If the child has helped with parameters, then there will never be a power struggle.

We want our kids to feel like we are helping them grow in their self-discipline, as we all have to do. Matter-of-factly saying, "I'm sorry, I guess I'm going to have to take your phone away for a couple of days to help you remember to keep our rules, because your safety is so important to us" might be a good approach, and then later, "I'm going to give this phone back to you, because I know I can trust you to do your best to manage it well."

Another great idea that a friend recommended for having more control and leverage over a new cell phone user was the idea of letting a child *borrow* a phone for a while. Rather than give a cell phone as a birthday or Christmas gift, instead the parents buy a phone and then allow the son or daughter to borrow it! This way they can set the rules and have better watchful control. This friend was adamant that phones as gifts can end up as a nightmare, so a borrowed one is a good idea, especially for a starter phone.

4. Setting Their Own Limits

Our young teenager had recently acquired a cell phone, though at that time, the phone was only used as an iPod (until an older brother left on a mission in a year and freed up a spot on our family plan). Mark and I told this teen, "We think you are old enough to make wise choices now, at fourteen. We're going to trust you with this." Mark did set up locks, filters, and parental controls on it, but occasionally I still worried about improper use of the device. For example, our family had a firm rule about only using the internet in the family room, but I would sometimes catch this teen using it in bed. At first, after several infractions, I felt like taking away the phone! I knew the dangers of the internet! But the Spirit guided me to persevere.

I talked it over with Mark and we decided to ask this teenager to spell out their own "Cell Phone Guidelines." I challenged this teen to write down a plan, and include what time they would finish for the day, where they would place the phone, etc. Listed was "9:30 p.m. phone is placed in charging station; Can be used for running early, but cannot then be used before morning routine and goals; All internet in Family Room: Won't be secretive," and so on. Both Mark and I read it over, then taped the signed list up in an inconspicuous but readily available place (behind the door of the hall closet).

A week or so went by, and I kept a watchful eye to see if the phone was in the charging station at night, etc. Once, this teen thought it would be okay to take a phone to the basement when the cousins had a sleepover there. So, I urged them to add to the list that exceptions needed to be okayed by Mom or Dad first. Things were going fine, until one day I saw this teenager playing a game on their cell phone. I reminded them that games were only allowed on Fridays, and that this applied to phones too. I asked that the consequence for slipping up be added to the list, that Friday game time would be lost if the rule was broken. It was effective to have the list be theirs, and to calmly suggest they revise it if necessary.

Though Mark and I continued to check up on cell phone usage covertly all the time, we had our teenager report overtly every week for a while and give us regular accounting at monthly interviews we already had in place. While giving our teen charge of their own phone, our goal was to give the message that this was important and that they must report on how well they were mastering the phone, rather than let it master them.

If we decide to give a cell phone as a gift, like my friend, we must do so with controls in place and a sharp eye. It would be well to have a message along with it that, "Dad and I feel that you are growing more and more responsible, and we feel like you are old enough to take care of a cell phone and to follow the family rules. We want to be able to trust you to use self-control with your phone!"

TV and Movies

1. Limit Them

My children used to habitually come home from school and turn the TV on first thing, after dropping backpacks in the family room. It was a struggle to change this routine. I even found myself thinking, "Oh well, it won't hurt for today. I have things I need to do, and this keeps them occupied. Maybe just one show." So first, I had to change my attitude. When my resolve to change and enforce limits was firm, I announced to my kids that TV day was Friday, when school was out for the week—only Friday. I explained to them that there were so many other things they could and should be doing in the afternoons and rehearsed to them the prophets' counsel to limit TV.

Even this did not work well until I did one more step. Helped by a prompting from the Spirit, I announced that if anyone came in and turned on the TV during the week, the whole family would lose their Friday TV watching. I had to enforce this only a couple of times. After no one watched that week, they started to quickly remind each other if someone forgot during the week! Gradually they developed some self-control!

I love it. Now, when someone turns the TV on during the week, all I have to say is, "Is this going to be your Friday?" "No!" they will answer and turn it off quickly. (They know that if they watch now, it will just be a short time, but on Friday a longer stretch is allowed.) Or, even better, a sibling will do the reminding: "Turn it off so we won't lose our Friday!" Actually, TV watching has gone way down, even on Fridays! We just have gradually grown out of the habit! Fridays have instead become a family movie night that we all enjoy together.

We must not hesitate to turn off something inappropriate—quickly. In fact, often we like to designate a "commercial police" to have a remote ready that lets them quickly turn off any commercials that show something we don't want in our home or in our minds.

2. Choose Shows and Movies Wisely

I teach my children not to surf channels. I tell them it's like saying, "Satan, come on in!" when they do that, since he can come into our home through inappropriate things they will find! Our family tries to plan what we will watch. When a certain series comes on, our favorite thing to do is to record the show. Then, we can choose when to play it, and every commercial can be fast-forwarded. This way we stop wasting a lot less time viewing what we really didn't want to see. Our system for the Olympics is to record the evenings events, then watch them at five the next evening, after an early dinner, so we could record that night's events at seven. We can watch them quite quickly by fast forwarding through the commercials and anything we don't have interest in. This particularly works well for Winter Olympics, since they come on during school days, so at seven, everyone can do their homework and duties, knowing they will see that night's figure skating or half pike the next night at five.

Plan movies too. I like to sit my children down for a movie when things get hectic. But I realized that even if a movie is good and teaches a good moral, it may not be the best thing to show to a child often. Most shows fill most of the movie with the conflict and the negative, with a very small section of the movie that is happy and positive. I try to make sure the movies we choose are "of good report," by asking trusted friends who share our standards or checking the movie out on a website. I plan to show a movie to my kids once, then talk about it thoroughly with them. We all talk about what we like and don't like. (Mark likes to comment on the acting.) We talk about what the characters learned and how they resolved the problem. Most of our focus is on the good results at the end of the movie.

I try to be extra careful that any movie we *own* is something that we really do want our kids to memorize, for we know that they take the lines they hear into their vocabulary. They will hear it over and over! But even more important, it will become a part of them.

> They learn the most from what we are.

What about at a friend's house? Whenever possible, we can check out what movie they will be seeing ahead. One of my daughters found herself at a friend's house with a questionable movie playing. She quietly went to another room to visit with other friends instead. A son wasn't afraid to speak up and let his friends know he couldn't watch PG-13 movies. Others may not have had the courage to speak up, but it worked well for him. His friends were good to pick movies he could watch too, or at least warn him ahead if not.

3. Consider Having Only One TV

Back in our college days, Mark and I were invited into the home of a favorite college professor. When we walked into a nicely furnished living room and then family room, we admired the homey feeling. We both noticed that there was no TV. There were bookcases, but nowhere could we see a television. After searching around a minute, we found a closed cupboard that must have contained the family TV, but it was not the focal point of the room. We determined then that in our future home, we too would have the TV be behind cupboard doors or at least not as a distraction to conversation in our own family room.

We realized that one TV was all our family should have, for it was impossible to properly supervise TVs that were in back bedrooms or the basement. We kept both the TV and the computer in a place near a traffic area of the house, where monitoring could be constant. We also set up a firm rule that kids could watch YouTube only when an adult was in the room. What our children see on a screen is important enough to always be visible to us.

It has been tempting to have another TV. In fact, at one point we were given a large screen TV for our basement! It was hard to turn it down and pass it on. I didn't want the pressure of having to police the basement nor the worry that anyone might be sneaking down to watch something. I liked being in the kitchen yet still able to see exactly what my family had on. Studies show that pornography addiction starts most often from something a child has seen early in their life.[3] We parents must be vigilant to know what our children are watching.

The Internet and Screen Time

1. Electronic Games

My friend who approached me about the cell phone gift told me that they planned to disable any games on her son's phone. Her family only did computer or electronic games on weekends, she told me, and they wanted to stick by those rules already in place. So they opted not to allow games at all on a phone. She would have to check his phone occasionally to see if he had added some himself, to keep this rule in place.

Here is a chance to teach exact obedience. One of our sons especially would rationalize more time than the family limit to play his game, or just not set the timer. But then we had a discussion about exact obedience, like that required on a mission. Obedience to all the many rules of the mission brings the missionary many blessings, and conversely, since missionaries need so many blessings (protection, the Spirit to help them teach, direction to those who are seeking), they receive them through their obedience. This son gradually learned to practice the exact obedience he would need later by being more careful to follow family guidelines exactly now.

Here again, we must be even more careful when our kids are very young. In fact, babies under eighteen months old should not have screen time at all. They cannot easily process what they see, and it can bring bad dreams. Plus the constant changing of the picture on the screen is one factor leading to attention deficit disorders, as shown below. Research shows that during this time of their lives, around eighteen months old, their ears are extra in tune to language development.[4] So for this season, it would be better for them to listen to the best of language, even scripture language, rather than put downs or sarcasm or crudeness that is often found on TV or movies.

2. Replace Screen Time

It is so tempting to let a screen "babysit" our children for a while or help them kill time. But really, there are other good things to do on a screen than just entertainment. There are books to read, puzzles to challenge minds, email communication. There is good music and teachings on Church websites such as lds.org, friend.lds.org, and youth.lds.org. One of the best things we can do online is family history or indexing. Kids can love the challenge and the joy of finding their ancestors and sharing with them the gospel ordinances. And even these good things should be limited in favor of being outside using large motor skills and inside using their imaginations.

3. Attention Problems

My daughters are so good at keeping the baby away from the screen! They wait to put on a movie until the baby is napping or in the other room. That is difficult to stick to—so it really helps to know the why behind it. Along with babies under eighteen months, screen time can negatively affect older children too.

Screen time from TV or video games is hard on a child's attention skills since it changes the scene so quickly. The child does not have the chance to focus on one picture for a sustained time but must refocus constantly, which is detrimental to developing attention skills.

The American Academy of Pediatrics says children younger than two should watch very little TV. The academy also says that after they turn two, they should watch no more than one to two hours a day. Instead, to increase attention skills, we can read to them or do puzzles and play games together. Showing lots of affection can help a child calm down and direct his attention.[5] Waiting at the doctor's office, little toys or books are preferable to screens for distraction.

"The kind of concentration that children bring to video games and television is not the kind they need to thrive in school or elsewhere in real life," according to Dr. Christopher Lucas, associate professor of child psychiatry at New York University School of Medicine. "It's not sustained attention in the absence of rewards," he said. "It's sustained attention with frequent intermittent rewards."[6]

Some studies have found that children who spend more time in front of the screen are more likely to develop attention problems. In a 2010 study in the journal *Pediatrics*, viewing more television and playing more video games were associated with subsequent attention problems in both schoolchildren and college undergraduates.[7]

The stimulation that video games provide "is really about the pacing, how fast the scene changes per minute," said Dr. Dimitri Christakis, a pediatrician at the University of Washington School of Medicine who studies children and media. If a child's brain gets habituated to that pace and to the extreme alertness needed to keep responding and winning, he said, the child ultimately may "find the realities of the world underwhelming, understimulating."[8]

Mark likes to tell our kids that they have such good brains, and that too much entertainment will make these brains lazy. In a movie, for example, everything is given them, rather than requiring them to put any effort into reading, picturing something, or figuring something out themselves.

May we all take care to wisely use these electronics that we have at our fingertips in good ways, and for developing self-control. May we be able to say of our kids "they are young, and their minds are firm" like Ammon's stripling warriors (Alma 57:27).

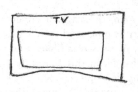

Dear Mom and Dad,

Even though I complain, I am really glad you care enough about me to limit my electronics and media. I am glad you don't let me waste my time or make my brain grow lazy from too much entertainment. Thanks for that.

Love, Me

Confident Parenting

One year, our son wanted to try freshman football at our high school. Practice was every day at 5:45 a.m., and they stayed on campus for breakfast and getting ready for school. I was anxious about the whole thing, as he would miss family scripture time every day—he wouldn't be fortified for the day! Not only that, but I had also heard about locker room talk, that it was less than uplifting! I prayed and then came up with a plan. I would wake early and read scriptures with him at 5:00 a.m., while he ate breakfast. I volunteered to drive the early carpool, and on the way, we would sing a hymn (with the hopes that the words would stick in his mind throughout the day).

Boy was it intimidating to sing with three sleepy football buddies in my car! It took confidence each day to have them take turns picking out a hymn. It takes confidence to be parents today! Our kids are so intelligent and bright! We have to be extra sharp. In fact, a clergyman told me that he has seen many parents who are scared of their kids! How can we grow in confidence as a parent?

We know that our children are really our spirit brothers and sisters. We are just called to come first and thus have stewardship over these amazing spirits. Even still, we can be confident in knowing that the family is the most important social unit in time and in eternity.[9] God has established families to bring happiness to his children, allowing them to learn correct principles in a loving atmosphere, and even to prepare them for eternal life. We are charged with carrying out this huge assignment of being the parents! But knowing these foundational truths will give us confidence in our roles as parents.

A child who understands that his parents are on his side and that they do what they do out of real love and concern for him, will much more likely be okay with the parameters we set and the teachings we teach. In fact, Joseph F. Smith teaches, "If you can only convince your children that you love them, that your soul goes out to them for their good, that you are their truest friend, they, in turn, will place confidence in you and will love you and seek to do your bidding and to carry out your wishes with your love. But if you are selfish, unkindly to them, and if they are not confident that they have your entire affection, they will be selfish, and will not care whether they please you or carry out your wishes or not, and the result will be that they will grow wayward, thoughtless and careless."[10] The answer is more love. There are many areas where we can grow to be confident:

1. Confident Enough to Set Rules and Limits

Ideally, our families set rules together. When the kids were little, we put the family rules to song, to get them into their head.

As they have grown, we have set limits and rules together in a family council. When a new dilemma comes up, Mark and I get together ahead of time to make sure we are on the same page. Then in a family council, we present the dilemma to everyone and discuss the need for limits. We try to help the kids see all sides of the issue, to listen to their point of view, and to reason with them, as well as express love and concern. We let them help make decisions, and help the family come to a consensus. Occasionally, there might be an exception to the family policy, but we call it an exception and it is rare. (See "Family Councils" in chapter 12.)

2. Confident Enough to Have Conversation

A wonderful place to share conversation is at the dinner table. It takes effort and sacrifice to get the family together to eat, but it is worth the effort. We can lead out by speaking up and then encourage them to also share tender mercies of that day, missionary opportunities, something embarrassing that happened, or a new joke! A victory or a challenge can be talked over. Current events can be discussed. This is where we exemplify our daily gospel living. If our kids feel like we will listen and empathize, praise and encourage, they will more likely open up in conversation.

Another way to have conversation is to have one-on-one interviews between parent and child. Here is where we tune in to specific needs of each child. Our hope is that the lines of communication remain opened. We can be confident in our asking questions, and they will grow confident that we understand them. Here we can express praise, and our belief in them. (See "Parent Interviews" in chapter 15.)

When we found that data had been added to our family plan for cell phones, we were suddenly in need of some concrete limits on cell phone usage. Although we had discussed *computer* boundaries, such as using the internet only in the family room, we now had to talk about when and where we could use internet on their cell phones. We decided together to add a filter to phones and we asked the kids to also only use the internet on their phones in the family room. We set limits on playing mobile games, and what time to stop texting. We added more to our list of interview questions, to ask about their screen time, especially on their phones. Of course, we explained the need for their protection and our concern for them.

Family home evening is a great place to confidently teach and discuss with our children. The wonderful thing about FHE is that no one is singled out for reprimand or correction. All of us are trying to live the gospel better. We all take turns teaching one another. (And everyone gets treats for just being a member of this family!)

"If you have any doubt about the virtue of family home evening," said President Gordon B. Hinckley, "Try it. Gather your children about you, teach them, bear testimony to them, read the scriptures together and have a good time together."[11] Here's why it is so important: "The study of the doctrines of the gospel will improve behavior quicker than a study of behavior will improve behavior."[12] With the confidence that teaching them the doctrines of the Savior will improve behavior, we can insist that nothing be more important than our regular family night. Our conversation about the gospel will grow, and so will young testimonies.

3. Confident Enough to Require Work

Our teenagers these days are busy! But it's okay to still require chores around the house and yard, scaled down if necessary to fit their busy schedules. We learned to require that if they ever couldn't do their chore, they were expected to arrange for someone to do it for them.

Teenagers feel good about paying their own way whenever possible. The things they pay for will mean so much more if they earn them. So we encourage that besides their chores, they also work for pay, such as yard work, irrigation, and a vacation service for neighbors—flexible work that they can fit in.

When our daughter was part of an expensive dance company, we had her help pay for it. She assisted a teacher in a younger class on Friday afternoons. I cleaned the studio for part of the cost, and she also helped with that whenever she could. I was confident enough to require this help, since I knew that because she had so much invested in it, she had to love it to continue. And she did love her dance classes and worked all the harder because she had helped earn them.

The home is the best place to learn to work, especially as we work beside them. Also, in the home is where individuals learn to someday provide the food, clothing, shelter, and other necessities they need. They learn self-reliance. They learn life skills. They learn so much from work—right along with learning about the gospel. (See "The Blessing of Family Work" in chapter 14.)

4. Confidence Because We Pray

I don't know how anyone can be a parent without the help of the Spirit! We gain confidence through prayer and the promptings that we receive from the Holy Ghost after asking in prayer for them! "We have boldness and access with confidence by the faith of him . . . of whom the whole family in heaven and earth is named" (Ephesians 3:12, 15).

If one of our children is struggling, Mark and I take his or her name to the temple, where we pray for how to help him or her. Sometimes our prayer is just to be able to love this child! It is a wonderful place to receive answers directly about that child. Then we can say, confidently, "I was praying about you, and these are the answers I got." Then, armed with our promptings, we give them evidence that we truly love them.

My son and his sleepy football buddies were less than excited to sing on the way to practice. But I could be confident because I felt this plan was a prompting from heaven. Also, I could proceed because I had explained my concerns and love for them. Since then, this son has thanked me for that season of sacrifice for him.

5. Confidence Because We Partner with God

Like Abraham of old, we have made a covenant with God, that He would be our God and that we would be His people. Let us claim every blessing of this covenant, even the blessing of prosperous, happy, secure families! We are promised that through obedience He will prosper us—this includes prospering us in our family relationships.

What if in our parenting, we mess up? Sometimes we totally blow it! Actually, this is wonderful! Being confident does not mean we don't own up to our mistakes. This is a chance to teach the Atonement of Jesus Christ—that because of the Savior, we can all try over and over again.

Isn't the Atonement wonderful? We can repent and show our children repentance. And truly, our children learn the most from what we are. Repentance and change are the essence of the gospel of Christ. Today we can start a path of partnership with God, trusting Him. Today we can begin to prosper in our families. Because of Christ, we can move forward with confidence, knowing that today is the first day of the rest of our lives!

Dear Mom and Dad,

I love it when you are confident. You are good parents, and I need you to confidently lead me and teach me and help me navigate through this life. Thanks for that.

Love, Me

Chapter 10
Discipline the Lord's Way

How does Father do it? I often ask myself in my parenting. We are blessed to have records of how God deals with man through the ages, as well as our own experience of His love and mercy. He uses eternal principles of giving commandment, showing mercy, and always loving us. May we examine His ways and use them in our homes.

Disciple Discipline

Loving a child is disciplining them. "Direction and discipline are . . . an indispensable part of child rearing. If parents do not discipline their children, then the public will discipline them in a way the parents do not like. Without discipline, children will not respect either the rules of the home or of society."[1]

When we have to discipline our children, what is it we really want to accomplish? Do we want to show them who's boss or demand their obedience and respect? I would submit that what we really want is to *teach them*. It makes sense to want to leave our children changed, rather than just subdued. This kind of discipline requires the absence of pride. It requires us to be true *disciples*.

A child's learning is the key. To illustrate, my son's math teacher recently told parents about his refreshing approach to wrong answers on a test. "My students can redo assignments and retake tests as often as they want," he told us, "since my goal is simply that they *learn the material*." Of course the goal in school is that the students learn. The object is not so much that they prove their deference to the teacher as much as it is to simply learn the material. While it is good and right to respect authority, they learn more when they understand the teacher rather than just acknowledge his expertise in that area. How great for us parents too, to have it our goal that our kids learn the principle we teach, no matter how many times they need to get it right. It takes a patient disciple as a parent to best facilitate this kind of learning.

The Lord Himself has outlined to us His pattern for discipline. He spelled it out through prophets, especially in Doctrine and Covenants 121. My neighbor calls this "The Lord's Law of Discipline." I like to think of it as "Disciple Discipline."

In Doctrine and Covenants 121:41–44 we read:

> No power or influence can or ought to be maintained by virtue of the priesthood, only by persuasion, by long-suffering, by gentleness and meekness, and by love unfeigned; By kindness and pure knowledge, which shall greatly enlarge thy soul without hypocrisy, and without guile—
>
> Reproving betimes with sharpness, when moved upon by the Holy Ghost; and then showing forth afterwards an increase of love toward him whom thou hast reproved, lest he esteem thee to be his enemy;
>
> That he may know that thy faithfulness is stronger than the cords of death.

We can apply this counsel, step by step:

1. We Must Be like Christ, Disciplining "by Persuasion, by Long-suffering, by Gentleness and Meekness" (v. 41)

A loving Master would never "pull rank" or use His authority or priesthood to power another into doing right. "We cannot force people into doing things, but we may love them into doing what is right, and into righteousness."[2]

How would Jesus correct little children? I picture Him with a child on His knee, stroking their hair, telling the child just the right story to show how important the right way is. He would gently persuade, with utmost patience and kindness. The child would be left wanting to do what's right, in order to be happy. There would have been absolutely no harm to their self-esteem in the process, and they would have ended up determined to try harder to be better.

We parents know all about long-suffering! How about being asked the same question fifteen times, or even living through a child's two-year-old phase? Parenthood is certainly training in patience and endurance, but the process is also a workshop for becoming Christlike.

A disciple follows willingly his master, loves him, and wants to be like him. As we discipline like a disciple of Christ would do, our children will more likely respond. The more we are like Jesus, the more they will want to be like us. Their respect for us grows as they watch us be obedient, kind, and forgiving, and Christlike in our sacrifice for them and in our undying, constant love. The Savior expected others to change and grow, and He loved them through the process.

2. They Learn the Most from Us When We Are "Without Hypocrisy" (v. 42)

Our children notice when we do not live what we expect them to live. We must model what we expect. Children will not learn honesty if they catch us in a lie. They will not likely learn to read scriptures if they never see us do it. But if they catch us kneeling by our bed in fervent prayer, they will have learned a sermon on prayer and will much more likely develop the habit of the daily prayer themselves. When our children observe us using will power to eat well or exercise, they will much more likely develop the self-discipline they see in us. "Parental hypocrisy can make children cynical and unbelieving of what they are taught in the home. For instance, when parents attend movies they forbid their children to see, parental credibility is diminished."[3]

"He that receiveth my law and doeth it, the same is my disciple; and he that saith he receiveth it and doeth it not, the same is not my disciple" (D&C 41:5). We must be careful to avoid hypocrisy, and model what we want them to develop. I understand that hypocrisy was the sin the Christ condemned the most when he was on the earth!

3. We Must Examine Ourselves to Ensure We Are "Without Guile" (v. 42)

We cannot deceive or trick our child into obedience or it will not be effective and lasting. Besides trickery, guile could mean having ulterior motives for their behavior change, such as making them obey us in public so that we will look good! Ideally, our motive must be their real happiness.

4. We Must Respect Their Free Agency, Avoiding "Unrighteous Dominion" (v. 39)

Forcing obedience is unrighteous dominion. Instead, we teach and we model the obedience we expect. "I teach them correct principles, and they govern themselves," Joseph Smith taught.[4] Of course, young children cannot govern themselves—they must be trained, but as soon as they are ready we can let them. That does not mean we don't have family rules and guidelines, but instead that we do not stand over a child with a ruler to get them to obey. The goal is for them to develop their own self-discipline one day.

When I was trying to teach my little ones to obey, I had this dilemma. How do I insist on obedience without forcing it? What I settled on was giving them a "commandment" such as: You need to put your toys away before lunch. Then I would simply walk away and wait for the obedience. If my child did not pick them up, I responded with, "Do it when you are ready, but I'll save your lunch on top of the fridge until you obey." He could use his agency to choose to obey or not and when to obey, but the reward did not come until after he had made the right choice. I would get out of the way but, in the background, still require obedience before the "blessing." God too can only send the blessing after the law is obeyed.

5. We Must Teach the Right Way to Live, Using "Pure Knowledge, Which Shall Greatly Enlarge the Soul" (v. 42)

I read a book recently, in which the father figure—in this case a clergyman—took in a preteen boy named Dooley, whose parents had been unable to care for him. Many times, Father Tim had been prompted to teach this boy to obey the rules at school and in the community. Yet, he just didn't follow through. At first, it was because poor Dooley had been through so much and needed a friendly approach. Father Tim had learned to love this young boy and he knew that Dooley had a good heart. Alas, he was so busy that he put off the discipline and teaching.

Then one day the unthinkable happened! Dooley and his best friend, Tommy, had gone to the construction site in town, where they had been told never to go. They played on a pile of lumber, and when it began to slide, Dooley was able to jump off, but Tommy slipped and the falling lumber pile fell on top of him, causing a compound break to his leg and a severe blow to his head that bruised his brain. Poor Dooley was so shaken up, since the whole thing had been his idea. He was forced to see his friend crippled from this accident, unconscious and in critical condition for days!

Father Tim berated himself for never fitting in that talk about obedience and rules. Now this young friend might have to walk with a limp the rest of his life. Father Tim made it a priority then! Along with an apology for not doing it sooner, he spoke to Dooley in no uncertain terms about the need to obey. Teaching a better way and explaining why, is the essence of good discipline.

"Obedience is the first law of heaven," Father Tim spelled out to his entire congregation. Then he laid out his strict expectations to his young charge. The two mourned together about the consequences to this friend. Dooley knew afresh the love and faithfulness of his guardian for him by his clear teaching.[5]

Once again, remember what Elder Boyd K. Packer taught, "True doctrine, understood, changes attitudes and behavior . . . quicker than a study of behavior will improve behavior."[6] From this we learn that teaching obedience is much preferred to going over all the behaviors that are unacceptable. We teach what we *want* to see happen!

> "We cannot force people into doing things, but we may love them into doing what is right, and into righteousness."
>
> —George Albert Smith

6. We Must Require Accountability, Which Will Help Lead Them to *Self*-Discipline "Which Shall Greatly Enlarge Thy Soul" (v. 42)

I, too, had a wake-up call at one point. Like Father Tim, I too had seen the good hearts of my children and so had been lax with my follow through. Yes, we had taught rules about cell phone usage and family guidelines, chores and expectations. However, I had become negligent in their enforcement, rationalizing away giving the set consequences, since they are such good kids!

We told our children about Dooley and the severe consequences to his friend because his father figure had neglected to teach him obedience. We apologized for being lax in some of our rules—letting important things slide. Then we talked to them about the dangers of rationalization. For example, we had a rule to put phones to bed by 9:30, but many times, a phone was not in the charging station until later. "Because we want you to be successful, good missionaries, we need to help you learn exact obedience and not rationalization."

"We are not planning on micromanaging you," we told them. "But instead, we are going to spell out exactly what we expect, and then at dinner, we will ask for accountability." In three areas—chores, phones, and games—we spelled out just what the family rules were and what we expected. Our plan was to ask *daily* about these items, then when we felt they were keeping the guidelines, we would only ask *weekly*, then *monthly*. If a new issue came up, we would add it to the list of accountable items. In spelling out the expectations, we were careful to ask their input, and then tweak it until they felt the expectations were doable.

On occasion (such as needing a phone for a homework question after 9:30), they would okay an exception with us. If ever they could not do their chores at the usual time (such as a rehearsal or a sports game that went late), they were to ask someone to do them in their place, thus taking responsibility for the task to get done.

We were careful to leave some things to their own good judgment, such as reading in bed. As long as they used good judgment, they could decide how long to read. We felt that they need to exercise their own agency in some areas of their lives, while being obedient and accountable in others. But if there were a problem, such as a pattern of reading too late and not being able to function the next day, we would have to take over for a while and have accountability in that area too.

We posted our expectations and accountability list in an area by the kitchen table that was visible and ready for our asking. When one of the kids could not answer with a yes, our response was, "Keep trying. You will get it!" (Or we might have to rethink an issue to make for better success.) There was a busy day here or there that we might forget to ask, but mostly, we established the accountability in order to teach exact obedience and the joy of answering. In fact, the kids would remind us to ask. "Yes, I did it!" became a source of pride. And it was leading them toward the goal of self-discipline.

Fred Rogers (Mister Rogers) said, "I think of discipline as the continual process of helping a child learn self-discipline."[7] (See also "Parent Interviews" in chapter 15 and "Missionary Prep" in chapter 17.)

7. We Must Correct, "Reproving Betimes with Sharpness" (v. 43)

Reproving does not necessarily mean belittling. It simply means correcting. Of course our kids need correction as they grow. I like to think of the imagery of taking a child's hand and turning them back to the path of happiness.

At times, anger tries to slip in. Anger is no good—it can make us say or do things we regret. Mark and I try to walk away from the situation for a few minutes to regroup or say a quick prayer to help regain our own composure and to come up with a plan for righteous reproof.

Betimes, as used in this scripture, means early or in good time.[8] It can also mean occasionally. If we deal with the situation quickly, then move on to positive interaction, the lesson will have been learned and self-esteem guarded. The message is that I know you can get over this and improve. We must remember that "preoccupation with unworthy behavior can lead to unworthy behavior."[9]

Once we had a son who played on the freshman basketball team. The coach made a point of jerking a player out of the game and to the bench the second he made a mistake. We noticed how counterproductive this was. For example, one player made a beautiful pass, and then a minute later, when he got the ball again, missed a shot. Sure enough, the coach yanked him out and put in a substitute. Nothing was said about the pass, but instead that player sat on the bench berating himself for missing the shot. These players grew more and more tentative, since they replayed their mistakes over and over after being sent to the bench after each one. Afraid of making mistakes, they lost their confidence. In disciplining our kids, we need to correct them, but we can get over it quickly, and then turn all focus on the positive. We can reiterate all that they do good and shower them with confidence that they will make right choices.

If we repeat what they did wrong over and over, they will be more likely to do it again! The more we say "Stop hitting your brother!" the more they hear the hitting part and get that in their brain. More misbehavior is *not* what we want, but a turning from the behavior. Tell them, "If you are frustrated, talk to him about it! Say, 'I want a turn with that toy when you are done.'" This helps them focus them on a solution, rather than the misbehavior.

Sharpness means promptness and exactness, not necessarily harshness. If a child eats a cracker on the carpet, getting crumbs all over it, we can immediately respond, "Food stays in the kitchen. We want a nice clean house," while bringing him (or his food) to the table to eat. "In our house, we only eat in the kitchen" is another good response that solves the issue quickly and positively.

Family home evening is a great time to correct. No one is singled out for reproof, but principles that we all want to live are taught.

8. We Must Listen to the Spirit and Act "When Moved Upon by the Holy Ghost" (v. 43)

All of us at times lack wisdom to handle a situation just right. Here's where we need help from the Spirit to know when to correct, the right words to say, how to be most effective. With prayer for the guidance of the Spirit, and with fortification from scripture, we will receive ideas that pop into our heads. (Or perhaps with the hindsight from later pondering, prayer, and study, we can learn how to handle a situation better next time!)

We may need to talk over consistent consequences with our spouse to figure out how we both will respond. But we must not despair if both spouses don't see eye to eye on discipline at first. Though consistency is ideal, a couple can choose to handle situations differently, as long as they both have the same goals. It took a good while, and lots of growth and study, for Mark and I to come to a consensus on how we would handle disobedience. The Holy Ghost worked on both of us for a long season.

Most importantly, each child learns differently, and we must have help to figure out what will help each child to see the need for change and be willing to make it. With help from the Spirit, a child's actions will change, and so will their heart.

When a particular child is going through a rough time with current misbehaviors, Mark and I like to "take that child's name" with us—in our thoughts—to the temple. We spend time pondering about that child's needs and the best course for us to take. We might each get a different approach we can take to remedy the situation, or we may be given the insight to be patient through this temporary phase. There is a special conduit within those walls and the inspiration comes.

9. We Must Continue "Showing Forth Afterwards an Increase of Love toward Him Whom [We Have] Reproved, Lest He Esteem [Us] to Be His Enemy" (v. 43)

Our kids need to know that we love them regardless. God loves us even when we make mistakes or sin. His love is constant. And in order to show them God's love, they first must feel our love, even and especially after correction and consequence. Brigham Young counseled, "If you are ever called upon to chasten a person, never chasten beyond the balm you have within you to bind up."[10]

Soothing words, extra hugs, time spent together, reminders of happy times and other situations the child handled well, are ways to show more love. We can apply the balm of reassurance that things will get better.

"By this shall all men know that ye are my disciples, if ye have love one to another" (John 13:35). When Father Tim had the conversation with Dooley to set him straight, laying out their plan for obedience, he began and ended by telling him how much he loved him. Love must be there for real change to take place.[11]

For example, I had a Japanese friend that lived in my apartment complex when we both had young children. When her son hit another child one day, I observed her gently pick up his hand. "See this hand, Davy?" she said, "This hand does good things. This hand must never hit. This hand is a good hand." And then the correction was over. If this active little boy did it again, she would patiently repeat her teaching. She was lovingly teaching her son by the way she corrected him.

10. We Must Let Our Children Know That Our "Faithfulness Is Stronger Than the Cords of Death" (v. 43–44)

Love is the key to disciple discipline, not to be confused with laxness—which can even become or seem like indifference or apathy. It is loving enough to want their happiness and expect the best. Love like that means sometimes difficult sacrifice. This is what builds the strong bonds, stronger even than death.

When I was a little girl, my worst fear was to disappoint my daddy. Why? Not because he would spank me or would scold me—it was because he loved me so much. Because of his great love for me and his belief in me, I was motivated to be the best I could possibly be. And when I messed up? "That's not my Leenie!" was my dad's response. "She wouldn't really do that!" He refused to think less of me. He still believed in me! His was the pure love of Jesus Christ, a supreme charity that raised me up better than any other motivation.

May we look to the promptings of the Holy Ghost to show us how to apply these principles best for each of our children. The struggle is worth it, and the consequences are eternal.

Dear Mom and Dad,

Thanks for expecting a lot of me and correcting my mistakes. Thanks for being firm, but thanks for doing it kindly and patiently. And thanks for modeling the self-discipline I want someday. This is my chance for real happiness when I grow up.

Love, Me

Evidence That I Love You

There are times when things get hectic and vision becomes obscured. For such times especially, our kids need to be able to easily bring to mind that we love them. This will happen best if we are constantly looking for ways to give them evidence of that fact. We know we love them, and they know deep down we love them. But for times when it's hard to remember that fact, we can constantly be giving them evidence:

1. Prayers

We can pray for our children by name, specifically, in our family prayers: "Help Michael to do well on his test." "Please help Cami to be able to make up with her friend." "Please bless Josh to be able to do his best on the mile run today." Kids love hearing their name, and they need the extra help from our prayers and the assurance that we know and care about what they are facing that day.

It means a lot when our kids find out they were in our prayers. "I was praying for you, and I had this idea." Or "I prayed about this dilemma and I just don't feel good about your going." Or even, "I know today is going to be tough, so I will be praying for you."

Sometimes we also have to pray to better love this child! "I want to be able to love this difficult child. Please, Lord, give me love for him." Our child can sense whether our love is genuine. If we fervently ask and are trying to be followers of Christ, we can be blessed with love for the child that is hard to love or is going through an exasperating season (see Moroni 7:48).

2. Send-offs

A good send-off to bed says I love you, such as "I have a hug for you" or "Do you need to rock with me a minute tonight?" We can take an extra couple of minutes to show our love, whether it be with a story, a song, a hug, a race to get on jammies, or a tooth-brushing party, as a quick connection and reassurance of our love before bed.

Likewise, a good send-off to school—such as "Remember who you are!"—tells them we care. A cheery goodbye helps your child face the day, armed with extra self-esteem. A family motto or an extra blown kiss says tons. One of my daughters loved it when I gave her an extra kiss for her pocket (a fist that I pretended to put in her pretend pocket). Another one asked for three hugs, so I crossed my arms over my chest and made a little "hug grunt" three times, then blew it to her, as she was taking off. "Take time to always be at the crossroads in the lives of your children, whether they be six or sixteen" was the counsel that President Ezra Taft Benson gave to mothers.[12]

3. Total Attention

To give evidence of our love, we can play a game they want to play, such as a board game or an out-door game of speed, ping pong, hopscotch, or marbles: "I'll take you on!" The kids absolutely love it when Mark will wrestle with them. For some kids, one-on-one time spent on an outing or doing a project is the ultimate "I love you." They know we are busy, and so when we make time to play with them, it is an extra effective way to show them we love them.

Our love is totally shown when we are willing to drop everything to tune in to what our kids say or what they need, such as, "You don't seem to be yourself today. What are you worried about?" I love it when I can do two or more things at once, but when a child needs our undivided attention, it's *not* the time to be trying to accomplish two things at once. We must turn and face them, getting down to their level and empathizing with their current concern.

"I've been thinking of you" is a wonderful affirmation of our love. The idea or advice that follows will be so much more likely to be well received.

4. Sacrifice

Every time we sacrifice to serve our kids, love grows. "I can arrange to be there" is a great show of love. Seeing you give up something for them speaks volumes that you really care. Sacrifice to show "an increase of love" gives our child evidence that we are not "his enemy" even when we have had to discipline and correct. A sacrifice we make helps them "know that [our] faithfulness is stronger than the cords of death" (D&C 121:43–44).

When we give up something we were doing and instead offer to help our kids with their chores, they will be so grateful. "I can see you're having a packed morning. Let me help you get this done." Other opportunities might be when we make a special trip to the store to pick up something they volunteered to bring somewhere.

5. Gifts

When we occasionally buy a treat our child likes or an item of clothing he or she may need, it tells that child again that we care. "I saw this and thought of you." My dad once found a key chain with my name on it and bought it for me. My name is unusual, and so when he saw it, he wanted me to have it. My mom knew how much I like to do crossword puzzles, so she got me a pocket crossword puzzle book. These were small items purchased many years ago, but I still remember them with fondness, since they were unexpected and so thoughtful!

6. Financial Help

Sometimes money can be evidence. When I was a teenager, I was so busy with academics and activities that I didn't have time for a job to earn money. At our home, there was no allowance either. So, when my mom helped me earn some much-needed money, I was so grateful! She was the block supervisor for newspaper boys, and she let me stack all the papers. For this job, I earned five dollars a week! If I had an after-school student council activity that ran past the 4 p.m. pickup, she would go ahead and stack them, and still pay me! I was so very grateful for this way to feel like I had a little cash!

My son had a similar need and no time because of music and sports. In fact, during the season, he had little time to do the yard work that usually earned his spending money. It was hard enough to just fit in his daily chores of taking out the garbage, so I set up a plan for him. I told him I would pay him one dollar a day for taking care of his face and having no clothes on the floor—habits I wanted him to develop! It was an easy way to earn a little spending money, but if he didn't do either of these, he had to pay *me* a dollar! I hoped this would be evidence that I love and care about his needs and wants, just as my mother had given me that evidence.

7. Boundaries Say I Love You

Sometimes rules that remain strong say I love you, and sometimes it's exceptions to them. Firm boundaries can give them security. But exceptions help them know that we have listened and understand their dilemma. The main thing is that they see how much we care. "I'm sorry if this is hard for you, but our family policy is no email account until you are twelve." Or "Maybe we can make an exception in this case. Let me talk it over with Dad." Both ways can work.

Our children need evidence that we love them, so that when times get rough and feelings get raw and Satan's whisperings get loud, our kids will have proof at their fingertips to counter all that. They need evidence that is easy to come up with in an instant, even during a crisis—concrete evidence we love them that can be pulled up at the end of the day, or at the end of their childhood!

Dear Mom and Dad,

I know that you love me. I know because I remember that time when you dropped everything to help me with my extra-credit project— with your help it turned out so good. Remember when you bought me that beautiful dress I wanted so much? Then there's the time you brought my paper to school, even though you had such a busy day! Thanks for all you do.

Love, Me

Hovering or Letting Them Fly

Our children are going to make mistakes. It is our job to teach them well, so that they won't have to learn everything from their own experiences but can learn to avoid their own problems. After having taught them thoroughly, there comes a point when we must let them try their own wings. They will someday need to leave our homes and make all their own decisions. While they are in our home, we must gradually get them to that point by balancing our control and gradually backing away to let them fly.

When our children are babies, we micromanage every detail of their lives. By the time they are two, most kids are telling us vehemently—even with tantrums—that they want to decide many things! So we start giving them more and more choices, *as* we teach them more and more. Of course, we want to train them to always do good. But part of this life *is* to "learn from our own experience." We must figure out the balance of when to let them go and when to take over the situation.

Joseph Smith counseled, "I teach them correct principles, and they govern themselves."[13] That is the pattern. It was Satan's idea to make us do right every time. For growth, we must have the freedom to choose. Consider some ways to balance caring with letting go:

1. Teach, Teach, Teach

"Principles are anchors of safety," taught Elder Richard G. Scott. "They are like the steel anchors a mountaineer uses to conquer otherwise impossible cliffs. They will help you have confidence in new and unfamiliar circumstances. They will provide you protection in life's storms of adversity."[14] If we are constantly teaching our children true principles, they will have the anchors in place to help make right choices or to learn from their wrong ones in our laboratory homes.

In the car is a great place to teach a captive audience. Going out for a smoothie provides a new, neutral setting for talking over the principles we are trying to teach. Sitting on their bed on a Sunday evening, or even a quick conversation in the hallway can be a chance to reinforce what we are trying to teach. "I was thinking about you, and I want to make sure you don't forget to ____" or "I was wondering how your situation at school worked out?" Or even lovingly asking, "Have we taught you to ____?"

2. Step Away Gradually from Micromanaging

As we teach well the principles of the gospel, we can back away from so much control. It's like a child learning to ride a bike. At first, we have a strong hold on that bike, as the child learns to balance and manage the pedals at the same time. Mark and I learned to provide a small bike that lets the child touch the ground and learn to balance that way. Gradually, we let go a little more and a little more. What a joy when the child can ride that bike on their own! We would be doing a disservice to hold on longer than necessary, or to leave the training wheels on after they don't need them—while helpful at first, they become a hindrance later on.

"When you are ready" has been a good phrase to help our children grow in autonomy. They help decide when they are ready to take a big step, such as when to wear underwear instead of diapers, when to start fasting, or when to get their driver's license.

Later on, our children may choose to make some large mistakes. "Parents, don't make the mistake of purposefully intervening to soften or eliminate the natural consequences of your child's deliberate decisions to violate the commandments" taught Elder Richard G. Scott. "Such acts reinforce false principles, open the door for more serious sin, and lessen the likelihood of repentance."[15]

3. Don't Hover like a Helicopter

Too much hovering is a hindrance to our children's growth. In the *Journal of Adolescence*, Professors Laura Padilla Walker and Larry J. Nelson report their study about hovering parents: "Helicopter parenting appears to be inappropriately intrusive and managing" in which parents make decisions and solve problems (i.e. with roommates, employers, professors) for their children, limiting their "opportunities to practice the skills needed to flourish in emerging adulthood, successfully take on adult roles, and in general, become a self-reliant individual." Helicopter parents have the best intentions "of strong parental concern for the well-being and success of the child," but this hovering proves to be harmful.[16] By the time our kids are young adults, they need to be able to live their own lives and tackle their own problems more and more.

4. Find a Balance; Be a Safety Net

One set of parents found that they were hovering too much, since they wanted to visit their college students' professors and go in to fix issues with roommates or employers. They decided to back off from hovering and instead become a "safety net."[17]

My youngest son had an online computer essentials class to get done during the summer before seventh grade. He chose to take a class in the summer so that he could take an extra elective that coming school year. I started out the summer urging him to get his class done and scolding a little too often when it wasn't happening. So I backed off completely, turning the entire thing over to him. (Okay, I occasionally gave him some incentives.) He knew the deadline and yet he chose to spend most of his time reading and relaxing with his brothers whenever possible. He did his chores and participated in family events, but his class was always his last priority. It was all I could do to not step in and manage his time for him! I could see that this was not going to get done before school started!

It didn't. He hadn't paced himself. We discovered that he could get an extension on the due date, but it was approaching. Well, Mark stepped in and mapped out times to get it done. Even on a family trip, Mark had him do several increments of online class between family events. Rather than fighting it, this son seemed grateful for the direction at this point. It was time for us to be the "safety net."

Looking back, I think the whole experience helped him. I could have started the summer off a whole lot better, with less scolding and warning, and more just teaching principles at Family Night rather than head on. (See "The Backdoor Approach" in chapter 5.) But at least now he manages his homework time a whole lot better than he did last year or last summer. Now, most of the time I can leave his homework totally up to him. I was so pleased when he did a science fair project with minimal help. He and a friend made a commercial for English with mostly their own motivation—we only had to step in to help the filming. He is gradually learning to fly.

There are times when we need to step in with extra tutoring in a particular subject. There are times when something is due and we need to cut out other demands on the student's time, so they can get it done. They need our support, especially in a crisis, real or imagined. But they also need to gradually learn to manage their own load.

One thing I leave completely up to this son is how to manage his music. I let him choose to play music while he studies. I wouldn't pick that, but I'm glad he chooses good songs. When he mentions to me that he's having trouble focusing on this paper he has to write, I might say, "Why don't you try turning off the music?" We teach the family about good things entering their minds, and we ask them if they listen to good music in our interviews. But we leave the decision about when to listen up to them.

The bottom line is to avoid "making too many decisions for your children, solving problems for them that they could solve themselves, and generally swooping in for the rescue."[18] There is definitely a balance of backing away and stepping in as a safety net that adjusts as the child grows toward total self-management.

5. Return and Report

Rather than micromanage our kids, we can have them show accountability. We can have them report to us on how they are doing at a specified time. For us it was chores, and they reported at dinnertime. Mark and I found ourselves reminding about chores way too often. Our kids were busy, and the chores were not getting done at the right time. We made the decision to teach them the principles of exact obedience and to spell out what we expected and when, and then to back away. Instead of so many reminders, we would consistently ask them to report. We would ask them at dinnertime how they did that day. In fact, we wrote down and posted what we would be asking. If they didn't get them done, they simply did the chores then. But they (and we) were pleased when they could answer that they had already gotten them done. When they became consistent with getting the chores done, we would no longer need to check daily. The plan was to back away from even reporting, turning the responsibility totally to them.

We haven't got there yet. It takes a while, but the kids are growing in taking responsibility. In fact, when he has forgotten to feed the pets, my son has texted me to please do it this time. That's so much better than forgetting entirely! A step in the right direction! I'll take it, and he has time to keep growing. We just have to be consistent with our plan and patient with our youngsters.

As our children grow up in our household, we would do well to gradually give them more autonomy a little at a time. The goal is for our children to leave us to serve missions or go to college on their own. The way to reach this goal is to train, to teach, teach, teach, to expect much, and to use our safety nets of FHE, family council, and interviews. Children need to return and report to us, until the time that they go off on their own.

Many young adults these days are having trouble making the break from home. They stay too long, not ready to face the world on their own. We can help with this process by refusing to hover. Gradually, we let them do things on their own so when they leave our shelter, they will "fly upon the wings of the wind" (Psalms 18:10).

Dear Mom and Dad,

I so need your safety net to get me out of the binds I get into! But thanks for letting me take the wheel every once in a while. I love it when you are pleased with me, and I love the chance to prove to you that I am growing up! Thanks!

Love, Me

Chapter 11
Live the Doctrine of Christ

One doctrine is so important that Nephi taught it as his dying declaration and the Savior gave it first thing upon His appearance in the Americas: "the doctrine of Christ."

Just what does this doctrine entail? Faith, repentance, baptism, receiving the gift of the Holy Ghost, and enduring to the end. On this occasion, after presenting Himself for each to handle, Jesus taught: believe in me (3 Nephi 11:32), repent (verse 32), be baptized (v. 34), and receive the Holy Ghost (v. 35), and endure to the end (v. 39).

These principles should be the bedrock of our lives and of our teachings. This is "the foundation of everything else in the Church. Like all that comes from God, this doctrine is pure, it is clear, it is easy to understand—even for a child. With glad hearts, we invite all to receive it."[1]

Rock Solid Faith

As my children have grown up and left home, they have faced intense trials. Each of these children is valiant, driven, and responsible. But for some, there have been major health issues, others have had significant financial setbacks, and still others have had heart-wrenching obstacles to their goals and plans. One family deals with a special-needs child who is difficult to understand and hard on family dynamics. Still others must room with or work with people who are unkind to them or even "despitefully use" them (Matthew 5:44).

One of my sons recently left home for college and then a mission. I think it gets harder each time, because not only are these younger children my "babies," but also I know more of what they might face in the world out there! Watching him go, I asked myself again, *Did I teach him enough? Did I do everything possible to teach him and his brothers and sisters faith and trust in God? Do each of them have a strong enough foundation?*

As I have watched from a distance, I have agonized for my grown children and their setbacks and discouragement. How I love these grown children, but now it feels too late to teach them the gospel! How do we parents help our children develop rock solid faith that will endure?

How Can I Build My Children's Faith When They Are Young?

When one of my sons approached me at the end of his junior year of high school when he was seventeen-years old, he was distraught. Three of his school friends had recently declared themselves atheists! These were boys from very religious families. One of the boys stood up in seminary and told the class that he had never received anything after praying for a testimony, so he decided to become an atheist. Another had given an autobiographic presentation in English class, and at one point told them: "This part of my life was the time when I figured out I was an atheist." A third young man posted his lack of belief on Facebook and received approval for "having the courage" to do so. And one of these young men had gone so far as to offer to help others *out* of religion!

I joined my son in feeling greatly troubled for his friends. "What can I do?" he asked me, with such sorrow in his eyes. I struggled with that question for a while and then found an answer in the scriptures: "Join in fasting and mighty prayer . . . for those who [know] not God" (Alma 6:6). I also thought of Alma the Younger's wayward season, when he led others away from religion. Then I read how the tremendous faith of his father's prayers brought a huge wake-up call for his son. I urged my son to fast and pray for his friends and to join with others to pray for them (Mosiah 27:8–10, 14).

President Dieter F. Uchtdorf relates, "Recently I was surprised and saddened to hear of an Aaronic Priesthood bearer who seemed to take pride in the fact that he had distanced himself from God. He said, 'If God reveals Himself to me, then I will believe. Until then, I will find the truth relying on my own understanding and intellect to light the way before me.'" He felt sorry for this young man, who had "unplugged the spotlight and then seemed self-satisfied in his clever observation that there was no light." Many, these days, excuse themselves from keeping the commandments and taking the steps to have a relationship with God, by "putting the burden of proof on God. Let me be clear, there is nothing noble or impressive about being cynical."[2]

As I thought more about this, I hoped these friends of my son would one day wake up and realize how much they need God. They had faith implanted in them from a very young age, and I still believe it will surface one day. The teachings of their parents are still there down deep, which brings hope.

How do we keep our children from this downward spiral of doubt? How can we build solid foundations of faith in them from the time they are very young? Here are some ideas:

1. Prayers from Babyhood

From the time my babies were newborn, I felt I should put prayer into their bedtime routine. As I held my new baby in my arms before putting them into a crib, I would offer "their" prayer in simple language. As they grew to become a toddler, I would kneel beside them at their toddler bed. This way, their entire lives from the beginning are filled with the knowledge that they have a loving Father in Heaven who hears them each time they pray.

My tiny ones learned early to fold arms and bow heads (even when they were too young to keep their eyes closed) before meals. I was trying to follow the scriptural admonition to train them, which comes with the promise, "when he is old, he will not depart from it" (Proverbs 22:6). I don't think toddlerhood is too early to teach them to use sacred words like "thank thee" (even when they repeat it like "tank we")!

For one stretch of time, I made a special point of helping my young kids to pray for others. Before the child's prayer, we would talk about how is in need, such as "Grandma doesn't feel well, so let's pray for her!" Or, "The neighbors lost their puppy—let's pray for them to find him!" This practice brought meaning to their prayers, which otherwise can be very repetitive.

As kids grow, we can help them gradually get their own answers. A place to start is to ask for help to find something that is lost. "Heavenly Father knows where it is. He will help us find it." Afterward, I remind that child to do their part and look everywhere. I search too (praying hard inwardly) and help my child to not give up hope. And again, I prompt them to give thanks when the item is found—to give God the credit.

As our kids mature, when they have perplexing decisions to make, we can suggest they pray about it. I like to kneel beside them when they need a special answer. I urge them to empty out their thoughts and open their hearts to receive an answer from God. I suggest that my child pray vocally first, and then I would too. Inwardly, I am gathering up all the faith I can muster to expect an answer! And I am saying my own silent prayer that I will have the right words to say in response. Receiving answers, even the ones that are a long time coming, is a wonderful connection with God, a huge step toward deep and abiding faith.

2. Share Stories of Faith

Another way to build faith is to tell stories of faith. We can teach the scripture stories and testify that they really happened! In a world that feeds them so much of cyberspace and fantasy, we must help them realize that there really is power from God that He uses to help mankind. There really was a young boy who slew a giant and an angel who shut the mouths of the hungry lions. Alma's people really were strengthened so that they could not even feel the heavy loads of brick or stone upon their backs. And Moses really was able to receive water from a rock! We can help kids apply the principles that these stories teach, though not negatively, such as "You should be more like Ammon!" but rather in a positive way, such as "Let's be like Nephi and obey without murmuring."

Everyone loves stories, and we can tell faith-promoting stories constantly. I like to turn every inspirational experience I come across into a story, whether it is from Church magazines, from a talk at church retold, or a childhood story of my own. "There was this family who had a cool experience," we can start, and then make the words simple for kids to easily understand. Missionaries often send inspiring letters that can provide us with stories. And there are wonderful stories of our ancestors that remind our kids who they come from and the faith these good people learned even through hardship.

At mealtime, we can talk about tender mercies that happened to us that day. Maybe we were protected on the freeway, were able to avoid a fire on the stove, or ran across someone we could help. Elder David A. Bednar testified that "the tender mercies of the Lord are real and that they do not occur randomly or merely by coincidence. . . . Each of us can have eyes to see clearly and ears to hear distinctly the tender mercies of the Lord as they strengthen and assist us."[3] I like to ask, "Did anyone have a miracle today?" so they will be watching for the daily tender mercies. If we tell them sincerely, with a feeling of awe for God's goodness to us, the stories from our daily experiences will capture their interest and build their faith in a loving Father in Heaven.

3. Sing Songs of Faith

It was way past midnight at the ward campout and my six-month-old son was wide awake. I needed to sing him back to sleep, but didn't want to wake up everyone in the tent or those in neighboring tents, so I wrapped him up and headed away from the tents to the smoldering remains of the campfire the night before, hoping it would bring a little warmth still. Then I began my most effective putting-to-sleep lullaby, "Silent Night!" No, it was not December but October! And though I had sung my very quietest, in the morning, a fellow camper remarked at someone's choice of lullaby!

Hymns and Primary songs are the best lullabies! They not only put the baby to sleep, but they instill faith as well. It is another powerful avenue to the soul. Words go to the left brain, but add music and they go to the right brain as well! Songs like "My Heavenly Father Loves Me" and "I Feel My Savior's Love" can become favorite lullabies as they teach faith.

4. Show Them God Daily

If a child has loving parents, it is much easier to visualize a loving God in Heaven. When we show them mercy, they can comprehend a merciful Father in Heaven who will forgive mistakes and allow do-overs. Richard G. Scott teaches, "Giving them confidence in your love can help them develop faith in God's love."[4]

We can also show them God is there when they are afraid. During a frightening thunderstorm, my daughter takes her anxious children on her lap, prays for them, and reassures them that Heavenly Father will help the fear get smaller and then go away. This helps God become a loving influence in their lives.

Nature provides a wonderful way to show our children God's goodness each day. My sister-in-law is good at this: "Wow, look at the sunset!" she constantly points out to her children or grandchildren. "What a gorgeous place God gave us to live!" Or, "Can you believe how detailed that little ant is? Somehow, he is so powerful he can sense food, like that piece of candy on the ground, and find it even though he may be many feet away from it. He can carry much more than his own weight! Aren't God's creations amazing?" My friend, a young mother of two, believes that "we need to help our children learn to see and feel God in the beauty and goodness around them. If they attribute their blessings to God and build a relationship with Him, they will have a hard time forgetting Him when others tell them there is no God."

To build faith, we also must take care to not blame God. My sister points out that she feels it's important that our children don't see trials, crises, and calamities always as the actions of God. They may see Him as harsh and unfeeling! Many disasters are just due to the physical nature of this life, and many trials are due to the bad choices of others.

5. Exemplify Daily Devotion

A mother's or father's daily scripture reading teaches children tons, especially when we draw from it in conversation with them! "I read something amazing today that really got me thinking." If these words are important to us, they will more likely become important to them, planting seeds and nurturing young testimonies.

Daily, there needs to be a connection to God. A BYU study showed that the biggest key to raising offspring who stay faithful is not where they live, nor how many friends they have of the same religion but instead it is the private practice of religion that makes all the difference. It's "not merely getting the youth into the Church, but rather getting the Church (personal testimony) into the youth." If a young person has learned to translate teachings into his own daily personal practice, he is much more likely to remain true to childhood beliefs.[5]

> Little seeds of faith in God can be planted daily.

What Is My Role When My Children Are Grown?

It is very different when our children are away from our daily influence. So much is out of our control! As I watch from afar when my grown children experience trial, I realize the Lord is refining and sanctifying them. I don't want to change the will of the Lord. Yet, if I do nothing, it feels like apathy and that doesn't feel right at all. So, I end up just worrying, which doesn't help anyone!

What should I pray for? I asked myself recently.

I knew from experience that I couldn't pray for people to change. They have their agency and must make that decision.

Though I shouldn't pray for people to change, I *can* pray that hearts will be softened and that ways will be opened for them. But what else should I pray for? Is it appropriate to pray for miracles to occur in the lives of those I so love? What if that interferes with the Lord's will or what He is trying to teach them? I do pray for the Lord's will to be done, but I want to do something more to help them through these tough experiences! What should I pray for?

I brought my question to a recent general conference, and I listened for an answer. This is the prompting that came: I would pray for my children constantly and add my faith by asking for miracles I wanted to happen. I would pray for their health to be restored and for their financial setbacks to be righted, their children to be well, and their paths ahead to be unfolded. I would use all the faith I could muster to hope that these would happen. But if the miracles I wanted were not the Lord's will, I would still be true and trust in Him. That was my new plan. It takes a lot of trust to be a parent!

Our older children as well as our young ones need us to confirm their faith:

1. The Blessings Will Come

One day, the Lord gave me just the right words to text one of my grown sons, who was going through some hard trials at college. It was a gift that opened conversation! This son loves beautiful, peaceful music, so I was also prompted to send him some inspirational songs via email. An occasional scripture that I found and sent to him made a difference too. I had hesitated to send those, wondering if he would feel I was preaching at him. But it made all the difference to send with it some love, such as "I was thinking of you when I came across this scripture," or "I am so sorry for what you are going through—hope this is an uplift." Besides my constant prayers and fasting for him, these little things reminded him of my love from afar.

Another of my sons was pushing through a lengthy situation with a boss at work. After I prayed for him one morning, the words came to my head: "He is being strengthened." I thought of the people of Alma in the land of Helam who were made to carry heavy burdens. Unable to even cry out in prayer, they prayed in their hearts and the Lord strengthened them. He did not take the heavy burdens away immediately, but He did strengthen them to be able to carry them without even feeling them. It was a wonderful miracle, that even while testing their patience and trust, God showed them without doubt that He cared. "Know of a surety that I, the Lord God, do visit my people in their afflictions" (Mosiah 24:14). Eventually, the burdens were lifted, and the people were led to freedom from this tyranny. I shared this idea that I'd been given with my son, and it gave him some meaning for this trial.

I have also seen little evidences that my other grown children are being blessed. They share with me some tender mercies and some breakthroughs, so that I can rejoice too.

2. To Love Them, Mainly Listen!

Mark and I have learned over and over again that our grown-up children mostly need a listening ear. My first tendency is to offer suggestions to their current dilemma! I want to get in there with them and fix this problem quickly! And though they try to appreciate my advice and to listen politely, they really are usually *not* asking for advice. They can figure things out for themselves.

What they do need is some empathy, and a safe place to vent. They need us to know that this trial is tough right now, but that they are trying their best to get through it. Often, as they talk through a current challenge, the steps to take begin to form in their own minds.

"You can do this! I believe in you" is the best message we can give, along with "This is tough! I'll be praying for you!" We can also remind them of other times they got through something hard, and reassure them that they will get through this too.

Mark and I remind each other: only give advice if they ask for it! And sometimes they do, but most often, they want to be independent. Though they need our support, they don't need our solutions! "When I call you, what I'm trying to seek," said one grown daughter, "is love." The answer is more love.

3. It Is Worth the Effort

Every prayer, all our fasting, and our visits to the temple in their behalf—all of it is so worth the sacrifice. We must never give up hope, nor feel that any struggle is in vain. In the end, these relationships are one of the very few things that we can take with us to the next life, and that affects our happiness forever. For me, it takes constant effort to remind myself to continue to trust God.

After all, our children of every age are "the most precious asset (we) have" taught President Gordon B. Hinckley:

> In terms of your happiness, in terms of the matters that make you proud or sad, nothing—I repeat, nothing—will have so profound an effect on you as the way your children turn out. You will either rejoice and boast of their accomplishments or you will weep, head in hands, bereft and forlorn, if they become a disappointment or an embarrassment to you. So lead your sons and daughters, so guide and direct them from the time they are very small, so teach them in the ways of the Lord, that peace will be their companion throughout life.[6]

Of course, some children will use their agency to wander. We should never give up but should administer even more love. If we have done all we can to train and teach them truth while they are in our care, we can rest assured that these teachings are still inside. We wait as did the father of the prodigal and welcome them back with all our love.

Every day matters! Everything we can do to strengthen faith within their hearts makes a lasting difference. How we hope our kids will develop strong faith and then make it through tough times as they grow up. We need the constant help of the Holy Ghost, prayer, gospel study, and trust.

The tender mercies will come, ways will open, and hearts will be softened. Through the Atonement of Jesus Christ, and with more of His love, truth will prevail.

Dear Mom and Dad,

Thanks for daily showing me that there really is a God in heaven and He has created all things for us to enjoy. I want to have strong faith like you do.

Love, Me

Glorious Repentance:
Turning Back to the Path Home

My son wrote the following story about what he learned as a young boy:

> After a tough but fun game of after-school sports flag football, my team was pretty happy with their win over one of the other six teams participating in the elementary sport. As I walked away feeling a little pride in our accomplishments, which was definitely portrayed in my body language, the captain of the defeated team swiftly spun me around and hit me hard in the lower jaw and upper neck.
>
> Struck with pain and shock from the blow, I quickly became angry at his aggressive form of bad sportsmanship. I was never one to try and seek revenge, but I felt myself get red with anger and frustration that I tried to contain.
>
> I composed myself a little and walked over to my mom, who had come to watch the game. After making sure I was okay, she quickly turned me around and told me to go make it right with him. I remember her scripturally imploring me to make it right "while . . . in the way with him" (3 Nephi 12:25).
>
> I was at first confused and even hurt by her response. I hadn't done anything wrong! He should be the one apologizing to me. I didn't want to go give him any more satisfaction for his actions. It was really hard for me, but with more persuasion, I decided that she was right.
>
> I walked over to him, stretched out my hand and said, "Hey Austin, I'm sorry." He took it and solemnly said, "Yeah, me too."
>
> As I walked back, I felt all the anger, confusion, and frustration leave. I did a lot of growing that day. I learned that competition is not worth the expense of a sour relationship. It helped me feel closer to the Savior as I realized His selfless love that He shows to everyone regardless of our actions. My testimony of the need for forgiveness and of the strength and power of God's mercy and the Savior's Atonement grew immensely from this experience.

Many think of repentance as "something miserable and depressing," taught Elder Stephen W. Owen. I know I did—in fact when I was growing up, I thought that it was shameful if you had to repent! But instead, it is "uplifting and enobling! It's sin that brings unhappiness. Repentance is our escape route!"[7] When we teach our families repentance and model it for them, we can help them see that repentance is a glorious gift given to us from our Savior's Atonement for our sins.

How can we teach that repentance is glorious?

1. Practicing Repentance

So, what about very young children who, we are told in the scriptures, are incapable of sinning and "need no repentance" (Moroni 8:8, 11)? I struggled with that concept. At times I knew that my child was definitely being naughty! Then I had an "ah-ha" moment to realize that they do have natural tendencies of greediness or anger at times—and they may copy bad behavior they see. They do wrongs but not sins, because they are not accountable for their actions, being innocent.

However, if my young child doesn't need repentance, how can I teach it? If we wait until they really need it, teaching remorse and repentance is much harder! So instead of telling a young child they need to repent, I decided to say, "Let's practice repenting." Then I can teach them how to feel much better after something has gone wrong. "Hitting makes us feel really bad inside! Why don't you go and tell your brother how sorry you are? Then, you could do something nice to make him feel better." Or "You must feel really bad inside. What could you do to make this better?"

Before our children are the age of accountability, eight years old, is the time to teach repentance. We can teach the simple steps of repentance, such as feel sorry, ask forgiveness, right the wrong, don't repeat the wrong,[8] and of course, the role of our Savior. My son used another way to teach this to kids while he was on his mission. He used the ABCs: A—Acknowledge our wrongdoings, B—Be sorry, C—Correct the mistake, D—Don't do it again, and E—Endure to the end. Simple but effective.

As our children grow, I like to teach that if Satan had gotten his way, we would be lost—one mistake and we would be doomed forever! But the Savior lets us be free to choose what we'll do, and not only that, He suffered so that we can repent and learn from it when we mess up. The ideal is taught in *For the Strength of Youth*: "Repentance is more than simply acknowledging wrongdoings. It is a change of mind and heart. It includes turning away from sin and turning to God for forgiveness. It is motivated by love for God and the sincere desire to obey His commandments."[9]

2. Turning Back to the Path

Like the prodigal son, "we all have to 'come to ourselves'—usually more than once—and choose the path that leads back home. It's a choice that we make daily, throughout our lives."[10] We can teach our children about the path back to God and our eternal home. President Nelson calls it "the covenant path." When we get distracted or make a choice that makes us step off the path, we need to hurry back, before we get lost! Before we come to the Father in prayer daily, and before we take the holy sacrament weekly, we should examine our lives. What did I do that took me away from God? What must I quickly correct? We are so grateful for this chance to fix our mistakes and turn back to the safe path back to Him.

To turn our kids back to the path, three words have been a favorite go-to line of mine: "try it over." They make correction simple. And while communicating that the behavior is not okay, these words do not belittle or even scold. They keep the child's self-esteem intact and tell them that I know they can do better. This is my best try at teaching positive repentance.

For example, if a child took a toy from his brother, I would respond, "Try it over." I expected a better way, and sometimes I would prompt them what to say: "May I please have a turn with that when you're done?" Then, I would wait to have that repeated. Some of my strong-willed children would not repeat what I prompted, so for them, I might say, "Figure out a nicer way to say this!" I have to determine the child's heart, because they aren't necessarily being obstinate but just reluctant to say something that's already been said! Further, some kids may actually think they *did* say it, because they heard it!

If a daughter blew up because her younger sister wore her new top without asking, I would say, "Try it over," to communicate that she should calm down and react better—that I knew she could do better than that! Later, however, when emotions were calmed down, I would remind the younger sister to always show respect by asking to borrow clothes first. But also, I might take the older sister aside and remind her gently how much her sister looks up to her and wants to be just like her—even dress like her! "She's figuring out who she is, and she admires you so much! Go easy on her, okay?" Talking to her like a grown-up is most effective, I have learned. But that conversation is later. At the time of the outburst, just my three words work best!

3. Helping to Bring Repentance

Sometimes kids are heavily into their own proud way and not ready to repent of it at all. At our house, if two children were having contention, to coax them toward repentance, I would come up with a job for them to do together until they "were friends." Most often, since there was always plenty of laundry, I sent both parties into the laundry room to fold clothes together until they figured it out. Sooner or later, in an effort to finish, the kids would usually start to see the other one's point of view and then be ready to repent and forgive—and "be friends."

In their family, Linda and Richard Eyre used a "Repentance Bench" to stop arguing and bring repentance. It was a designated bench, where two people sat when they had had a quarrel. Here they must stay until they each had figured out what *they* (not their sibling) had done wrong. When both people had figured out their own wrongdoing, apologized, and given each other a hug, then they could leave.[11] It was an effective way to bring about an introspection, an apology, and peace to the household.

4. Godly Sorrow: Our Goal

What we want is for our children to feel sorry. "If they feel remorse, you have succeeded."[12] The scriptures call it a "broken heart and a contrite spirit," and this is what we want our children to learn to feel—humility and regret. "And whoso cometh unto me with a broken heart and a contrite spirit, him will I baptize with fire and with the Holy Ghost" (3 Nephi 9:20). A good spirit is restored when we or our kids feel godly sorrow and so can truly repent.

Sometimes it takes a quiet conversation together that first validates a child's feelings but then points out the other person's point of view, thus bringing on the contrite heart. "You must be mad about your tower being ruined. He must have thought you were done with those Legos and wanted to try to make something just as good as yours," we might explain after little brother has wrecked a Lego creation. "He so wants to be just as good as you at building! And when you pushed him away, it really hurt his feelings! Do you think you can understand? How could we make that right?" Then, when there is understanding and then a feeling of sorrow for their reaction, a hug or a thoughtful gesture can heal wounds and bring peace.

5. The Apology: Confessing

Our kids had a "system" for taking care of confession and apology. When our older boys were saying good night to each other from their beds, one would call out, "SORRY FOR ALL THE CONTENTION!" Someone else would yell, "LIKEWISE!" and then the next brother would yell, "LIKEWISE" and the next would also yell, "LIKEWISE!" After a few weeks of this nightly process, they all just dropped the "sorry" part and simply would yell out just, "LIKEWISE!!!"

Later on, our younger boys developed a code to yell as well: "C.C." Or maybe it's more accurate to write it, "SI SI!" Apparently, this is an answer to two unsaid but understood questions: "Would you forgive me for all I have done?" (Yes! Or *si!*) and "Would you forgive me for *all I will do in the future?*" (*Si!*) I guess that about covers it!

So the question I am asking myself is, "Did I teach my kids repentance?" Or did I just teach them *efficiency?*

6. Making It Better

"Turn to God, and do works meet for repentance," we read in Acts 26:20. I take that to mean that we must do things that show we are repenting. We must teach kids to rectify the situation, or, in other words, to make it all better!

My brother-in-law had his feuding kids dance together! This would inevitably end in laughter, with friendships renewed! Dancing and laughing together were the works that showed all was forgiven.

One of my daughters was about eleven when she snuck in and ate an entire box of treats we had left up high on the "don't touch shelf." She didn't think anyone knew, but she felt bad and wanted to make it right. So she came to me for jobs to earn money, then got permission to ride her bike to the grocery store to buy a new box. Oh, what joy and relief she felt to make up for her sin. She turned and repented!

7. I Forgive You

When our kids were folding clothes together in the laundry room, if needed, I might call in: "It's time for someone to say, 'I forgive you!'" The two would eventually start to see the other one's point of view and be ready to repent and forgive—and be friends.

Besides "please" and "thank you," there are three more mannerly words that are wonderful to teach: "I forgive you." These words can be modeled and taught, even before kids feel the emotion. Trained to say "I forgive you" after someone says, "I'm sorry," kids will have a habit in place and the feeling behind it will catch up later. We can model the words for one to say after another apologizes, and it will create peace and heal wounds. ("I did it, and I'm sorry!" is another good phrase to train in to their vocabulary early!)

What a huge blessing we give kids when *we* apologize to them for our mistakes and misjudgments, and quickly forgive theirs. We teach repentance and forgiveness best by doing it sincerely in our own lives, by sharing our struggles, and by using the Savior's gift.

After a child has repented or has forgiven someone, there is cause for a small celebration! Saying "Good for you!" recognizes that they did something hard but so good. "Don't you feel good inside?" helps a child feel what we want them to feel! They did something very good in repenting of a mistake—or forgiving another's mistake! While we don't want to make too big of a deal about it (some children might hit *again* in order to have another repentance celebration!), we do want to reinforce the good effort and the good feelings that come from doing what's right!

8. Clean Again!

How wonderful that we only have to focus on one week at a time! Each week, we can start fresh after repentance by taking the sacrament. We can teach our kids that it is almost like being baptized again, because we can be clean again just like after baptism.

However, ideally repentance can be daily, as one little boy showed by repenting along with nighttime prayers each night (See "Baptism: the Gate, later in this chapter). This truly is the *good news* that the world needs to hear, to know that Christ came and paid for our sins so we could repent and try again. Repentance is a glorious blessing—one we can all use daily!

9. The Atonement of Jesus Christ

"Without the Redeemer, . . . repentance becomes simply miserable behavior modification."[13] "We can try to change our behavior on our own," said Elder Owens, "but only the Savior can remove our stains and lift our burdens, enabling us . . . to turn our hearts towards our fellowman" and to Him. "The joy of repentance is the joy of being clean again, and of drawing closer to God."[14]

Mark is a loving father, so it is easy for us to visualize God as a loving Father, so ready to forgive. For others, it may be harder. But all people can come to know the goodness of God, or who God actually is. A missionary currently serving in Mexico determined she would try to re-teach those who saw God as vindictive and revengeful. "God isn't an executioner," she taught, "He's a dad. He makes it completely 100% possible for us to win! Even, maybe even especially, when we're 'wandering from the fold of God.'"[15] Elder Scott taught, "By understanding the Atonement of Jesus Christ, you will see that God is not a jealous being who delights in persecuting those who misstep. He is an absolutely perfect, compassionate, understanding, patient, and forgiving Father. He is willing to entreat, counsel, strengthen, lift, and fortify. He so loves each of us that He was willing to have His perfect, sinless, absolutely obedient, totally righteous Son experience indescribable agony and pain and give Himself in sacrifice for all."[16]

Let's paint for our children a picture of a merciful, loving God who waits to receive us when we repent, even celebrating with us like the father of the prodigal son! "Repentance is a divine gift, and there should be a smile on our faces when we speak of it. It points us to freedom, confidence, and peace. Rather than interrupting the celebration, the gift of repentance is the cause for true celebration."[17]

Dear Mom and Dad,

You have taught me to say "I'm sorry" since I was little. Now, I am learning to really feel sorry, to want to turn back to the path toward Jesus. Thanks for giving me this gift of trying over when I mess up!

Love, Me

Baptism: The Gate

It was a bit noisy at the baptism. Lots of cousins and friends had joined the new eight-year-old on his special day. In fact, as she watched him, his grandma wondered, *Does he really "get it"? His sacred ordinance of baptism took less than a minute today. In all this busyness, can he possibly internalize the covenant he made and his new responsibility? Does he understand what a great blessing this is?*

The next night, Grandma was in this grandson's bedroom, tucking him in for the night. He had said his prayers and climbed in, when all of a sudden he exclaimed, "Oh, Grandma! I forgot to repent!" She wondered about that—he'd only been baptized one day ago! But he climbed out of bed, knelt, and prayed, "Heavenly Father, please forgive me of my sins so that I can stay clean. Amen." Then, his little sister called out, "I didn't repent either!" to which he answered, "You don't have to. You're only six!" Grandma smiled. He sure "got it!" His parents had taught him well, so he knew that he had been washed clean through baptism and he had faith that he could now stay clean by constantly repenting.

We parents are preparing our children from the time they are born for the important step of baptism. Before age eight is a special time for children, with no temptation from Satan. Yes, they pick up wrongdoings from the world around them, and they too deal with the natural man. But sins do not form in their hearts from temptations of Satan. It is the perfect time to teach the gospel.

Baptism is one of the most important things a child can do, and we must teach him that. We can show him in the scriptures that baptism is the *gate* which must be opened to commence in the path back to Heavenly Father (see 2 Nephi 31:9, 17–18). No one can get back to Him without being baptized. It's the first step, and it's that important! In fact, that is why we do this ordinance in the temple for those who died before they had the chance to hear the gospel, so that they too can be baptized and return to Heavenly Father. Here are some ideas for teaching this ordinance:

1. Fears Concerning Baptism

Some little children are afraid of being baptized. Some might be afraid of going under the water or have other fears. Parents should leave the lines of communication open and be approachable on this topic. We can reassure and address the fears if we know and understand them.

I had myself been afraid of going under water before my baptism. So, I reassured my very young child that he wouldn't be baptized until he was ready. I made sure to take him swimming and let him get used to going under water before age eight. As my children were approaching eight years old, I was so grateful to the Primary in my ward. They presented a baptism preparation booklet to the seven-year-old kids at a visit to their home. Inside were some activities and some stories copied from the *Friend* magazine about baptism and receiving the Holy Ghost. Most of them dealt with children who had one fear or another as his or her baptism approached. For example, one story was about a boy who was afraid that the sins of the children baptized before him were left in the water! Another story was about a little girl who was very afraid of all ghosts! I so appreciated this tool to help me spend time with and talk to my seven-year-old children as they got ready for their special baptism day. Later, when my younger children turned seven and there was no longer this resource, I reused previous booklets and searched to find stories myself for these children. Today, stories about baptism and the gift of the Holy Ghost can be found at lds.org.[18] It helped the preparation for baptism be a sweet time.

2. A Little Bit at a Time

I wanted to make sure my son was prepared for baptism. Our family had regular scripture study and family night, but I didn't really know what this youngest son had picked up and what he had missed. So I decided to teach him a little bit every night. I would lay down beside my son on his bed and just talk to him. We would review the fourth Article of Faith night after night until he knew it well (knowing that the bishop likely would ask him to recite it in the baptismal interview). We regularly went over the baptismal covenant: the promises he would make and the promises the Lord makes in return.

One of the best ways to prepare children for baptism is to start taking them to baptisms at a very early age. Our families can attend the baptisms of cousins and friends from Primary, so our kids see what will happen and be ready. Our kids will feel comfortable and start to get excited about having this beautiful day themselves.

Inviting others not of our faith to the baptism is a great idea for a missionary experience. Special teachers and friends, knowing the excitement a child feels for this special day, may choose to come support him. Baptisms are Spirit-filled occasions, so it is wonderful to allow our friends to have that experience with us!

3. Teaching Helps

I used the acronym TAKE to help him know the covenant he would make: Take His name upon us; Always remember Him; Keep His commandments; and Endure to the end. I also added the elements of the baptismal covenant found in Mosiah 18:8–9, which remind us that we promise to "mourn with those that mourn; yea, and comfort those that stand in need of comfort, and to stand as witnesses of God at all times and in all things, and in all places." Then I emphasized the wonderful things God promises us: to give us the constant gift of the Holy Ghost, to forgive us when we repent, and to give us eternal life! I tried not to overwhelm him with too much at once by taking a little piece at a time to talk over with him. A silent prayer beforehand helped me to tune in to him and to have the words that would help him best understand.

My son especially responded to the concept that now that he was going to become a member of the Church, he would be joining Jesus's team! Just like he put on a soccer jersey for his soccer team, he now was "putting Jesus's name on himself" by being baptized. This team name was not written on his shirt but could still be as obvious to people that he was like Jesus, that he was on His team and doing His work. The other team was Satan's team, and they would be trying to beat us constantly. But we must be true to our team and help conquer Satan.

During the year before their eighth birthday, it is good to hold family home evenings where children can ask questions. Mark likes to show them just how he will hold their arms and let them practice bending their knees as he helps them go under the water. Family home evening is also a good time to ask the older kids to tell what they remembered from their baptisms. Mark and I share our special memories as well. Every member is reminded of the importance of their ordinance and the need to renew the covenant every Sunday by taking the sacrament.

4. Keep It Simple

Our bishop gave us wise counsel in relation to the proceedings of the baptism day. He told us to keep it simple and focus on the ordinance rather than just on the child. This helped us not to stress about too much extra fluff but to emphasize that which was most important.

One of my daughters was extra conscientious about things. At her baptism, the ordinance had to be done over since it was unclear whether part of her had gone completely under the water.

I feared this daughter might be totally devastated from this or feel humiliated about having to do it twice. So, at the first possible chance, I said to her, "Isn't it wonderful that they did your baptism twice?!" She looked up at me somewhat incredulously. "They wanted to make absolute sure that it was done right! You're lucky!" At that, this daughter's expression turned from bewilderment to contentment. "Yea, I guess you're right!" Talking it through had helped turn that detail of her baptism from negative to positive in her mind, right then and every time she remembered it later! In fact, I encouraged her to write about her baptism in her journal to capture the good for her to remember.

5. Renewing Baptism with the Wonderful Sacrament

Sometimes, a child is determined to stay so clean after his baptism and so feels devastated when he goes ahead and makes a mistake! *I blew it!* he may think. Parents can be available to reassure their newly washed-clean child that when he or she has made a mistake, there is still the sacrament to allow us to be clean again! "Isn't the gospel wonderful?! Didn't Jesus do a wonderful thing for us, when he suffered so we can repent!"

We parents can also emphasize what a privilege it is to become a member of Christ's Church. After being baptized, our kids are old enough to be a really good example of those who believe in Christ. We can stress how good our kids have felt when they chose the right and that the gift of the Holy Ghost will help them choose the right in the future. Taking the sacrament will help us remember Jesus, so we can always keep the Holy Ghost with us.

Baptism is such a big deal. It is worth all our efforts to prepare our kids, to walk them through the ordinance's meaning, and to tune in to any special worries each child might have or reassurances they might need. May we help their baptismal day be one they cherish and remember their entire lives.

Dear Mom and Dad,

I'm excited about my baptism, but a little nervous too. Thanks for the time you take to teach me all about it. Soon, it will be my turn to open the Gate back to our Father in Heaven!

Love, Me

The Holy Ghost: My Best Friend

"If the Holy Ghost is one being, how can he help everyone at the same time?" one of our kids asked once. "It's like the sun," was the answer I came up with. "It is one body, but we all can feel it at the same time. Some may step into the shade, or even go into a dark place, and not feel its warmth or see its light. But it is still there for whoever chooses to be in places where it can be felt." Mark gave a second analogy, "I can send out a message to all, via radio waves," he told the kids, "but not everyone will receive it. The message is right here—even everywhere—but only those who are tuned in will get that message. So it is with the Holy Ghost."

Actually, we were talking about the influence of the Holy Ghost, that everyone may feel, since everyone born on this earth has access to the Light of Christ. But after we are baptized, we are confirmed and told to receive the constant companionship of the Holy Ghost. It's like we are given our own wonderful flashlight that we get to have with us always. We must keep it with us, and we must turn it on, or it's no good to us. But what a wonderful best friend is the Holy Ghost!

"The Holy Ghost is the third member of the Godhead. He is a personage of spirit, without a body of flesh and bones. (D&C 130:22) He is often referred to as the Spirit, the Holy Spirit, the Spirit of God, the Spirit of the Lord, or the Comforter. . . . The gift of the Holy Ghost is different from the influence of the Holy Ghost. Before baptism, a person can feel the influence of the Holy Ghost from time to time and through that influence can receive a testimony of the truth. After receiving the gift of the Holy Ghost, a person has the right to the constant companionship of that member of the Godhead if he or she keeps the commandments."[19]

I have often realized that I couldn't do parenting without the help of the Holy Ghost! "For behold, again I say unto you that if ye will enter in by the way, and receive the Holy Ghost, it will show unto you all things what ye should do" (2 Nephi 32:5). It is interesting in that chapter that the scriptures *tell* us all things we should do, and the Holy Ghost *shows* us all things we should do! I make a point each morning in my prayers to ask for the Spirit to help me that day, since I need that help constantly to know what to do! What a marvelous blessing it is to have a best friend beside me in all my daily dilemmas, with ideas, truths, comfort, and peace. But one of the greatest things about this spiritual best friend is that it can also be a best friend to our children. We can introduce Him to our children, and help this friendship happen.

We certainly don't have to be perfect to have this wonderful friend around, I have learned for myself! But we do have to be trying to qualify. "This is the grand privilege of every Latter-day Saint . . . that it is our right to have the manifestations of the Spirit every day of our lives."[20] He cannot stay where there is discord or darkness, however, so we have to work to make an atmosphere where our best friend will be comfortable to stay.

We can help our children want to keep this best friend. When it's their turn for family prayer, my kids have picked up a phrase I like to use: "Help us do nothing to offend the Spirit in our home today." We want the peace of the Holy Ghost in our refuge from the world. But also, we want to take him with us wherever we go.

One time I needed the help of the Spirit. I had just taught a Primary lesson to a class of five-year-olds. I was packing up afterward, and I discovered that I couldn't find my keys. The kids were being helpful, searching for them with me, then one of them said, "Sister Ellingson, we need to pray." "Yes" was my reply, but I hesitated. I had looked everywhere in that small classroom; there was simply nowhere else to look! What would these little children learn when the keys didn't show up?" Then, I berated myself, "Where is your faith?!" So I mustered up all the faith I could find, and said, "Yes, we should pray." We did have a simple prayer together, and a couple of minutes later the Spirit moved me to check a spot I had already searched several times. We found the keys! The kids were delighted, and I was even more so, for not only had the incident indeed strengthened their faith in God, but it had also strengthened mine!

Here are some ways the Holy Ghost can be our very best friend:

1. The Holy Ghost Testifies of God the Father, and His Son, Jesus Christ

He gives us messages from Them. "When we reverence deity, we are filled with the Holy Ghost" is the way my neighbor put it.[21] In the play "My Turn on Earth" there are real messages from heaven. As the characters are figuring out how to navigate this life, little pieces of paper drop from heaven, each with a message written on it. Often the message is a scripture that corrects their behavior or helps them with the next steps they are going to be taking.[22] This is a great visual about help from above through the Holy Ghost.

2. The Holy Ghost Comforts and Brings Peace

Little children can experience great sadness. A loss of a pet, a move, an abrupt change in their lives or any other trial can leave the need for comfort. We can turn our grieving children to prayer for the comfort from the Holy Ghost that Heavenly Father sends. We can help them recognize the sweet, comforting feeling and know its source. Our love coupled with love from above can bring them peace.

3. The Holy Ghost Brings Things to Our Remembrance

Sometimes we may wonder if the principles we are teaching our children really stick. Did that child who was messing around during family night really learn anything? I would submit that if we tried our best to bring the Holy Ghost there—through song, through prayer, through truth taught with love and concern—the concepts are indeed planted in their hearts. And the Holy Ghost will bring them to our child's remembrance when they are searching and need to draw deep for truth.

Here too, the home is the workshop. When children have lost something—like I and my keys—we can turn them to prayer. Sometimes, this takes great faith on our part, that we really can find this treasured item amid all the places it could be. We must believe that God does care and He does know where it is. Here is an opportunity to share that faith with our child by kneeling together and asking in faith. And God will help, by sending ideas to our minds through the Holy Ghost. Even if help is not immediate, we can teach them sermons by not losing hope and by expressing our trust that God knows what is best for us, and He will help us at the right time.

We often need to have help remembering things as well. I have a poignant memory of sitting in high school geometry class. I was taking a test, and there was a tough question that I just could not figure out. The tenseness grew as I grappled with the problem—it was worth a lot of points on this test, and no ideas were coming as to how to solve it! Then I remembered to pray. I humbly asked for help to remember what I had studied. And it was amazing: I listened and the concepts came back to me. I still remember the amazement and relief and the gratitude that came to my heart that the Holy Ghost would bring these things to my mind. "But the Comforter, which is the Holy Ghost, whom the Father will send in my name, he shall teach you all things, and bring all things to your remembrance, whatsoever I have said unto you" (John 14:26). I have shared this experience with my kids, and we have coined a phrase for when they have a test at school: Remember T. P. (Test Prayer)!

4. The Holy Ghost Testifies of All Truth

Whenever we teach the gospel to our kids, at family home evening, at scripture time, at casual conversation around the kitchen table, or during a ride in the car, the Holy Ghost can confirm the truths that we are teaching. The Holy Ghost can fill our hearts to testify to each of us that these are indeed true. We can bear testimony, formally or in casual conversation, that we know these things are true, and we can help kids to recognize that the peaceful feelings they have inside are from God, through the Holy Ghost.

Our job is to provide chances and places for our kids to make this connection with God. We can take them to sacred places and help them to be still and listen for those sacred feelings, as best as we and they can. The Lord will help our righteous desires, and He will help us get past the opposition that always comes when we are trying to put together these special opportunities. He will make up the difference, and the kids will feel even more than we even think they do.

Mark and I put together several trips to sacred spots in order to help our children to feel sacred feelings from the Holy Ghost. It was not easy, and kids got tired and hungry. But we did our best to make it meaningful. We prayed for a sacred experience and for the opposition to be quelled. At the end, when one son came up to us and said, "My testimony has grown on this trip," it was all worth it!

Before one of the boys left on his mission, we took the family up a mountain overlooking Phoenix. It was dusk, and after a short hike, we sat and watched the lights of the city turning on below. We wondered about all those people who lived in all those places. We talked about how each one is beloved of our Father in Heaven, and many are searching for more truth. The Holy Ghost would help our new missionary to find them, to bless their lives, and to bring them closer to Christ. It was a choice moment to think and feel.

5. The Holy Ghost Gives Us the Words to Say and the Best Thing to Do

When someone asks us a hard question or when we are just out of ideas as to how to address the current dilemma, the Holy Ghost is our best friend. Whenever we need the right words to say, a quick prayer will bring help from the Holy Ghost. I have learned clearly that we do not have to be perfect to qualify for this help. When we are trying to do our best to read the scriptures, pray, and desire it, heavenly help will come. "Treasure up in your minds continually the words of life, and it shall be given you in the very hour" the right words to say (D&C 84:85) is a promise of help from the Holy Ghost that we can count on.

Reading the scriptures brings us the help of the Holy Ghost, which gives us words to say. There was a season when I had five little kids under five! It was extra hard to fit in scripture reading, but when I did—even opening them up when I slipped away to the bathroom—I found that I was blessed with the Spirit. I found that I was blessed with the Holy Ghost to give me better words to say, help to pause a minute when things got hectic, and power and strength to give more Christlike responses. What's more, it was interesting to me to notice that when I got my minimum daily requirement in, it usually applied to the following day! How I needed that extra help. How much it blessed me to better be the mom I wanted to be to my precious, needy little ones.

6. The Role of the Sacrament

How wonderful to regroup each week when we partake of the sacrament! What a great chance to repent, become clean again, and try again for a new week of help from above to be our best. I had been listening to the words of the sacramental prayers for all my life, when one day it hit me: the more I remember to try to be like Jesus, the more I will have His Spirit (the Holy Ghost) to be with me! It was a formula I need to apply each week.

Before we go to church, I like to remind my children occasionally that now is the time to look over our lives, to remember anything we need to repent of, and take care of it so we will be ready to take the sacrament. We have talked about this in family home evening, but a reminder at just the right time will help them put this practice into their lives. They will better stay on the path if they repent, remember the Savior's Atonement, and receive the Holy Ghost weekly.

7. Listening and Following

Many, many times I have realized that I had had a little thought about how to handle something better and had not acted on it! It was hindsight that showed me that the Holy Ghost had been trying to prompt me! So I decided to change my daily prayers. Along with asking for the Spirit to be with me that day, now I also ask that I will listen carefully and follow it!

8. Gifts to Parents

I have come to realize that the Holy Ghost is a parent's best friend especially. Some of the many gifts the Spirit gives to parents are:

- The Gift of Noticing: The Spirit helps us to notice the good intentions and good actions our kids do, so we can encourage them by reinforcing and praising these tiny steps in the right direction!
- The Gift of Seeing: The Spirit can help us catch the tiny signs that our children give us, clues about their inner workings. Really seeing my child's goodness and innocence happens best for me sometimes when they are sleeping!
- The Gift of a Mighty Change of Heart: The Spirit can help us do a 180-degree turn in our hearts and minds, from total despair to deep gratitude, just by the way we look at something and the way we decide to think about it!
- The Gift of Redirecting: The Spirit can help us be able to totally change a child's focus. With help, we can better direct them to a better thing to focus on.
- The Gift of Letting Things Slide: The Spirit can help us react like water on a duck's back, letting some things simply slide off and not penetrate our heart or mind.
- The Gift of Absorbing: The Spirit can help us totally absorb the bad thing that happened, and not let it grow. It can stop with us, dissipate, and disappear rather than doing harm to us or to anyone else, if we give that bad thing to the Savior. We can lay it at the altar, and let Him take it from us.

- The Gift of the Right Words to Say: What a wondrous gift of the Spirit to be given just the right words to say! Feelings can be soothed, self-esteem can be bolstered, and love can be received when we have just the right phrases come to our minds.
- The Gift of Follow Through: Sometimes we come up with a great idea, but when things become tough, it is hard to see the plan through. The Spirit can bring the push we need to simply continue through rough patches and on to victory.

All these and so many more gifts combine to make our lives full and sweet. What an amazing gift is the Spirit in our parenting!

Dear Mom and Dad,

I'm so excited to get my own constant best friend after I am baptized! Thanks for teaching me about the Holy Ghost and showing me in your own life the precious gift of a constant and true best friend.

Love, Me

Enduring to the End: Be a Finisher

The end seems like a long way away—especially to a young child! Good thing God has separated life into pieces for us, in that we have rest and renewal every Sunday! But life happens, and every one of us has heavy burdens to carry and seasons of intense opposition and trial.

Elder Leonard D. Greer, our Area Seventy, gave us a new perspective about enduring to the end as part of the doctrine of Christ, when he taught in stake conference. These doctrines should not be pictured as a horizontal line, he taught, in which we have faith, then repent, then get baptized, then receive the Holy Ghost—all of those happening quite quickly—and then comes a *long* season of enduring to the end. It's not like that at all, taught Elder and Sister Greer. Instead, it's like a circle. We develop faith, which is shown by the action we take; we repent of our sins, not just once but constantly; we are baptized and we renew this covenant by taking worthily the sacrament; and we receive the Holy Ghost over and over as well. Then we press forward to endure whatever comes our way. Which leads us to more faith, and the circle repeats over and over, spiraling us upward toward God. Enduring to the end is one of the important steps that builds upon the others and propels us higher.[23] We must help our children be able to endure to the end and grow in the process by helping them learn to be finishers. Here are various ways to teach that concept:

1. Press Forward

Nelson Mandela was a leader of the apartheid movement in South Africa, working to dismantle segregation and enduring twenty-seven years of imprisonment during his struggles, but later receiving a Nobel Peace prize for his efforts. He once reflected on being a saint and simply described a saint as "a sinner who keeps on trying."[24] We all must keep on trying. We are taught the importance of enduring in 3 Nephi 15:9, in which the Savior tells us, "Behold, I am the law, and the light. Look unto me, and endure to the end, and ye shall live; for unto him that endureth to the end will I give eternal life."

When I think of someone who is pressing forward, I think of someone who is pushing onward despite blustery winds that blow the other way. We can teach our children that the trials or winds of life can be tough to navigate through, but they can also be good for growth: wind moves sailboats, generates energy, and allows kites to fly high! When we push through the hard times, we will grow, and our children will see us enduring well. They will learn the most from our examples.

Our pioneer ancestors bravely navigated their trials by focusing on hope. They pressed forward, through terrible trial, to push their handcarts and take their family to safety. They endured, and in the process, they grew. Like them, we too want to get our families safely back to heaven. We must endure trial and keep up our hope, and not just hope—a bright hope. "Wherefore, ye must press forward with a steadfastness in Christ, having a perfect brightness of hope, and a love of God and of all men. Wherefore, if ye shall press forward, feasting upon the word of Christ, and endure to the end, behold, thus saith the Father: Ye shall have eternal life" (2 Nephi 31:20).

2. Be Finishers Along the Way

As we were taught, enduring to the end is not just a one-time long and miserable event. There are many chances along the way to practice our endurance by being finishers and teaching our children to follow through as well. Long-term endurance is built on many short-term goals. We can teach our children endurance by dividing a large task into pieces, like planting one seed at a time until the whole garden is planted or picking one weed at a time until the whole garden is weeded. We can expect them to see a project through to the end, like sweeping up after you mow the lawn. (A nice water fight at the end is wonderful too!)

Many projects start out fun. They are new and exciting. Finishing them to the end is not always so fun, but it is such a great skill to teach. Cleaning up, returning items, giving thanks for the help, and tying up all loose ends are important things to expect and to insist upon. We teach follow-through best by doing it ourselves.

One of my sons was a junior in high school when he decided to build a float for the homecoming parade. As he was part of the Teenage Republican Club at school, he and friends built a huge elephant. He built the massive body, but then was stuck on how to construct the head. In fact, the elephant remained headless for a week or two because he couldn't figure out how to make the shape correct with the frame underneath. He was focusing so much on creating the perfect product that indecision impeded his progress. Mark told him to just try it, just start, and he would figure it out as he went. Enduring at this point meant to just move, to start. Don't be afraid to fail and keep moving.

The elephant received a head at last, and the project came together wonderfully. This was not just an elephant; it was a cool elephant: it had a trunk that shot both candy and pressurized water out of its movable trunk! It was amazing, and so fun for our son to be inside and run his creation. On our path of endurance, we have to overcome tendencies of perfectionism and focus instead on steady progress.

After it was all over, it was hard to dismantle the float because it meant the end of their good times with the now-legendary elephant. But the kids returned the trailers and cleaned up. They were finishers.

3. He Is Not Just at the End

Our Savior walks every step with us, not just at the end. His Atonement includes His grace, or the enabling power to help us through our trials every step of the way. His hands are outstretched to us, but He will not force His divine help. He invites and waits, and He longs to help us through the hard times. "Behold, I stand at the door, and knock: if any man hear my voice, and open the door, I will come in to him, and will sup with him, and he with me" (Revelation 3:20).

My son taught me that the "daily bread" of enduring to the end is not about doing your best. We will never totally do our best in this life. It means to keep trying, relying on the Lord, and changing daily. Sometimes enduring even means walking blindly with God, with an imperfect understanding of the destination or resolution of our problems. That's the secret. When we have no idea how our mountain of problems in going to be solved, we just demonstrate some faith and keep trying to move in a positive direction. It's about letting go of the need for control and simply relying on the daily bread. Enduring to the end means waiting on the Lord. "We endure in faith to the end one day at a time," taught D. Todd Christofferson. "It is the accumulation of many days well-lived that adds up to a full life and a saintly person."[25]

We don't become perfect parents overnight, but we always "try a little harder, to be a little better."[26] By the same token, we can't demand perfection from our children, but we can celebrate the positive progress we observe.

4. Draw Conclusions and Learn from Them

"And thus we see" is found so often in scripture (see Alma 28:14 for one), before a summary of what the people had just learned. It is good to have closure, especially with negative experiences. We learn from them, and then we put them away and move on. Writing in my journal helps me to learn more and to feel closure, so I like to help my children write—or dictate for me to write if they are too young—their experiences in their journals too. It was when my young son wrote about his experience at a temple open house for a talk in Primary that he cemented in his heart the fact that he had felt the Spirit there. This experience was foundational for his testimony.

5. Don't Just Endure—Grow

"God cares a lot more about who we are and who we are becoming than about who we once were." As we repeatedly live the doctrine of Christ, "exercising faith in Him, repenting, partaking of the sacrament to renew the covenants and blessings of baptism, and receiving the Holy Ghost as a constant companion to a greater degree . . . we become more like Christ and are able to endure to the end, with all that that entails."[27] As we press forward to endure, we can keep trying to grow to be a better and better person.

Sometimes enduring to the end means holding out to the end of our families. It might seem like the younger ones get spoiled with more luxury, but it's a challenge to give the younger ones the same teachings and opportunities we gave the older ones (when we had more energy)! There is a temptation right now for me to turn to career and work, but I've realized that the youngest children need their mom at the crossroads, just as their older siblings needed me when they were that age. Though I can do other things, they are my highest priority and they need to feel it.

6. Pick Flowers Along the Way

One of the hardest seasons for Mark and I was when we had twin sons in the ICU after their premature birth. Since it happened as we were in the process of moving out of state, we were in limbo, with no job, no home, our belongings packed up. But mostly, it was so hard to watch our tiny babies lose weight day after day and to have to be separated from each other and from us. I just knew they would thrive if only we could get them home. But enduring this time, staying in my sister's temporarily vacant trailer, we connected with second cousins who lived nearby, and celebrated Grandma's birthday. Our sixteen-month-old daughter learned to swing on a nearby swing set and we decided it was okay to eat our bottled fruit that we had saved for a rainy day! We did our best to pick flowers while enduring a "treacherous" journey.

May we change our view of enduring to the end, if need be. Some even choose to call it "enjoying to the end!" May this be a process of circling upward toward heaven and our Savior, knowing that his enabling power is with us each step of our journey home. We can enjoy the path and the scenery along the way, picking the flowers, and knowing He will help us get where we want to end up. "Behold, I am the law, and the light. Look unto me, and endure to the end, and ye shall live; for unto him that endureth to the end will I give eternal life" (3 Nephi 15:9).

Dear Mom and Dad,

Thanks for your efforts to help me be a finisher. It is a good skill and I want to use it to endure to the end of this life. Thanks for helping me access the grace of our Savior as we go.

Love, Me

Chapter 12
Stick Together as a Family

*I*n order to be a unified family, we must work to all be on the same page. Tools to make this happen are effective family councils and family home evening. May we use these tools to the fullest, to grow a family that is cohesive, loyal, and together.

Family Home Evening: Go Ahead and Have It!

It was getting later and later on a Monday night, and Mark had still not come home from work. He had a deadline to meet and couldn't get home sooner. But my kids were getting sleepy, and soon I would have to put them down to bed. What about family home evening? I wanted my kids to grow up knowing that we *always* had FHE! Now what? I'm sure I prayed about it that night before crawling in myself. Well, the next morning I looked at the kitchen table where Mark and all the kids were sitting, quietly eating their cereal. I had an idea! With his okay, I read a story from the *Friend* as the family ate. I summarized it and explained the principle taught. Then I said, "This is our family home evening this week!" So we *do* have it every week! I felt so relieved.

Why is this such a big deal? Because family home evening is a big deal. It is obedience to a prophet's counsel, yes. But it is also a wonderful tool to teach the gospel to our families. For one, no one is singled out for a reprimand or a need for this lesson. We are all trying to learn and live the gospel. For another, it's teaching doctrines that changes behavior! "Preoccupation with unworthy behavior will lead to more unworthy behavior. That is why we stress teaching the doctrines of the church."[1] When we are having trouble with pride, for example, we should teach humility. When we need less contention, we can teach peace.

Family home evening is not easy. Not only are there busy schedules, but also there is the short attention span of the little ones and sometimes the lack of enthusiasm from the older ones. But we can catch the attention of the younger ones with object lessons and role-plays and activities, and we can keep the attention of older ones by having them teach part or all of the lesson, drawing from their own experiences.

Sometimes it is tricky to teach various ages—but interactive lessons draw in everyone.

"Would you come stand on this chair?" I asked a young son one family night. That got his attention—and everyone else's! I handed him a kite, there in the family room, and asked him to "fly it high"! I turned to another child, "Would you please be the child who is holding the string to fly this kite?" as I handed this one the kite string. I then proceeded with the story that they were acting out, about a little girl who loved sending her kite higher and higher into the sky, letting out more and more string to let it dance in the wind. "I wish my kite could fly away free," the little girl said. "It's this string that is holding it down!" She begged and begged her dad to let her cut the string. So finally he did! (I got some scissors and cut the string. That brought a gasp from the whole family!) As soon as he did, the kite came crashing down! (I whispered to the child holding it up to let it go.) This is just like obedience, I told our kids. Obeying rules and commandments is like the kite string: It may seem to be holding you back, but in reality, obedience keeps you up, and lets you be happy. It is when we disobey that we crash to the ground and cannot be happy.[2]

Object lessons and role-playing are wonderful ways to teach little kids—and big kids too. When we tell something, our kids only use one of their senses to hear it. But whenever they can engage more senses to see, hear, touch, move, even smell and taste, the better the learning. My neighbor's son will never forget the story of Samuel the Lamanite, because he got to help act it out. When he was six or seven years old, he was so excited to be assigned to be the rock in the story. Turns out the one playing Samuel the Lamanite stepped on the "rock" to get to the top of the table, where he warned the people. Yes, this little boy was a rock, who stood still like a rock—a very important part of the story! And from then on, he remembered the story vividly!

Every Monday night, without fail, at dinner my teenagers ask Mark and I two questions: "What are we doing for family night tonight?" and "How long will it take?"

1. Planning FHE: "What Are We Doing for Family Night Tonight?"

Sometimes, at this point, Mark and I look at each other (with no idea yet what we are doing that night)! And even if we do have something planned, I don't want to just say, "We're having a lesson." So, my usual answer is, "We are having a wonderful family night tonight!"

Talk It Over. Ideally, Mark and I would have talked it over ahead of time. Maybe on Sunday or before, we'd have discussed just what our family needs to learn. But if that didn't happen, I liked to call Mark at work during his lunch break and discuss our ideas for FHE. That way we are on the same page. He then can introduce, and I can put together what we talked about! Mark leads out on family night, to have a song, call on someone to pray, and announce the lesson or activity.

Schedule. It works well for some families to set up a monthly plan for their family nights, such as the first Monday, Dad teaches; the second Monday, Mom teaches; the third Monday, one of the kids teach; and on the fourth Monday, the family does an activity or a service. This way, everyone knows ahead. We have to be flexible, for example, when a good opportunity to join with other families opens up or an invitation to go swimming with cousins for FHE, but a skeleton plan helps. Other families take turns choosing the song, prayer, lesson or activity, and treat. But these are not necessary if a family needs to have it simpler.

Lessons. In the current "Come, Follow Me" program, our teens teach their peers often. In the "Duty to God" and "Personal Progress" programs, they are required to share what they have learned as well. In each case, they will have studied a certain topic and come to understand it better. Suppose a teenage daughter just gave a lesson in Young Women on feeling the Spirit. How natural is it for her to then present what she has learned to the family? Parents can emphasize to her how much the family—particularly the younger siblings—needs her valuable insights and experiences feeling the Spirit in her life.

While it is ideal to ask a teenager *ahead of time* to teach the family night lesson coming up, it doesn't always happen. If need be, we simply excuse that teen from doing dishes that night, in order to go prepare his lesson. A stake leader advised us to use "For the Strength of Youth" regularly, so we often assign our teenager to choose one of the standards to present—say honesty and integrity— and give their own personal insight about and experience with being truthful and trusted. They will learn the gospel better as they are teaching it! If a teen is reluctant to teach, they might respond to an invitation to share, such as "Would you share a time you had a prayer answered, to help us teach this to the younger kids?"

2. Priorities: "How Long Will It Take?"

When my teenagers invariably ask this, I remind myself that it's not that they are being rebellious or complaining; they are just busy and want us to be efficient. Regrettably, they do have other things that fall on Monday nights at times: team sports, study groups, rehearsals, homework. While we have them move commitments whenever possible, it is sometimes a delicate balance to respect some of these things that they cannot change, such as commitment to a team, while keeping family home evening a top priority in our lives. The prophets have counseled us to have family home evening, and we can be confident before the Lord when we follow prophetic counsel. But what do we do when conflicts come up?

Use Dinnertime. Everyone has to eat! When we are gathered at the table, we can begin the lesson while they are eating, if necessary, or quickly remove dirty dishes and keep everyone together for the song and prayer and lesson.

Move FHE to Sundays or Another Day. Some families, especially those whose kids must be at a mandatory sports practice, simply move family night to Sunday. Without the weeknight conflicts, they have time to be together unrushed. This is definitely a better choice than no FHE at all!

Go Ahead and Have It! Families can be flexible as needed, but we are sure to tell the kids, "This is our family night," to give them the security of knowing that our family is obedient and consistent. We may have it in the car, but we have family home evening.

3. Activities: "Let's Have Some Fun!"

It can be tricky to plan a fun activity for both older and younger kids to do together, but it can be done. Little kids and grown ones alike enjoy a big beach ball! It can be used in a game of volleyball or a different sort of baseball. Kickball is another game for all ages, as is charades. Board games can be played with teams—a big person teamed up with a little one. One night we had fun making paper airplanes and throwing them off of the bleachers at the high school!

Service is another great family night activity. We have taken our kids down to the church to pick weeds. The "grandma ladies" at the nursing home need visits and hugs and songs. Somebody's car may need washing. Around our area there is a need to pick citrus, and then we can donate it to the food bank! Our own family members may need service, such as a teenager running for student council who needs help making badges or signs. Once we delivered wedding invitations for a family who needed our help. The children can help the family be on the lookout for service needed among the widows or any neighbor or family member!

4. Family Night Treat: "Yum!"

To a kid, the family night treat is a big deal. Come up with something, even ants on a log, crackers with something spread on top, frozen grapes or bananas, etc. to call your family night treat for that week and celebrate family!

Remember, all members get a treat just for being a member of the family! This is not the time to teach about eating all your food before desert—teach that on Tuesday or Wednesday or all the rest of the week, but not with the family night treat!

5. Building Testimony: "This Is a True Principle."

The Lord always provides at least two witnesses that something is true and to confirm all His words and ordinances. "In the mouth of two or three witnesses shall every word be established" (2 Corinthians 13:1). Family home evening provides an important second witness. Teachers at church try their best to teach our children each week, but our teachings at home are even more important. When our children get both witnesses that the gospel is true, they are more likely to understand it and believe it. What a great plan, to have different ways to reach our loved ones.

Family home evening is also a wonderful place to strengthen and bear testimony. Each time we teach a principle, we can bear testimony of it. We can encourage our children to testify of the things they are teaching. And, sometimes, we can all share testimonies. They grow by bearing them, and the home is a safe workshop for learning how to bear testimony and growing in our courage to do so. All testimonies are accepted, and we parents teach the most by our example.

Family home evening is a great time to get together and talk and play and laugh and eat and learn something together. It will be a cherished memory of our families, if we put in the effort to go ahead and have them, and to make them fit our family's needs! The little one who is rolling around on the floor is getting more than we realize! And the teen who is impatient to get on with his other activities can be one of our family's best teachers!

Dear Mom and Dad,

I feel like the gospel is important when you take time to plan a lesson and teach me it. It makes me feel good when you help our family be obedient and be consistent in this. I will try to do better to support you at FHE. It is amazing to feel your love and your testimony.

Love, Me

Counseling Together in Family Council

When I was a young girl, I loved family councils! We didn't call them that back then, but I remember sitting around the kitchen table and talking together about a new situation we needed to discuss. How good I felt when I spoke up with my point of view, since everyone listened and took my ideas seriously.

One of our most poignant family meetings was when my parents had received a call from a lawyer, offering us a baby to adopt! We already had a large family, and we knew of families who were struggling to have children, but the call made it clear that if we didn't adopt this child, they would go to the next family on their list. So my parents asked us, "Should we give this child a chance to have the gospel?" It wouldn't be easy; there would be challenges. What did we think? It was unanimous! We all wanted to provide this baby a good home and a family to be sealed to. My parents called my older sister who was away at college, and she agreed wholeheartedly. We were so excited and so pleased to have a voice in this very important decision.

Fast forward to our own family. Mark and I set up family councils too. We decided to let our children join us when they became twelve years old. That way, they would look forward to coming, and would see it as a privilege they earned. Each child was excited when they were finally twelve to see what family council was all about. We held ours in the basement, a different place than family home evening. Mark and I planned ahead what we would discuss, and we kept notes, so we could go back and remember our previous decisions. Eventually, these notes became our Family Policy Book, which has proved to be an amazing blessing to our family.

My daughter and her family once had a family council in which they brought up a problem to discuss and to get everyone's input. She and our son-in-law explained the issue and everyone commented. Their seven-year-old was especially attentive, asking about things three different times. Later, after the meeting was over, this young girl came up to my daughter and said, "When you talked about our problem and solved it, it made me feel happy—actually good inside." It was sweet that such a little girl could feel the Spirit and feel secure, as the family counseled together. Consider the advantages of holding family councils:

1. Counseling Together

"Please remember that family councils are different from family home evening," taught Elder M. Russell Ballard. "Home evenings focus primarily on gospel instruction and family activities. Family councils, on the other hand, can be held on any day of the week, and they are primarily a meeting at which parents listen—to each other and to their children."[3]

Family councils are a good time to establish family rules and policies. Kids need limits; they are much more secure with consistent boundaries. In the family council, we can present the current family dilemma and why we need to discuss it. We can help the kids see all sides of the issue, and even if they are reluctant, help them understand the need for limits. It's important that we listen to their points of view and give them ample time to talk things over. Family council is a great chance to reason with our kids and express love and concern. If we let them help make the decisions, helping the family come to a consensus if at all possible, every member is much more likely to support it. Even kids who end up with earlier curfews, for example, will feel good about what was decided because they can look forward to later curfews in the future, as they grow up and earn more freedom.

For Mark and I, it is ideal for us to have discussed the current topic for family council as a couple privately beforehand, to see how we both feel about the issue for discussion. If we disagree on it, that is the time to work out our differences. We are able to stop, think, and even pray about the issue, so we can guide the family discussion unitedly.

2. Growing in Trust

As we counsel, we must make sure that we trust our kids as much as possible. We must *not* put across the attitude, "I know you're going to mess up, so we are going to make sure you don't." Instead, the message that must come across is "We care about you. We trust you, as much as you earn it, and as you grow older we can give you more responsibility and freedom to do more on your own."

New issues that come up in the family during regular conversation or at the dinner table can be saved for the next family council. Everyone will rest assured that the family will discuss this fully soon, so they won't have to stress about it right now. In the meantime, all members could be thinking about it, searching the scriptures, and praying about the issue too.

Family councils are a good time to make plans for family safety. One family council, we came up with a key word that the kids could use if ever they needed to let us know they were in a tense situation, even if they couldn't spell it out on the phone. If, for example, they were at a party where it just didn't feel right and they needed us to come pick them up right away but didn't have time to elaborate further, they could simply say, "I'm done now."

When kids are approaching adulthood, they need to be given more freedom. They will soon have to make these decisions for themselves, without us, so we should start giving them the chance to use that freedom while still in our home and learn for themselves to make wise choices. For example, we decided as a family not to watch PG-13 movies. But we wrote in our Family Policy book that at age sixteen you can "use your own judgment, but we strongly suggest you follow family guidelines." We have worked to teach them to guard what goes into their minds and to choose only that which is "of good report," but we feel that there comes a point where they must choose for themselves. We know of kids who were so restricted that once they left home, they made all kinds of poor choices just because now they could! The key is to teach them early the reasons for good choices and then let them use their agency.

3. Writing the Decisions Down

Over the years, we have taken a three-ring binder with sheets of lined paper and written down the family policies and decisions that were made in our family councils. This binder book isn't fancy or particularly organized. It just has pages inserted as situations and decisions have occurred, but it has become our compiled Family Policy Book, the result of lots of questions and pondering. These policies have worked well with our family. Other families will adopt their own family policies, with decisions that work best for them, their children, and their circumstances.

For example, in our family, this is written down about when our kids get a driver's license:
After three months, you may drive with music on.
After six months, you may drive with friends in the car.

The kids know that we want to limit the distractions until they are more confident drivers. We have pointed out accidents that have occurred to a distracted driver. They know we only want their safety and everyone's! As new drivers have come along, they may not like these policies, but at least they know that the siblings before had to also go through this and it was decided on for everyone's safety. Also, when friends say, "Now that you have our license, you can take us all home!" the new driver can answer, "No, actually I can't until I've been driving for six months."

An issue used to come up each Halloween about whether they should stay together as a family or let the kids go out with friends. Years ago, we talked it over and decided on a family policy:

• Age 0–11: Stay with family. Visit grandparents together.

- Age 12–15: You can go with friends in the ward boundaries, then join family.
- Age 16–18: You can choose to get with friends in a home, but avoid being out in a car very much, since there are so many kids around.
- Age 18+: Practice what you've been taught!

After the Halloween policy was in place, there was never a problem. Each year, someone got out the family policy book and figured out the rules for his or her age. It was already decided, so no one rehashed it!

4. The Family Policy Book

One summer, we were offered the use of an aunt and uncle's old boat. We wanted to enjoy this opportunity safely and yet not have the boat be too big of a distraction from our regular duties. We wanted to promote modesty and safety with this new experience. As part of the next family council, we set some new family policies relating to the boat that we wrote down in our family policy book.

- Our Goals
  - » See some neat sights
  - » Let everyone learn to drive a boat
  - » Teach everyone to water ski
  - » Only go if we feel good about it
- Our Rules
  - » Make sure everyone is safe
  - » Sunscreen is mandatory
  - » Shirts over swimsuit
  - » Life preservers for all

With these guidelines in place, the season with a boat was a successful, happy time for all.

I don't remember who introduced us to the Family Policy Book, but it has been a wonderful tool for family peace. It is a place to put all decided rules and limits, for anyone to refer to as needed, eliminating anyone having to remember them all from month to month, year to year.

For example, in our Family Policy Book are our decisions about what age a daughter can use makeup or choose if she wants pierced ears, when the kids can get an email account (and that parents can read the emails), and our policy on sleepovers (only with cousins).

I had long had a dislike for guns in our home. But with nine sons, I quickly learned that little boys will pretend almost anything is a gun—even a piece of bread! Mark wanted our sons to be good marksmen. But I had heard of accidental shootings when guns were out in a home. In fact, we knew of a young man who had shot virtual guns in games so much that he didn't hesitate to shoot a real gun with tragic consequences. So, when we talked this all over in family council, with give and take and lots of reasoning together, this is what we wrote down: "We are builders, not destroyers. 'Thou shalt not kill' is a commandment. There is no repentance for killing. Using a gun to hurt gets in your mindset; it is hard to distinguish reality. We do not hurt people. But we do need to learn strategy and protection and defense. Marshmallow guns, water guns, etc. are not for hurting, so can shoot at people. Other guns should shoot at targets. Pretend guns, such as rubber band guns, should be for 'tag,' not 'killing.'"

So in our home, you can own your own water gun at age four; slingshots at age four (we had to put those in for the little ones); BB guns at age eight (only after reading all the directions and setting up a safe target); Airsoft or pellet guns at age twelve; and a "22" at age fourteen. After this was all in place, our boys actually had less interest in guns. Yes, they do play guns ("shooting" at "bears" or "bees"). But real guns we leave in the attic and we only get out when we go camping or to the desert for target practice! The bottom line is this: I felt much better writing all this down! Another family will come up with totally different rules about guns, but it was sweet for ours to come to a consensus about what we think about and set rules about them.

In our family policy book, we have quite a bit about dating, i.e. at what age they can do boy/girl activities (fourteen), at what age they can double date (sixteen–eighteen), and when they can single date (after missions). We wrote out part of *For the Strength of Youth* about pairing off: when it's okay or not okay. Our kids can date a person not of our faith one time, then they must invite him or her to church. At my insistence, we added "no hitting your date with paintballs!" (It happened once, and the poor girl came home with welts! I couldn't stand for my gentleman sons to do that!)

5. Exceptions

Occasionally, there might be an exception to the family policy. If a special situation or extenuating circumstances arise, Mom or Dad may make an exception to the policy. When our young scouts had an intense desire to learn to build fires, for example, we altered our policy to allow lighting fires when Dad was there. But we made the decision carefully, and we emphasized that this was an exception. For the most part, once something is entered into the book, it stands.

6. Revisiting

While nothing has to be rehashed, sometimes it is important that a policy be revisited. When a younger child was not present or doesn't remember the family council that developed a certain family policy, there could arise a need to explain the reasoning and the principle behind that policy. For some, it may not be enough that everyone else has had to abide by this rule, but they may require a detailed explanation, so they can realize the whys behind the rules. Once it has been talked through, each can feel secure and protected. Or the rule can be changed or discarded, if things have changed.

7. Synergism

Synergism is defined as "the interaction or cooperation of two or more organizations, substances, or other agents to produce a combined effect greater than the sum of their separate effects."[4] It is so wonderful when the whole family works together on an issue until a good plan of action has been figured out. Perhaps there has been compromise, but the new plan is something better than anyone would have come up on their own. M. Russell Ballard calls this, "strength in synergism."[5]

I love the example of one family who had a problem with their pets. The parents were ready to get rid of these expensive, messy animals, but were concerned that while the kids were giving them less and less attention, they may still be attached to them. "We held a family council to decide what to do with our pets. Emma, our nine-year-old, had two parakeets. Michael, our ten-year-old, had a gorgeous reddish-orange bearded dragon. We loved these pets; we would hold them on our shoulders and take them on walks. But unfortunately, our kids were becoming busier as they got older, and I had noticed the pets sitting in their cages more often." These parents were both "shocked to discover how much the pets were costing us. We wondered if the pets really gave us the same amount of enjoyment they used to and if they would be happier with other owners."[6]

So they planned a family council. Beforehand, they told each member of the family about their concerns and how they wanted their input about this issue. They asked each child to think about it and pray about it, and to bring their ideas to the family meeting. When the family council was held, the parents heard the kids' lists of pros and cons, then their suggestion. "We decided Michael would let his bearded dragon go to a new owner and that Emma would keep her birds for now. Initially this idea sounded unfair to me—to let only one child keep her pets. But it actually was our children who realized that Emma still needed and loved her pets and that Michael admittedly viewed caring for his pet as an obligation. The birds had each other for company and weren't as lonely as the dragon might have been, and the dragon was certainly more expensive. The solution made sense, but my husband and I never would have come to this conclusion without counseling with our children." The children may have resented the decision had they not been included in making it. The parents were blown away by the plan the kids had helped come up with. It was totally different than what they had thought, and it surprised them, but it turned out to be perfect![7] The synergy between all members together made for just the right outcome.

Elder Ballard taught that "great spiritual power and inspired direction" can come from family councils, and that they are "vital . . . to the accomplishment of the mission of the Church."[8] President Russell M. Nelson gave us a glimpse of how the leadership of the church counsels together: "Though we may differ in our initial perspectives, the love we feel is constant. Our unity helps us to discern the Lord's will. . . . We listen prayerfully to one another and talk with each other until we are united. Then when we have reached complete accord, the unifying influence of the Holy Ghost is spine tingling!"[9] May we strive for such an ideal, as we use this amazing family tool to bless and guide our families with more cooperation, unity, and peace.

Dear Mom and Dad,

I love it when my point of view is wanted and listened to in our family councils. Thanks for valuing my input and considering my feelings on any subject. I love it when we all talk together. And I'm glad I can check the Family Policy Book to make sure I am treated fairly!

Love, Me

Thine

My Will
I toss around as if it's boss
I want it my way! I shout
Or none!
And thus it becomes my love and my loss
But then I give loving Brother my hand
After all, they are thine
And thine is the light and the peace
I think I'll have a talk with thee
About home

Chapter 13

Encourage Greatness

*W*hen our kids make a mistake, it is our job is to encourage them to try again and keep trying. There is greatness within them that will come with time. We all get second chances on our way to this greatness, thanks to our Savior Jesus Christ.

Reaching for School Success

Children spend so much of their childhood in school! We should get a feel for what happens during their days and how we can help them succeed.

Their whole lives, our children will need to reach for success. School is the first big measurable challenge. What is our role in helping them find victory in their daily school experiences? To provide the best chance for success, we must form a connection of support from home, teaming up with the school to provide what's best for our student. It is our job to be the advocate for our student, especially since classroom sizes are often way too big.

School must be important to us parents. We must take an active interest and find ways to be in their classroom to view firsthand the goings-on. We can help figure out the best approach for our child while still being positive about the teacher's policies. It all starts with good routines in our homes, such as these:

1. Be a Sergeant

A schedule of early bedtime, healthy habits, and a good breakfast helps so much to facilitate success at school. Sometimes we have to be a sergeant to limit TV or insist on a good routine. A system for getting homework done at a good time is a big boost and a place for it is important too. A balance of extracurricular activities—not too many—also helps. Our students need some down time, to be outside for a while or to just be at home and unwind and talk with us, so they can better tackle school work with more interest and energy.

- **Enough Sleep.** I was wondering why one son had become so negative about school, and I had been praying about it. This young boy was simply not getting enough sleep at night! Night after night, he stayed up with older his high school–aged brothers and sister, who had concerts or homework to keep them up. I decided to set up a study room in our home, away from the little boys' bedroom, so that I could read his bedtime story to him and his brother earlier, with the older ones out of the way. I tightened the reins on his bedtime, appointing Daddy as "Bedtime Police." Happier student! Problem solved!
- **Breakfast.** A good breakfast is a big deal. Sugary breakfasts bring an immediate high of nervous energy, then an abrupt downhill plunge of no energy when the sugar is used up and the body needs to draw from other nutrients to digest it. This high and the low that follows are both detrimental to sitting still and concentrating in class. A breakfast of grains and fruit is much better at keeping the energy at an even keel throughout the morning until lunch.
- **Homework.** It's a fact of life to have to do homework. My friend knew her kids had to do homework directly after school. She found if she was firm in her expectations at the

start of the year and required homework immediately after a short snack time, the kids would quit fighting it. On the other hand, I tried to set up a regular homework session each afternoon, first thing. But I found that some of them especially needed to get out and play! They had used up all their patience sitting still and conscientiously making that pencil do what they needed it to do, and now they were done! I found that when I let them eat a good snack, then play all afternoon, they were happier. So, I let them move homework time to mornings. The family got up early so there was enough time to get it all done. This change made for a lot less struggle.

After seeing several students go completely through the school system, Mark and I have learned that we should let the child learn early on to take the lead on homework. As early as reasonable, our goal was to have the children learn to be self-directed. I coaxed my children into taking charge of their own schedule, simply by not managing it for them. I even let them pay the penalty of missed recess if they didn't get it done. The natural consequences they faced while they were young helped them internalize and determine to do better. Later on, when grades mattered much more, the lessons had been learned.

2. Be a Cheerleader

I try to give a cheerful send-off to school. But some days I have to really fight back the urge to scold. Really, it takes a little more effort and a little more love to forego the scolding and have them leave thinking they are great and can conquer the world that day. For example, one day my son and I, in the car on the way to school, were talking about being late. "I'm never late!" he announced to me. On the tip of my tongue were the words, "What about the fifteen tardies last semester?" But at the last second, I was able to switch to "Yes, you *are* getting better at that!" I was so glad the Spirit helped me change my response. He really had been working harder on that, and my response left him to take on the day with a better view of himself and more confidence. Both of those sentences were true—I am glad I chose the upbeat one!

"Find donuts!" is another send-off I like to leave them with. When someone gives you a donut, you could either look at the yummy donut and thank them for it, or you could look at the hole and complain that this donut has a hole in it! This outlook helps them be positive.

3. Be a Team Player

Schoolteachers have so much pressure on them! There is new curriculum, new electronics, non-English speakers, and too many children in the class! Besides all that, teachers have their families at home to worry about, and their own health issues. We can teach our children to empathize with the teacher, pray for her, for her family, and for the students to be more polite in order to make her load lighter.

We can team up with a teacher, to work together to meet the needs of our child. It is good to expect our child to follow the rules in class and help the teacher. Of course, there must be a balance between expecting great things from our own child and helping them meet their own needs too.

Thanking a teacher, and even praying for them, is such a great thing to encourage our students to do. If our kids have the attitude of empathy and gratitude for the teacher, they will be developing an attitude of reaching out to others, rather than "It's all about me!" Handwritten thank you notes are ideal, and if we help them brainstorm, letters can be specific. Teachers treasure personal thank-you notes.

4. Be a Loving Listener

A child brings various papers home and we can make sure we see them! We can find good things to praise such as, "I like the way you made this T," or "colored the sky," or even "remembered to write your name at the top." Or, "This is an especially good part of your story!" Talk about the day right after school, and again at the dinner table with Daddy. (See more on the "Daddy Report" in chapter 1.)

Channels of communication need to be wide open when it comes to school. We need to hear about what they are learning, what they are feeling, what their friends are doing. Whenever possible, we can try to be our kids' first teacher about truths and values and right and wrong. (See "Teaching Them First," in chapter 8.)

5. Be a Detective

Our children are not always open about what happens at school. Sometimes it takes some detective work. We can ask good open-ended questions, and keep asking, to find out what they are learning and what slant is being presented. We can take care to look over the notices, newsletters, and flyers being sent home. When we volunteer in their classroom, we can better see the classroom dynamics and the needs of our child.

We need to watch our kids interact with their friends. My sister-in-law used to position herself where she could even listen in to their conversations! She found out a lot that way. Any clues we pick up will help us know what is on their minds lately and know what topics to bring up in personal conversation or at the dinner table. There need be no apology for lovingly probing to find out how we can correct attitudes and trends. Of course, we don't want to micro-manage but just be aware, interested, caring parents.

When our children had a new friend who was not a good example or influence for them, Mark and I were worried. We decided to teach them about the influence of friends and that we can decide who we want to be like. "Trust no one to be your teacher nor your minister," we taught them, "except he be a man of God, walking in his ways and keeping his commandments" (Mosiah 23:14). We can reach out to everyone in friendship, we emphasized, but choose wisely the ones that we want to be like. Only let friends who are Christlike be your mentors or teachers. We were specific about this friend, urging them to be nice to him, but to be aware not to adopt his ways. We applied this to teachers at school too. We can learn what they are teaching, but not adopt their attitudes and philosophies if they are not a godly person or have different values and beliefs than us.

6. Be Available and Interested

One family home evening growing up, my dad showed us kids a special chair at his dental office. "This chair is for you," he told us. "If ever you have a hard time or an important question, you can come sit in this chair. I promise that I will stop my work and come talk to you." I didn't anticipate needing this kind gesture. But one day, my friend told me something shocking. So I went down to my dad's office and sat in his chair. True to his word, he finished up prepping a patient quickly and came in to sit down by me. We talked, and he didn't overreact but made it simple for me. He told me the best way to be a friend but keep my distance too. For him to stop working was a powerful show of love for me.

7. Be an Advocate

It is our job to see that our child's needs are being met at school. There is no one else to tune in to our son or daughter's specific requirements. We must have the courage to speak up, politely but firmly until things are worked out. Sometimes it might mean a different teacher or even a different school, but these decisions have to be worked out carefully and prayerfully. As we are firm and persistent, we must also be polite.

My friend's little girl—I'll call her Sophia—was struggling at school. As this mom watched and prayed, she realized that her Sophia, an active and creative child, was so bored with all the busy work each day, and again at night. She was very tired of all the repetition. As she wrestled with what to do, this mother came to realize that it was her job to get her child the best education to suit her. She was the one to promote what was best for her child! She arranged to meet with this teacher, carefully explained about her daughter's needs, then proposed her plan. It included no more homework, that Sophia would keep up academically, and that she would provide extra practice if needed. Journaling would substitute for the busywork. The plan also included one day of the week at home. Every Wednesday, they would learn practical skills and give Sophia a rest from academics and a chance to be creative and do things with her mom. Her classroom teacher was a bit reluctant, but she let this mom give it a try. And Sophia soared. Her grades went way up, and she was so very happy! School became a good place, and home became a wonderful place!

8. Be a Coach

A positive voice from home helps kids see their potential and work towards it. But sometimes we have to intervene. The Spirit will help us to know when. Some of our kids were overachievers and needed to relax a little more, so we taught them to tell themselves, *It's going to be okay!* Others needed a constant nudge to push harder and better reach for the grades they were capable of. It takes discernment to figure out the right kind of encouragement to give—and all effort deserves praise!

Our kids may need some tutoring in an area. It may be that an older sibling is just the one to help, if we can't make that happen ourselves. Or we may be able to find tutoring at school. The student must know that we care, and that we are on their side.

Dear Mom and Dad,

Things go wrong at school sometimes. I'm so glad you are there for me, to listen to my worries and help me with my setbacks. I am lucky to have interested, involved parents like you!

Love, Me

Every Child Is Gifted

Several of my children had a very special third grade teacher who taught them that every child is gifted. They learned to view all of their fellow students in that classroom as excelling in different ways. If one of their friends was not so good at math, they knew that she was an amazing artist. If another had trouble spelling, they knew that he was on fire when it came to science. Thanks to their teacher, they learned to embrace the diversity of everyone's gifts.

Then, several years later, our sixth-grade son told Mark and I that the extended learning program that he participated in was changing its name to the "Gifted and Talented Program." "This bothers me," he told us. "*Every* child is gifted!" We were so delighted with his attitude! And we agreed: intellectual gifts are *not* the only gifts!

Some children are word smart, others are math smart. Some are picture smart, music smart, or people smart. Still others are body smart or even nature smart. Parents have a job to do here. We must figure out our child's inclinations! What does he love to do? How does she naturally tend to spend her free time? It may take some investigation. What a gift we give our children when we notice and validate something that they are good at or love to do: "It's so great that you love to be involved with people." Or "I noticed how good you are at sharing your feelings." (See "Teach them Who They Are" in chapter 3 and "Validation and Reassurance" in chapter 9.)

Then, we need to help each child embrace their own gifts and not feel bad about the things that come harder to them. Yes, they can grow and develop in all areas, but they can feel good about what they are extra good at! After the ongoing process of discovery, we can then provide expression for these talents. We could give a child with artistic inclinations a wonderful art set for Christmas. We could take a child who loves nature on camping trips and find books for them to peruse, and so forth. Also, we will understand better what makes them tick and what they need.

I have two little granddaughters who are a month apart. When they were both two years old, one day they came over to my house. I noticed that one of them could talk up a storm, using grown-up words and expressing herself amazingly well. The other one could jump with both feet at the same time and run and dance with amazing coordination. Though they were exactly the same age, they had different tendencies and things they could do well. When one struggled to play hopscotch, I would remind her how good her picture was. When the other said, "I can't do that!" I would remind her how well she had done at something else. Both could feel good about themselves!

"To every man is given a gift by the Spirit of God" (D&C 46:11). I feel bad that schools usually emphasize only one or two of these areas of learning. But I am grateful for a special teacher who taught us to celebrate many different ways to learn, which variety of gifts fill our planet with progress in discovery, the arts, and new knowledge, not just intellect. If we parents will instill in each gifted child of ours the gratitude for and expression of their own talents and gifts and those of all mankind, they will draw closer to God and feel His goodness to all His children.

Dear Mom and Dad,

Thanks for making me feel like I am okay just as I am, and that I have my own special gifts. Thanks for helping me learn in the way I do it best!

Love, Me

It Takes Time:
Growth in Responsibility

It seems to me that there is an awkward stage for every child that usually hits about age eleven to thirteen. Puberty starts and things go crazy. Along with the bodily changes, emotions run high, with no recognizable pattern. Faces break out and hormones hit. Voices change, and with the change seems to come a need to use that new voice constantly! And what comes out isn't what used to be typical!

Our child is stuck in a "no-man's-land," not really a child anymore but not ready to be an adult yet either. Not only do clothing sizes not fit in either category, but also everything else doesn't seem to fit as well. It takes time, and lots of patience, for everything to even out. We must pour on the love during this phase, even if it is resisted.

Another important milestone at the age of limbo is that our children quit taking our word at face value. They stop believing something just because we said it. Instead, they start to question everything. It was good for me to recognize this huge change, so that I could put more effort into teaching all that I wanted to help my subsequent children believe while they readily accepted it! We try to teach the gospel before baptism at age eight, but we also keep teaching the concepts they will need for life and teach them early! Remember the "five years before they need it" rule! (See "Teaching Them First" in chapter 8.) At age ten, we need to prepare them for age fifteen with the grown-up teachings they will need for high school and beyond.

During this challenging time when toddler-like tantrums hit, we can ride them through knowing it takes some time to get through this stage. (See "Talking Out Tantrums" in chapter 6.) When our children want to be treated like a grown up but aren't taking much responsibility yet, we can rest assured that it will come. It just takes time.

How can we help the process?

1. Help Them Feel Stewardship

There was a time when I was pondering how the Lord handles work in His kingdom. I came to realize that rather than give us jobs, He gives stewardships. He gives us responsibility over a portion of His work. Mark and I decided to try to duplicate this gospel approach in our family. We wanted to communicate to each child that the family was counting on them to accomplish their stewardship. Carefully, we chose a job well-suited to each child, then one by one, we spoke with them, telling them about their new stewardship and how much the family trusted each to do their part. "We are counting on you," we told each one, "to keep our house free from germs by taking care of this bathroom for us" or "by seeing that the dishwasher is always filled or emptied so we have clean dishes."

"If you don't follow through, it will be hard on all of us," we emphasized. "If you neglected taking out the garbage, for example, our home would start to smell. If you forgot to wash out the garbage can on Saturdays, mold or germs would start to grow and might make someone sick. And if you forgot to take the garbage to the road on Fridays, the whole family would be in a bind with no place to put all our garbage for the next entire week! Our house would not as readily be the nice place where the Spirit can dwell." We tried to help each of our children feel the importance of their special part.

After implementing the new plan, at times it would still be hard on us all if one person didn't come through. Though some of our kids needed a little reminding at first, we tried to let our kids feel the consequences of forgetting, to teach them the importance of their stewardships. We might let them go a week without room in the dumpster, then praise the garbage taker-outer when he remembered the next week!

One of our sons inadvertently neglected the little chicks we were raising, at one point leaving them in the sun. Mark and I both did not catch it in time either, so all of them died! The boy was heartbroken at what he had caused. Never again did we see this son neglect an animal! He had learned a life-or-death lesson.

2. Attitude Shift

Over time, attitudes begin to change as our children grow in responsibility. Suddenly, we started to hear, "Would you take care of my chores for me when I am on this outing?" or "Thanks for doing my chores!" *My chores* is what they said! Even though they needed help to do them that day, we were delighted with this wonderful shift in attitude. The work had become theirs.

3. Babysitting: A Gradual Responsibility

This "tween" season is the time to teach and to expect responsibility. But it must be expected gradually. For example, babysitting younger kids is a hugely important responsibility, which must be learned in increments. At first, we could watch as our nine- or ten-year-old changes a diaper or feeds the baby several bites under our supervision. We could ask the child to watch over the baby while we quickly shower or take this important call. After a while, we could leave that child to watch the baby while we run a quick errand and see how things went while we were gone. We can build from there.

In our community, a child is not legally old enough to babysit until age twelve. However, I had authorities tell me that within a family there must be the training. We cannot expect our tween kids to suddenly know how to do it when they turn twelve! We must be teaching responsibility in increments way earlier than age twelve. In fact, until my oldest turned twelve, we hired a babysitter but expected this daughter and her sister to do lots of the babysitting. We found ourselves giving them the instructions about dinner and bedtime and what the younger kids could watch, rather than the sitter. It was a great understudy role, in which they did the acting! And when age twelve finally came, babysitting was no sweat. Not only did we not have to pay a sitter any more, but our sitters were experienced and ready to take it on. We had them take turns being in charge, with the full responsibility resting on one, the other there to assist.

4. Growth in Work Ethic

Our family works out in the yard a lot. For each one of the kids, there has come a season when, on a Saturday morning work session, they are found sneaking back to bed or going over to the swings when they should be hoeing weeds with the others. They pick the easiest part of the yard to mow and forget to sweep afterward. They want to be with the older ones but certainly don't carry the same load, nor the same work ethic. While coaxing them back on task, or getting them outside to work again, Mark and I have learned to relax a little. This child will grow to be a good worker too;

it just takes time. In fact, six months later, we will usually notice a good stretch of sustained work from this former slacking child, and look at each other and smile. With time, this one learned responsibility too.

There comes a real shift when our youngster starts to join in the work all on his own. What a great change it is when they choose to come help—and stick with the task! We can be lavish with the thanks and the praise for willingness and work well done.

5. Managing Their Schedule and Schoolwork

While keeping a watchful eye from a distance, we parents can gradually turn over to our kids the responsibility for their schoolwork. With support and with time, a junior high–aged student will grow in their ability to keep up in all the subjects. At first, we may have to help them keep track, but this is an important time to shift it to them. High school grades are much more important for getting into college or getting a scholarship in the future. So junior high is the time to step away—when slip-ups are not so costly. With time, encouragement, and trust, a student will move toward setting homework time, setting his own alarm to get up early, and pacing himself through projects. Each one's responsibility clock may be different, but the goal is to back away and, while still supporting, allow growth in managing their own.

For example, when a science fair project is coming due, we can start helping our student by brainstorming an idea early. We can help provide the needed presentation board and take them to buy the materials needed. We can express interest and give advice but be clear from the start that this is their project. After they do their own typing, we can proofread and even help cut out write-ups. But the learning and applying the science concepts and the putting them down is theirs. The creativity is theirs. Though we free up segments of time, the accomplishing of this project needs to be theirs, as much as possible. There will be many projects ahead throughout this child's life, and now is a good time for them to start owning them and gradually reaching for the self-control and time management to get them done.

6. Grow in Trust

Remember young Enoch, who questioned the Lord for choosing him. "I . . . am but a lad, and all the people hate me; for I am slow of speech," he told the Lord (Moses 6:31). But the Lord knew his potential and trusted him. With time, Enoch grew to be a powerful leader, so effective that His city qualified to rise to heaven!

"I'm going to trust you" is a wonderful message to give our young person. When they have our trust, they will more likely work hard to keep it! Even if they let us down at times, we can give another chance and be willing to trust them again soon. When Mark and I have occasionally gone out of town, we have asked our ten- or eleven-year-old to collect all the mail. Then, at eleven or twelve, we have trusted them to water the flowers (an important thing in Arizona summers!). At about twelve or thirteen, we have them cook meals, and at thirteen or fourteen they could even be trusted to irrigate the yard at just the right time, and turn it off so neighbors get their turn. Trusting them in little things, like washing the car, will lead to trusting them in big things, like driving the car!

We must expect greatness while allowing growth, and realize that takes time!

Dear Mom and Dad;

Growing up is not for wimps! It's really hard sometimes! Thanks for being patient with me and for letting me take lots of time to transition from a kid to an adult. And especially, thanks for your great example of responsible adulthood!

Love, Me

Second Chances: Mercy and More Love

School was almost out for the year when one evening I was working on the computer. My sixth grade son called from across the family room, "Hey, Mom! Do you want to see my web presentation? It's your last chance to see it before it erases." "Sure!" I said, though I kept typing. So he brought the laptop over to the counter near me and opened it up. It was a web presentation about the island of Fiji, and I turned to look at it with him. He started, but I immediately pointed out a misspelled word. "The teacher doesn't care about those," he said. But I countered with reasons he needs to do excellent work and fix any errors. He went on, but when he paused for a second, I went back to my typing for a bit—after all, I was almost done! Then I could give him my undivided attention, I told myself. "Mom. You're not even looking!" he exclaimed. "Yes, I am. You were busy for a minute," was my reply. So, he went through the rest of it, and I asked questions about it and told him how well he had done. And that was that.

The next morning, I woke up realizing that I had really messed up. This boy's high school–aged siblings were getting so much recognition the past few days, and what about him? He had sat there in the audience with us over and over while they were given various honors. His presentation on Fiji was my chance to give him a little recognition! I felt awful. Why didn't I go and sit next to him on the couch and really experience his view of Fiji with him? Why did I immediately try to fix mistakes, rather than point out all the amazing photos and setup he had done! I *knew* to do that. I had learned this lesson time and again on his twelve older siblings! Still I messed up.

So I prayed for a second chance. "Please, let me figure out a way to give this son the praise he deserved," I asked in prayer. Then an idea came! I woke up Mark, and told him the story. "Would you help me?" I asked him. "Would you look at his presentation this morning, and make a big deal about it? I'd be so grateful." So later after breakfast, I said to Mark, "You've got to see this presentation on Fiji! It is amazing!" He came over and gave his undivided attention (like I should have). The Lord gave me this second chance to praise and build up the good in my son.

I am constantly asking in prayer for second chances! It's often early in the morning when clarity comes to me. That's when I realize the need for another chance to set things right and apply more love.

Mercy is an amazing principle to apply often:

1. We All Make Mistakes

Many times, I have had to pray for another chance to run into a certain person who I could have treated better. Often it is after they are gone that I remember their name, or remember something I should have asked about, or realize a better way I could have responded. That's when I pray to have another chance, and I've noticed that the opportunity to interact with them again comes, so I can try to be a better instrument in the Lord's hands the second time around! Our children will see our efforts and will learn mercy and kindness.

2. Children Make Mistakes Too

Sometimes we have to stand firm and follow through with consequences that are in place, but there is also a time for mercy. "Blessed are the merciful, for they shall obtain mercy" (Matthew 5:7). We need it, and there are times we need to model it. It just takes some promptings and wisdom to know when.

My daughter had been working with her little four-year-old girl, who still had struggles with potty training. During one such season of relapse, my daughter grew so frustrated. There was a Mother-Daughter Tea Party coming up that night, and she told her daughter, "You can go if you can keep your underwear nice and dry all day!" She reminded her over and over, but late afternoon, there was an accident! What should she do now? Her little girl had been so excited to go with her sisters and mom to this special event. But she had messed up again! She had cried and cried after the accident—truly remorseful. (She hadn't had her nap that day either.) "Don't leave me," she begged.

After mulling over what to do for some time, my daughter finally took her little girl on her lap and talked to her gently for a little while. "I know that you didn't mean to, and I know that you can do better. Do you need one more chance?" she quietly asked her. "Oh yes!" was her relieved reply. And she had a wonderful time that evening and in the long run, it was okay.

Older children need mercy as well. A mom I know had a blow-up with her thirteen-year-old son on the way to school over being on time. This was a volatile one, and she was left feeling angry and fretting all day over it. She knew she should apologize, but this son didn't respond to apologies or even thanks recently. "Yeah," he would answer when she tried, untouched.

In spite of her busy day and in answer to prayer, this mom received a prompting. *Make him some cookies,* was the thought that came to her mind. Every day without fail, the minute he got in the car he asked, "Is there food?" and there never was. She never had cookies waiting after school either! But that day she carved out time to make him his favorite snickerdoodles, and took them warm on a plate with a glass of milk with her to pick him up.

When this teenager approached the car, she could tell that the incident from that morning still bothered him too, but when he saw those cookies his whole countenance changed. "He softened like butter," she told me. Rather than being closed, he talked to her about his day all the way home. And the next morning, she could change her approach about being on time—and this time he was not closed off. She had partnered with God to use something that meant love to him, to put a deposit in his "love bucket" and heal the relationship breech.

3. Both Justice and Mercy

I truly believe in follow-through. We parents need to mean what we say and follow through on consequences, so our kids will believe us and realize we are serious. But sometimes, we can tell them, "This is an exception." There is a time for mercy and second chances. "Mercy cannot rob justice," we are told in the scriptures (Alma 42:25), but sometimes, there is a way for both!

My friend had a daughter whose room was a disaster. She told her daughter that she couldn't go to the party that night until it was cleaned up! But this teenager was having an emotional day. She kept putting it off until it was time for the party, and she still had way too much too do. She sat on the couch and bawled. My friend went and sat by her. She smoothed her daughter's hair for a while and gradually, this daughter opened up to her and they had a good talk. Then, the mom said, "C'mon! I'll help you with that room!" She was late to the party, but she was in much better spirits, and her relationship with her mother was better too.

When my kids are trying to meet a deadline but just don't quite finish their chores on time, I have learned to let them "plead diligence." If they were truly diligent at trying to get done, they could have the reward, and finish later.

I had a grandmother who was also a voice of kindness and mercy. When I was in despair, she believed in me. When my family was all upset about something major that went wrong, she was the voice that said, "It will turn out all right!" I held on to that voice! I cherished her belief in me. When all kinds of things go wrong, a parent or aunt or grandparent can be a huge blessing of comfort and optimism.

This is how my great-great-grandfather kept his word but was merciful too:

William J. Flake, who founded Snowflake 135 years ago, believed a deal is a deal. A handshake was as binding as a written contract. In 1878, he bargained for the land and water rights of James Stinson in the Silver Creek Valley. The purchase became the town site for Snowflake. With a handshake, Flake agreed to deliver, over three years, Utah grade cattle—200 cows, 150 two-year-olds and 200 yearlings. In exchange, Stinson agreed to sell the land, the water rights, farm equipment and six mules.

In 1881 when the last cattle were delivered, Stinson wanted to keep a special saddle mule. Flake said, "No, the mule was in the trade and now belongs to me."

Stinson acknowledged that was right and invited Flake to cut five cows out of the delivered herd, so he could keep his special mule. Flake told him, "No, a deal is a deal and the mule is mine. Pull off your saddle." With tears in his eyes, Stinson pulled off the saddle and bridle, patted the mule on the neck and handed the end of the rope to Flake and walked away.

William J. Flake stopped him and said, "Stinson, we have done a lot of business in the past three years. For a long time, I have wondered how I could show you my appreciation. I want to present this mule to one of the most honest men I have ever met." Stinson saddled the mule and rode off without a word.[1]

4. A Time for Mercy

When one of my sons was in high school, he had the chore of cleaning the bathroom. I had been extra frustrated with my kids for not doing their chores during the week, so I came up with this plan: Every day that they didn't do their chores during the week, they had to spend ten minutes doing that chore before they could go out with friends on Friday night. "Even if you only spend five minutes a day cleaning part of the bathroom, that is enough." I told him. "But if you do none at all, that is the consequence." So that next Friday night, this son was in the bathroom, catching up on five days of not doing his chores. He had five 10-minute sessions to catch up, as per our policy. He tried to reason with me that he had been so busy, and this just wasn't a good rule. But I wouldn't budge. I needed him to learn responsibility!

It wasn't until later that I grasped the whole picture. This son had planned to stay home that weekend night, since his friends had planned a movie that was not totally appropriate. I'm sure that had been a tough decision for him! How did he spend that evening instead? Doing fifty minutes of bathroom cleanup! I should have praised him up and down for that choice he had made! I should have taken him out for a hamburger or gathered the family to play a board game with him instead. I must have apologized and told him how proud I was of him. I still feel so badly that I didn't realize this was a time for mercy! I know it's never too late for a parent to apologize. May the Lord give me many more opportunities to praise and build up this valiant son for his good choices.

When we parents fall short, we can pray humbly to ask forgiveness and for another chance to handle things better. I know our loving Savior will open up a way for us to try it over. After all, that is why He suffered the Atonement for us, so that we can repent and have many chances to learn and grow and become more heavenly in our interactions. More love from Him gives us more love to give. "May [the] Spirit ever guide you," taught Elder Faust, "[to] reach out to others in love and mercy."[2]

Showing mercy does not always mean we do not require as much. We must still have high expectations. "I will be merciful unto your weakness," says God. "Therefore, be ye strong from thenceforth" (D&C 38:14–15). He is merciful but expects better. And His kindness is everlasting. Likewise, even with kindness and mercy at times, we can make sure to let our kids know they can be great! May we be blessed with the wisdom to know when to stand firm and when to be merciful.

Dear Mom and Dad,

Sometimes I need to pay consequences, so I will learn from my mistakes. But sometimes, I need mercy, and I need to see mercy given. Thanks for making exceptions and giving me extra chances. I grow to love you so when you rescue me. And I grow to understand the mercy of God in the process. You're the best!

Love, Me

Chapter 14
Yes Provide, but No Free Ride

*I*t is valiant to provide for one's family and meet their needs. But as they grow, our children can learn to do their part. They can gradually contribute to the family through work and provide for some of their own needs. In doing so, what they will receive will mean so much more to them! At one point, we decided that our kids could earn five dollars by baking a batch of bread, and needless to say, all the kids have learned to make bread! (In fact, several of the children have become better than me at bread-making!) When they work, there is less a feeling of entitlement and more a feeling of gratitude for what we provide.

The Blessing of Family Work

Early on, kids think work is fun! When the vacuum is a curiosity to them, we can let them try vacuuming the room. When they want to sweep but can hardly hold the broom, why not let them try it? Some of my kids are fascinated with the spray bottle and washing the windows with it. Some of my kids loved pouring soap in the toilet and using the toilet brush to pretend to "make soup!" We can praise good effort, and we can try to connect cheerful feelings with working as we do it together.

I took a class on family work from a professor, Kathleen Slaugh Bahr, who did her graduate research on ways daily household work may influence family relationships and the growth and development of children. Among the ideas that stayed with me were how sending children outside to play while a parent does the inside work may result in missed opportunities to teach and relate to children that come from doing the work together. Another example I remember was how the kinds of thinking and problem-solving a young child learns at school may differ from what they might learn at home. One example was of peas. In school, the teacher may ask, Are peas a fruit or a vegetable? What color are peas? What shape are peas? At home, the teaching will be more practical, and the conversation may be more like: What should we fix for lunch? Sorry, marshmallows are not an option. How about sandwiches? Grilled cheese? Oops, we are out of cheese. Tuna? We have tuna. How about grilled tuna sandwiches?

Both kinds of learning are important, but as in this example, the learning at school helps a child put things in categories, while the learning at home prepares a child for life. Skills for life are learned through the interaction processes that accompany the work. And work can be a huge blessing in any life.[1] Here are some thoughts about work:

1. Teaching Kids to Work at Home Is Incomparable

My daughter wanted to start teaching her one-year-old to work. So every day, she said to her baby, "Let's do service!" Then together, they would go and water a flower, or straighten the books. They might pick up a piece of trash outside their apartment or pick a weed. In this way, work is viewed as helping someone, a great attitude for little ones! Working at home is a wonderful service to our families.

When another daughter of mine had young children, she also wanted to help them develop the attitude of helping the family. So, when her children asked to watch a movie or have a popsicle or whatever, she would answer, "First, do one thing to help the family." Her child would look around and find a wastebasket that needed emptying or a floor that needed sweeping and do it. She might have to help them at first, but soon they could do it alone more and more. With this approach, they realized that there was much work to do at home, and they could help!

Working together brings a different sort of family bonding. All work that is done well brings contentment and fulfillment, especially when it is done together. One summer our young boys were determined to earn money. Together, they began a trash barrel–moving service for neighbors on vacation. Later on, they added yard work, cleaning pools, and irrigating. When our daughter had an expensive high school choir tour to help pay for, she started a homemade pizza business. Every Friday and Saturday night, she and a friend would make homemade pizza and deliver it to hungry, grateful neighbors. Her younger siblings helped, and they watched her amazing example of work. She and her friend learned a lot, and gleaned much business experience in the process. And my daughter felt good about paying her own way to the costly trip.

2. Weeds and Work

I detest weeds! But I am thankful for them too! No matter how many you pick, there are always more to pick next time. My kids know that every Saturday, there will usually be weeds to pick in the flowerbed or in the garden. We don't have a farm, where lives depend on the crops to survive, to teach the essential need for work. But we do have a pet or two and usually a flock of chickens that require constant attention in our hot Arizona sun—or there are dire results! And always, there are weeds! In fact, Mark researched how many times "tilling the earth" or "tilling the ground" is found in the scriptures. It's there 175 times, which makes us think that growing things is important to the Lord.

From our kids' earliest memories, Saturday work has been a part of their week. It's just what we do—we have to get ready for Sunday. Usually, the work consists of little more than weekday chores. For example, if the regular chores are taking out the garbage all week, on Saturday they rinse out the wastebasket too. Or if they vacuum one room per day during the week, on Saturday they vacuum all of the front rooms. We expect bedrooms to be cleaned and clothes to be washed and put away, ideally making sure the Sunday clothes are ready (the expectation but not always the reality). And don't forget weeds to pick! We may not have a farm to raise our kids on, but we do have plenty of weeds!

Weeding the garden does not require much skill—although we do have to teach which plants are not weeds and what will happen if the kids don't get the root. But usually, while weeding we can talk. We discuss a movie or book someone just read or a school event or a favorite memory. This is a good opportunity to teach tolerance and understanding for the younger one who is trying every possible way to get out of the weeding and play instead. ("You used to be like that," the fault-finding person is reminded!) There are many lessons to learn from weeds—like to pick them early before they get out of control and difficult to pick, which is very much like changing our habits!

I'm not quite thankful for the morning glory that grows prolifically in one part of our yard, wrapping around the flowers or grapevines and squeezing the life out of them! But there are lessons to learn from them too! In fact, one family home evening, since the weeds had gotten out of control and Saturday had been too busy to tackle them that week, we all went out to weed together. Each person was assigned to come up with one life lesson to learn from the weeds. It was amazing the amount and the variety of analogies the kids came up with. After this FHE full of work, we had an extra good family night treat!

> "Children are like an investment. You have to invest early if you expect a large return."
>
> —Elder Shayne M. Bowen

3. Shadowing an Older One

Young children will not just do their job well and regularly from the start. They usually need Mom or Dad or an older sibling to work alongside them for a while. One season, I paired an older child with a younger child to help the younger one learn to do his chores well (and for the older one to learn some patience). Working alongside a child teaches them until gradually, they are able to do it on their own.

When it was my young son's turn to feed the family's crop of chickens, I resigned myself that I would be feeding them each day with him. I knew it was tricky to reach in and change the water and to feed the squawking chickens without letting them out. It was not my favorite thing to do, but I figured that he would be learning. Gradually, he could do more and more, and even devise ways to get it done easier. By the end of that season (our kids did the same chore for that entire semester), on days when I was extra busy, he could do most of the job alone.

Each child has his own time line on when he is ready to work hard. As the child leads the way in taking more and more of the responsibility to get the job done well on his own, the better he feels about himself in the process. With praise, he will learn to be proud of his work.

4. Show Kids the Family Budget

It's a great idea to map out the family finances and discuss the budget. This helps our kids learn to better appreciate Mom and Dad's work. Mark and I found that in family home evening or family council, if we would spell out the family income and spending plan, our children were more willing to turn up the air conditioning and use fans (or turn it down and use sweaters), to turn off lights, to conserve water, and to help out. The children were amazed at how expensive it was to run a family. Here is a good chance to teach tithing as well, when they see us budget to pay our tithes and offerings first.

We use a two-week plan for buying groceries, so we can save money by going to the store less. We use the fresh stuff first and the frozen foods the second week—our children laughingly call it "feast week" and "famine week." But after seeing how much the family's food really costs, they support the plan and wait for payday for "the good stuff" to be replenished. They actually help to pace our ingredients, so they'll last. I like to have each child take a turn to cook. They plan ahead for ingredients, learn new skills, and are more willing to eat their concoctions. What's more, they appreciate my cooking better and are more thankful for the food that we can buy.

In our cousins' family, the father had been out of work for some time. The teenage boys, though they lived in an affluent area where kids had all kinds of "toys" provided, learned to pay their own way. What's more, they started a family landscaping business. One of the boys even postponed his college for a year, helping get the family business off the ground before turning it over to his father. What fine young men these boys have become. Paying their own way and sacrificing for the good of the family built character.

5. Provide Good Discussion about Work

One time when I was stressed about many pressing duties, I was talking to my mother. Her advice to me was, "Have your kids help you." If they understand, our children can and will help. They feel the responsibility to help the family if they are trusted with why things are difficult at present.

We need to provide explanations and really talk over things with our kids. If we ask them to do an extra good job cleaning the basement, we should tell them that there's going to be company staying soon and we want them to be comfortable. If we ask them to sweep or vacuum, we could explain that the any extra crumbs left could attract bugs into our house! Or that sand on the rug actually cuts the carpet fibers and damages it. We could teach that water hurts the wood and polish helps protect and let it be beautiful a long time. Every time we teach our kids to help out and why, we are bringing our family closer as friends and helpers forever.

6. Work Brings Happiness

While all work usually includes some drudgery, there is also much in the way of satisfaction for a job well done, and joy in accomplishing a valuable task. Later on, working to earn their own money and pay their own way will bring pride and confidence.

Work is where we learn new skills. It is a wonderful outlet for creativity. Ether 10:22–28 mentions work eight times. In verse 27, for example, it reads, "they did work all manner work of exceedingly curious workmanship!" They were creative in their work. The footnotes on the page for the word *work* read "skill" and "art." Work helps us learn skills and creative arts. In verse 28 is the consequence for all this work: "And never could be a people more blessed than were they, and more prospered by the hand of the Lord."

I remember Sister Julie B. Beck saying that she really wanted her kids to learn to work, but since they were a rather small family, there wasn't a lot of housework, and since they didn't live on a farm or acreage, there wasn't a lot of outside work. So she decided that her children would be required to focus on music. They had to practice and become serious piano students. This was the hard work that she provided for them. And in the process, they learned a marvelous skill that brought them a lot of happiness. They also learned the law of the harvest.[2]

In another family, which we meet in the book *My Dad Was a Carpenter*, the author tells of straightening tons of nails. He spent hours hammering those bent nails back into shape. His father didn't need to reuse those nails, he realized much later, but he needed to keep Kenny busy and to teach him to work![3]

From the time Mark was nine years old, he was like an only child. His six brothers and sisters were all much older and had married and moved out. When he was fifteen, his mother and father bought a home in the mountains. This home had literally tons of junk strewn all across the acre of land that required hauling away. It still had old food in the cupboards and was completely rundown. Mark and his dad spent several entire summers redoing every part of that home and yard. There was a huge lawn to mow, fencing to paint, and more junk to haul! This project took Mark away from mischief! He thought his parents were buying a cabin getaway, but instead they were raising a boy. To this day, Mark has the skill of fixing anything; he knows how to work hard and tackle a big project. I am so grateful for wise parents that provided this for him!

7. Work Is an Antidote for Mischief and Unbelief

I have wondered why Alma and the four sons of Mosiah went about doing great mischief and creating doubt in those around them. Could it be that with the rise in power of their fathers, they had much affluence and therefore, no need to work? Without work, there is need for something constructive to do. In fact, there may seem to be no need for God: *"All is handed to me, so who needs God to provide it?"* If they had had to work hard, however, there would have been no time for doing damage. Instead of doubt, there would have been the need of constant prayers for help with the work, and better prosperity. It was later on, when these young men were zealously working to repair the damage that they had done, that they were filled with love for the people and desire to share the gospel on missions!

My neighbor, a father of eight, had lots of experience with young people. Once he shared what he had learned, that if young men do not work, they will deny the faith. I thought about that a lot. Young people need to learn the self-motivation to work, the self-discipline required to do a job well, and the self-esteem that comes from paying their own way.

Work is a key to family success and happiness. I love John Bytheway's analogy of a family tandem bicycle to show the need for each member's work. The "family bicycle" has as many seats as there are members of the family. Each person pedals to help the family move forward and especially to go uphill! If any one member chooses to coast, the whole family is affected and can't move forward nearly as effectively. If one puts on the brakes and quits, the family suffers tremendously. But if everyone gives it his all, the family soars![4] We need to pull together as a family, and work is a wonderful tool.

Dear Mom and Dad,

To tell you the truth, I don't like to work. Work is hard! But I guess I like it when the work is done, and the house or yard looks nicer. I guess I am glad that you make us do chores. (Even though some of my friends don't have to do any!) Since I want to be like you someday, I am going to work hard like you do!

Love, Me

Resourcefulness and Resilience

Our children will run into dilemmas and situations where they will have to be resourceful. We can provide opportunities to develop this skill and the ability to face things with optimism and courage. Each will need to learn that with resourcefulness and resilience, creativity and persistence, "I can do hard things."

In providing for our children both the necessities and experiences, we want to give them enough but not too much. We want them to learn to be resourceful. And since our children learn the most from what we are, when we are resourceful we can let them participate:

1. Provide Chances to Help

Previous generations were good at fixing and reusing and "jimmy-rigging" things together to make them last. They cooked and sewed and mended the old clothes. By making the effort to pass skills of resourcefulness on to the next generation, we are helping our environment and helping our kids.

Whenever we try to do something good, like help our neighbor with his lawn or bring flowers to someone who is sick, we can bring our kids along to sweep up the grass clippings or help carry. When we reuse a container or fix something broken, a child could help wash out a pickle jar or hold the screwdriver. It is usually easier to do it all alone, but by letting the kids "help," we teach invaluable lessons.

2. Provide for Their Wants, but Not All of Their Wants

"By not satisfying every immediate want," said Elder Robert D. Hales, "we obtain . . . the more desirable reward," that of resourcefulness, satisfaction, and skills.[5] I have been grateful that we don't have the means to grant every want, thus teaching our children that not all are necessary. In our family, there are lots of us, so we limit a child's sports camp or season to one per year. If a child wants to do more than one sport, he must pay for it. This system weeds out all extra sports except the ones desired the very most. In addition, we have found that when the newness wears off, the kids attend more willingly lessons they have chosen and are helping pay for. When our daughter's dance classes became expensive, in addition to our cleaning the studio to pay for it, she started assisting teaching the younger dancers. With this ownership in her dance, she never had to be urged or hardly reminded to go.

When our young son wanted to take kung fu like his friends, I set up a plan for him to earn it. The teacher agreed let us pay for each class separately. It was quite expensive, and I didn't know if it was just a passing craze, so I made an extensive plan for him. Five items had to be completed before I gave him the money for each class, including a lesson of typing, an exercise in cursive writing (both things I had wanted him to learn), a song on the piano, and two extra jobs. Kung fu did not come super easy for him, but he stuck it out and worked hard to earn each class. At first, he did not always get everything done on time, and as per our agreement, he didn't go that time. But I did not push him, nor did I give in to his pleadings to go anyway, and he figured out a way to fit it all in. Since then, he has usually made it on time. And he's sure proud of that yellow belt he earned!

3. Provide for Their Needs, but Not All Their Needs

Parents must see that children do not go hungry or naked, but as they grow older, if we let children earn their own way at times, they learn satisfaction, skills, and appreciation for what they have. Paying their own way feels good.

Kids can help earn their clothes. In an attempt to keep our children busy during summer months, Mark and I had them set goals for the summer. As the kids daily worked on these goals, they earned points, which translated into money for school clothes and supplies at the end of the summer. Each child kept track of the points on a calendar, one point per day for meeting their goal and one point per day for doing all their chores. Right before school was to begin, we counted up the points and handed out cash in envelopes (the youngest kids' envelopes in my purse to take to the store). It was money we would have spent on school clothes anyway, but the kids could manage the amount they earned and make the choices. The more diligent each had been, the more they had to spend. It was a long-term reward. In fact, I learned that I didn't have to remind or nag as much each summer day, for as they grew older, the children learned to see ahead better. They wanted more money for school supplies at the end, so they were sure to accomplish their jobs and goals each day. Also, I noticed that the kids usually wore the clothes and took better care of the items they purchased themselves.

4. Provide Rewards Carefully

Showering children individually with lots of praise and sincere compliments builds self-esteem. When we use things for rewards, we must take care. There are not always immediate rewards in their lives. On missions or in college, there is no candy bar for a good job. Many of the rewards from providence come much later. Children can learn to feel good about accomplishments and wait for rewards.

If we were to give a dollar for an A grade, for example, the dollar would be the reward, instead of the self-satisfaction of doing a good job. If we gave a piece of candy for doing a chore, when the candy stopped, the chore would stop too! If a daughter drew a wonderful picture and got a quarter, she would expect one for the next picture too. Our praise for something well-done is the best reward. And to give more praise, we can tell Daddy or let the child call Grandma to tell what a wonderful thing they had done!

It is imperative for our young kids to learn to delay rewards. When they are in the mission field, for example, there will be long seasons of work before they see the results, with no one passing out tangible rewards along the way. They must learn to provide their own pat on the back for a lesson well taught, and to pick themselves up again after the hard days of work. Mark and I have learned that planting a garden is a wonderful tool in teaching children to wait for their rewards. A seed planted will not sprout for days, and then will not provide fruit for weeks. But the rewards do come, and it is good to learn to wait for them.

5. Develop Attitudes of Resourcefulness and Resilience

I recently became aware of a program called "Days for Girls." It addresses a need in third-world Africa for feminine hygiene. Without pads, as soon as a girl's period starts, she must quit school and sit on cardboard during those days she has her cycle. This program has come up with some discreet reusable pads that clean up in very little water in a ziplock bag. It is literally giving back a life to these girls!

This program made me think: if the girls here found themselves without feminine hygiene products, would they be resourceful and thrive anyway? Or would they shrivel up in a corner, and in a sense "curse God and die?" It is their frame of mind that will get them through times of hardship. We can help them now, little by little, to be resourceful and to make do.

When something breaks, we can find a way to fix it and reuse it. Rather than going out and buying something we need, we could look around the house and find an alternative. If we don't have the exact ingredient a recipe calls for, we can try something else instead. And when things go wrong, we can work to be optimistic, prayerful, and determined to conquer the opposition.

Our children will experience disappointment, discouragement, and trial. What a gift we give them if we teach them to be resourceful in facing a problem and resilience during them. Sometimes those traits are within. Remember Alma's people? When the wicked Lamanites took over their city and made them carry heavy burdens, and then threatened to kill them if they prayed, they turned to praying in their minds. They continued to have faith, and received a wonderful miracle, that they couldn't even feel the load upon their backs. "The burdens which were laid upon Alma and his brethren were made light; yea, the Lord did strengthen them that they could bear up their burdens with ease, and they did submit cheerfully and with patience to all the will of the Lord" (Mosiah 24:15). Elder Bednar pointed out that it was *they* who were strengthened rather than just the heavy loads lightened. "The challenges and difficulties were not immediately removed from the people. But Alma and his followers were strengthened, and their increased capacity made the burdens lighter. These good people were empowered through Christ's Atonement to act as agents (D&C 58:26–29) and impact their circumstances."[6] The miracle was inside of them.

I once heard a follow-up story about that miracle that I love to share to help my kids see that we can apply the scriptures to our own lives and receive the same miracles and blessings. There was a young man who lived with his family in the difficult times after World War II. His family did not have enough food to eat, and one day they heard that potatoes were available out in the country. This boy was sent to go find them and bring them home. He had to walk far out in the country to locate potatoes for his family to eat, and though he was delighted to finally find some, he couldn't carry the heavy burlap sack full! It was too heavy for him! What should he do?

If he left it there, someone else would take it! His family needed that food desperately and they were counting on him! As he struggled with this problem, the story of Alma's people came into his mind. If the Lord helped them carry heavy burdens, He would help him too! With prayer and with faith, that boy was able to lift that heavy sack of potatoes and carry it all the way back home. He could do it! He still had a heavy load to carry home, but he was strengthened to make it light. This boy had been taught, he had listened, and he had developed faith that he could access when he needed it.

6. Provide Happy Memories

Joyous occasions can go along with the teachings. These can be simple and inexpensive. Even in hard times, we can join together to solve problems and still be happy. It's hard, but with wisdom and help from above, coupled with more love, we can grow in resourcefulness and help our families to grow as well.

Dear Mom and Dad,

Okay, I realize that I am lazy at times. But thanks for trying to teach me to be resourceful! I am learning it, even if I complain. Thanks for letting me provide some of my needs and wants, and for caring for me enough to want my success!

Love, Me

Chapter 15

Make Teen Connections

*W*e want to be close to our teenage kids as they go through this difficult stage of life. We want them to come to us with their dilemmas and challenges. It is we who want to be their support, rather than some immature, inexperienced friend who doesn't care about them nearly as much as we do! So we must make connections that will bring us together and keep us close.

Walls Coming Down

Adolescence can be a volatile time! In this arena like no other, the answer is more love. We must love them enough to be patient as they mature, ride out the storms, and be there for them regardless. They must have evidence that we truly love them. (See "Evidence That I Love You" in chapter 10.) Trust must grow. And we must make connections to solidify our love and support in their lives.

Often, we parents find that there is a wall between us and our teen that is blocking all these things. How can we tear down this wall in order to open up love and trust, communication and connection?

1. Find Common Ground

We must find an opening in the wall that our teenagers put up. Actually, this idea is from a wonderful article I found about connecting with teenagers. When there is a figurative brick wall that is between you and your teenager, teaches Brad Wilcox, expert in working with young people, you must "find the loose brick." Figure out something that you and your teenager have in common—be it skiing, cooking, shopping, art, even the same TV show, or the same book, and use that to gradually tear down the wall and build an open relationship. A dream of theirs, a skill they want to acquire, or an interest, such as motorcycles, sports, food, computers, horses, guitars, skateboards, journal writing are more possible common interests. Do that thing together, talk about something new in that field, or even talk of happy memories of doing that together. Use it as a springboard to a new positive conversation.[1]

I was sitting at the sewing machine one Saturday afternoon fixing something while my daughter was in the room folding clothes. She had saved up her chores all week and therefore had a lot of laundry to fold, and she was frustrated about it. I felt bad for her and looked for something to talk about, to get her mind off the mundane chore. *What do we have in common?* I asked myself. I started to tell her the plot from a girly movie I had just seen, in minute detail, and my evaluation of it. She loved it! When I was done, she told me the plot from the book she'd just read. We found a common love, and that afternoon became one of our favorite memories!

Other children have responded to my interest in their current subject matter at school, my offering to edit for them, or my accompanying them on the piano. One son likes it when I use his expertise in electronics. Another son who lives away from home connects with me at the grocery store, asking for advice on how much or what kind of thing to buy. Some of my skinnier kids need me to alter their clothes to fit better. Other times, when I am at a loss, the Spirit helps me come up with common ground to make a connection with my teenagers.

2. Listen, Truly Listen

Listen until your teen is done talking. Then ask questions so they will talk longer.

- Perhaps go to a different place to talk and listen, one that is free of past baggage or negative conversations.
- Perhaps talking with one parent would be more effective than with both, as they may feel outnumbered.
- Invent "necessary" car rides, just the two of you, in which there are no distractions.

Ask questions and truly listen. Make sure the questions are not leading questions that you already know the answer to. Sincere, open-ended questions, in which there are no right answers, are the best because they send the message: I really want to know how you feel.

I have resisted texting at times, but I've had to admit that often, texting is the best way to reach teenagers. In fact, I have had some really great conversations with my older kids through text that I wouldn't have gotten any other way. Face to face is better, but we must embrace their language. Mark and I have learned that we may need to start with texting to break down barriers, which may allow more personal conversation later. It is harder to show emotion or tone with a text, but we must do our best to convey love and sincerity to open up future avenues of communication that may be better.

3. Stay Calm, Especially in Voice

A quiet response will be so much more effective than a loud one, especially if it is void of all sarcasm. We can state the facts and show concern. It would be best to let unkind responses just die, and not get to us. A "soft answer turneth away wrath" (Proverbs 15:1). We must make sure our answers do not belittle or blame, since criticism makes love die. It does not work well to bring up past mistakes; simply forgive. Take every chance to guide and teach truth, rather than be critical.

I watched my younger sister go through a serious problem with her throat that required surgery. Afterward, for quite a while, this sister had little or no use of her voice and was required to speak only in whispers. But what I was surprised to observe was that this sister's six active children also began to be soft spoken. The tone in their home was peaceful. It was remarkable for me to watch, but it reinforced the idea that children learn what they live and learn the most from example.

One season, I too found power to give calm responses. I noticed that the times when I was reading the scriptures regularly, even if it were only a small portion every day—were the times when I had the most power over my reactions. My responses to my kids were better, because I had been given the gift of a minute to compose them. In that minute, the Holy Ghost could remind me of my love for that child, even though they might be exasperating at the moment. In the scriptures, I came across 2 Nephi 26:16, in which "he [Mormon] was given power that he may whisper." Power to whisper! It is just what a busy mom in a hectic day needs—help to "lower our voices a few decibels," as President Hinckley counseled.[2]

We must resist the tendency to overreact. Rather than being emotional, we must teach truth and help our teenagers see the long-term consequences for poor choices.

> A professional counselor asked one mother, "Suppose your son came home and said, 'I have a friend who is taking drugs.' What would you say to him?" The mother paused for a moment and then said, "I'd probably tell him to find another friend." This mother may have missed an important opportunity with her son. When a child tells you about "my friend's problem," there is a possibility that your child is struggling with a similar one. Young people drop hints to test our reactions. If we are hasty, harsh, and judgmental, our children may not want to open up any further.[3]

Again, we must resist the tendency to respond sarcastically. "The negative effect of using sarcasm is that people can't then share tender feelings for fear that you will be sarcastic with them," says educator and clergyman Scott Rapier. "Too often, even though we often pretend that it doesn't bother us, sarcasm hurts. I think we quietly wonder if the negative comments said in the name of sarcasm is how people really feel about us. It erodes confidence and trust. We want our teenagers to feel like they can open up to us. Sarcasm will block that. Even if your teenager speaks sarcastically to us, we would best respond in a sincere, adult voice that builds relationships."[4] (See also "A Look at Sarcasm" in chapter 7.)

4. Apologize When Needed

If we tell our child sincerely that we are sorry for past conversations that didn't work out well, it will help bring down walls. We as parents are learning too, and sometimes make mistakes. We must model repentance.

I have learned that when I apologize sincerely, the mood softens. I have also learned to avoid comparing one child to another, but to communicate that I value each for who they are, regardless of what mistakes they have made. Since saying "I'm sorry" is a good heart softener, we could use this even if we don't think we were really at fault. "I'm sorry I have upset you," or "I'm sorry we are at odds," or "You're right, I haven't been very good at _____" are approaches that help bitterness to melt.

5. Be a Parent Regardless

Our teenage children do not need us to be another friend; they need us to be their parent. We must avoid being a chum, because during the growing up years when they are in our home, they desperately need us to be a parent. We can be friendly without trying to be popular with them and their friends.

We must set guidelines, limits, and rules. Our teen needs boundaries that are not too strict, and not too lenient. They need limits, even if it just so they have someone (you) to blame for the things they cannot do with friends. We should prayerfully decide these as a couple, and as a family, and then write down family rules and curfews for all to remember.

The key is to also express love and concern, while holding firm boundaries. "I love you enough to want to guard and protect you and keep you safe," should be the message we always give with the limits. "I am also willing to sacrifice my time and comfort to help you be safe."

One of my daughters often asks me, "Mom, would you tell me that I can't go to this get-together tonight? I have a paper due tomorrow." I would then respond as directed: "I'm sorry, but you may not go to the get-together tonight, since you'd better get your homework done." Sometimes, this same daughter asks me, "Mom, tell me I can't wear this top." Or even, "Mom, tell me that I have to go to bed right now." It is a little bit comical, but really, it shows me that she is using good judgment but still needs boundaries that I can provide.

Teens can be a huge challenge, but we must remember daily that deep down, we love them dearly. The Spirit will prompt us the best way to show more and more love at this difficult time in their lives.

Dear Mom and Dad,

It's tough being a teenager! I have so much I am facing, and I need to be able to talk about these things. Thanks for letting me open up and for loving me enough to listen and not overreact. I can tell that you truly love me.

Love, Me

Parent Interviews: Accountability

My daughter-in-law grew up having regular interviews with her father. "I loved them!" she told me. "I felt like I could talk to him about anything!" In fact, she feels like her once-a-month chance to talk to her dad are some of her favorite memories. What a wonderful connection with her father.

Mark and I have also had a great experience communicating with our kids through interviews. Mark likes to do interviews on the back porch swing; I like to have us both sit on my bed. We start with a prayer, and our first question is usually, "What is on your mind?" Our kids know they will have this chance to talk with us regularly. (See also "Confident Parenting" in chapter 9.)

The goal is to listen carefully and be positive and accepting in tone, while still telling them we expect a lot and encourage them to continue being the good person they are. We talk as long as needed over their current dilemmas, and then come the standard questions.

We decided to make a list of questions to ask our kids at each monthly interview—much like a temple recommend interview—so they would know what they will be asked. I typed our list up, modifying it as needed, and I keep a copy in my drawer and one posted for them to see. We felt like this would be a deterrent from doing some things, knowing they would be asked about it, and a motivation to do some things for the same reason.

Some ideas for interview questions:

- How are your prayers?
- Are you reading the scriptures?
- Do you honor your parents?
- Are you completely honest?
- Do you strive to take the sacraments worthily?
- Are you paying your tithing?
- Are you getting along with your brothers and sisters? Do they know that you love them?
- Do you have good friends, who make you want to be your best? (We encourage them to be friendly to all, but to choose as their closest friends those of all faiths who will uplift them.)
- Are you listening to good music?
- Are you able to avoid bad pictures? Movies? Bad jokes? Cheating?
- Do you avoid offending the Spirit in all that you do?
- Do you treat all girls/guys with respect?
- Are you avoiding pairing off before your mission or college?
- Will you decide ahead when you are going to kiss? (The little ones giggle on this one!)
- Are you striving to be more and more like Jesus?

At one point, new situations came up regarding electronics, so we counseled together with our family of teenagers about what questions would help us use them appropriately. We added these to our list:

- Tell me about your recent electronic usage.
- Have you seen any suggestive or bad images or words on the computer? (Or when was the last time you saw something bad on the computer or phone?)
- Are the books you read about reality and goodness too, not just fantasy or violence or science fiction?
- Are you using YouTube only in the family room? No internet in your room (laptop or handheld)? Is your browser remaining off outside the family room?
- What is your texting limit?
- Are you living a transparent, open-book life?
- Do you feel good about your electronic usage?

We end with another open-ended question, such as "Is there anything else that is on your mind? And of course, "Do you know how much I love you?"

When Mark had a demanding calling, which required a season of extra busy Sundays, I took over all the interviews for a season. It was a sweet time with my kids. I would share with him in private later what I had learned from each child. Other times, we have come up with a schedule of who interviews whom each Sunday of the month. Occasionally, we talk with a child together, but sometimes this feels like our child is outnumbered, so for interviews, we keep it one-on-one, and we trade off doing the interview and then sharing what we found out with each other.

The kids love their interviews—I don't think I've ever had a child hesitate to have one. For the most part, they want their turn. I remember one time when an interview started to turn a bit confrontational, but I just reassured my child of my love and support and we worked out the issue. Another time I could tell a child was in a bad mood, so I ended the interview early so that it could end on a happy note. Some touchy issues we save for family council and our Family Policy Book (see chapter 12). But those have been rare. Month after month, for many years, the kids have readily come—even instead of a Sunday nap—and are so willing to talk. They love the connection, and they welcome the accountability.

Most of the time, our kids don't really want us to fix their problems as much as just to be a sounding board or even a place to vent and gain empathy.

If our children know they will be accountable, they will have more incentive for choosing right. Just as we report in to our church leaders each time we want to have a renewed temple recommend, our children can also report in during parent interviews. What's more, here is a regular time and place for them to talk over anything they have been wondering about and unload any of their current worries.

One of our sons shared with me the effectiveness of casual interviews in his life: "One of Dad's best tactics for me was when he would come sit in my room on Sundays during high school. He never called it an interview—he would just ask about things that were important to me and I would open up as little or as much as I felt like. He expressed his love for me by caring about what I cared about."[5] Interviews can be casual, even unplanned, when there is the need for that modification. If we are around our teens a lot, they will open up when they are ready.

Casual interviews can bless immeasurably. Many, many times—usually at night—I would approach my dad and say, "Can I talk to you?" He was doing something else at that moment, but he never turned me away. "Sure, Leenie!" he answered, and then he let me pour out my young heart to him. I remember once when I came crying bitterly, "Dad, I think I lost my smile!" He fought back the laughter and reassured me it would return! How I love him for that—for getting me through my pressing concerns and loving me so in the process. I hope my kids feel a portion of my love for them when I regularly make time to talk one-on-one with them.

Dear Mom and Dad,

I am so glad you care about me! You have busy lives, but I feel valued when you stop and take time out for just me. I love your validation of what I am going through. I love your encouragement to keep trying to reach goals and do the daily important stuff!

Love, Me

The Power of Touch: "Skin Hunger"

Everyone needs to be touched. It's part of being loved. Some yearn for it more than others, but our skin was designed to be stroked and patted and hugged and squeezed! Even those who claim to not be "touchy-feely" usually like a mild show of affection, like a hand on a shoulder or a quick side hug. Mark refers to our skin as having electrons that need to be shared with one another! That may or may not be true, but skin can be vibrant and there sure is some kind of wonderful exchange when hands are held or an arm is stroked or a hug is given. We need to give our children the gift of touch.

This human need to be touched was shown me in an amazing way when I had my premature baby twins. It was incredible! Each time I put my baby twins down to sleep, one on each end of one crib since they were so tiny, I was amazed when they woke up! There they were, touching each other with their heads together, nestled one above the other. They were almost intertwined—just as they had been in my womb! They were four-pound babies, who had been born almost eight weeks early. They had spent almost two weeks separated into two hospital incubators. But they needed and longed to be touching each other, like they had inside me. How could it be possible for them to scoot or even move? But it was so, time and again, that though I placed them at either side of the crib, they were together, touching when they awoke.

Consider these reasons for more touch:

1. Babies Need Touch and So Do the Rest of Us

Babies can die without touch, as poor overcrowded orphanages have seen. Though the staff at such places can feed them all, some babies simply die, since they are not able to hold each one enough! Everyone, but especially a baby, needs touch. (See "The Godly Power of Attachment" in chapter 2.)

When I was a teenager, my favorite thing to do when I walked in the door was to pick up my baby brother or sister! No matter how my day had gone, here was an instant source of happiness and love! Blessed to be at the start of a large family, who adopted several children at the end, I always had a baby sister or brother to love! And they loved me back—unconditionally! It was a huge blessing to me and to the baby too. My problems melted away and the world seemed good again.

In a completely different situation, my friend's daughter suffered some severe postpartum depression after her last baby. What did the doctor prescribe? Two things. One, that she play the piano every day—something she loved but had mostly given up. And two, that she hold her baby! Isn't that obvious? Well, in her depression, this mom had given the baby to an older sibling or dad to care for most of the time. To heal, she—as well as her baby—needed that touching time. And the two-step plan worked.

2. Children Need Touch

One of the five basic "Love Languages" is touch. A simple touch on the shoulder or arm or back blesses a child immensely.

> Studies indicate that many parents touch their children only when it is necessary: when they are dressing or undressing them, putting them in the car, or carrying them to bed. It seems that many parents are unaware of how much their children need to be touched and how easily they can use this means to keep their children's emotional tanks filled with unconditional love. . . . Parents need no special occasion or excuse to make physical contact. They have almost constant opportunity to transfer love to the heart of a child with touch.[6]

Of course, some children need more touch than others. I have a son who has always loved to feel soft things. At the grocery store, he often goes over to touch the stuffed animals and points out an especially soft one to me. For Christmas, this young son gave his older brother the very best thing he could think of—an extra soft body pillow! Some of our children have climbed on our bed often at night, hungry for some extra time on our soft bed and an extra hug afterward. Most of our kids have longed for time to wrestle Dad on the family room floor. Some initiate a group hug for the whole family whenever possible.

Another son doesn't seem to ever need extra touch. But yet, this is the son who from the time he was a little boy, without fail, made it a point every single week to give me a kiss and a hug after sacrament meeting before he left for his class. He too needs touch. When he left on his mission, I sure felt a longing for that weekly hug! Although it wasn't the only hug we had each week, it was a special one that belonged to just me and him, in a special place at a certain time. For a good long season, it was ours.

Some may need it more than others, but all need touch. When I catch myself trying to save time by blowing a kiss to a child, or calling out "I love you, good night!" from afar, I remind myself to take the extra minutes or seconds to go ahead and go to each one with a hug. It is totally worth the extra time, since it tells each child another way, besides words, that I truly love them. May we sense what touch the members of our family need, and provide it and more just in case, regularly and often.

3. Marriages Need Touch

At one point, Mark and I decided that no matter how tired either or both of us were each night, we would spend a few minutes touching. Stroking an arm, holding a hand, or caressing a face is plenty, but it is necessary. (And an occasional foot massage is heavenly!) Though we were used to praying together and saying "I love you" before bed, we discovered that we needed a little touch each night as well. (When we are not up to more.) This decision has blessed our marriage so much.

Once, I happened upon a newspaper article about *Skin Hunger*. "Touch each other often," it affirmed, for "physical intimacy helps make marriages strong. *But non-sexual touching does, too.*" The article talks about "using non-sexual touch to facilitate bonding and countering the stress of daily living with frequent gestures of caring." It shows a survey that validates that these elements keep married couples happier and marriages more secure. "The simple act of placing a hand on your partner's shoulder or arm, or holding hands when you walk or watch TV can release oxytocin, the hormone that is responsible for trust and attachment, which glues couples together. Touch is so important to our emotional well-being that behavioral scientists have coined a phrase that describes what we experience when we don't get it: skin hunger. . . . A pat on the back, a squeeze of the hand, a hug, an arm around the shoulder—the science of touch suggests that it can save a so-so marriage."[7]

4. The Wonderful Hug

When I used to take preschoolers to visit a care home, I would urge them to give hugs to these "grandmas and grandpas," who don't get one very often. I found that most little children are happy to give hugs readily and freely! What a precious gift is a hug!

I understand that sometimes the elderly go to get their hair done weekly *not* just to look nice. It might be the only touch they get all week, and they long for and need it. I feel bad for those who are alone, without a person to pat them on the back or give them a hug. The rest of us can be aware of this need and appropriately provide a touch with our hello or a shoulder embrace with our goodbye.

For those who are sensitive about giving hugs, there is the wonderful side hug. It is simply one arm around another's shoulders as the two persons stand side by side. We encourage our daughters to give side hugs, for they are totally appropriate and give the right message of mutual affection and appropriate touch.

Jesus healed the blind man with his touch (Mark 8:25). He used his hands to help this man have the faith to be healed by feeling them over his eyes. The woman with an issue of blood also used touch to be healed. In fact, she had faith that if she could just touch His clothing, her ailment would end (Luke 8:43–44). With His love, we can often be instruments in the hands of the Lord to bring healing and blessing to others. With His priesthood, we can request "the laying on of hands" to bless others (D&C 20:41). Loving touch is powerful.

How grateful we are for our wonderful bodies of flesh and blood that God has given us for this mortal existence. We are so blessed to have skin that is vibrant and full of electrons to share! Let us give them away appropriately and liberally, and by so doing, make family bonds strong and secure.

Dear Mom and Dad,

Thanks for all the kisses and hugs. I may squirm and even object at times, but I really do love them. I like to feel secure that you really love me just as I am, and I feel this when you touch my hand or pat my back or give me that extra hug.

Love, Me

Chapter 16
Be a Lioness at the Door
Protecting Our Homes from Evil

I love the image that Sister Julie B. Beck used to describe a mother who is vigilant as a lion. She is determined to protect her family, so much that she is at the door watching carefully at what comes in her home. Nothing harmful will get to her family! She makes no apology for her fierceness because there is too much at risk to those she loves fiercely! We have enemies beyond our door that would hurt our families and we can confidently refuse to let them in! Together with our family, we can build a fortress home, guard and protect it, and always administer hope and help if someone is harmed in any way.

Sister Beck emphasized that this lioness "guards that gate, and things matter to that family if they matter to her." The things that are important to her will happen in her family. "This means that there has to be some prioritizing." We must focus first on the things that are essential.[1]

Protecting Their Purity: Guarding Our Children from Evil

"Stop, drop, and roll," we teach our children if ever they encounter dangerous flames. We must also arm them with a plan for if the dangerous sight of pornography assails them, such as **"Turn it off, turn away, and tell**." "See this button here?" we can show even our very young children the on the front of their screen. "Just push it, quick as you can, if ever there is anything inappropriate that pops up on your screen! Turn away. And be sure to always tell *us* what happened!"

Even on the computers our children use at school, they have to be careful and ready. I overheard of some incidents at the elementary school in which the kids had inadvertently accessed something inappropriate, despite the filters and blocks. "Push the button quick," we can tell our kids, "then go tell the teacher. It's okay to not do the assignment if you need to turn off something bad!" At home and wherever they go, we want to provide our kids protection and a safe haven where all is wholesome and where things can be talked about openly. Consider some ways to protect and guard our children:

1. A Lesson on Avoiding Pornography
Who has a body? (Funny question! We all do of course!)

Are our bodies good or bad? (Good! Heavenly Father created them!)

Which is better, a girl body or a boy body? (Another silly question. Both are super!)

Because our bodies are so wonderful—even temples—and were created by Heavenly Father, He asks us to keep them covered.

Sometimes we see pictures of people who don't. These are bad pictures. Sometimes these bad pictures pop up on a computer screen or a phone.

There was a young boy named Connor whose friend gave him the letters to put into his computer to see something cool! It turned out to be a bad picture and he felt terribly inside! He turned it off quickly, then went

I Will

*T*urn It Off
Turn Away
Tell

to his room—he didn't want to tell anyone. Later, when he was saying his prayers, he got the feeling to tell his parents. They helped him.[2]

2. Courage to Set Limits

After we have taught them about avoiding porn, we must set rules and limits, and if we are consistent, enforcing limits will get easier. Persistence in making sure that each device has filters is good, but we must also be vigilant in checking up on what they are watching and games they are playing. We must be sticklers about the content of the TV, movies, music, and internet. It is wise and necessary to check out ahead of time what is actually in a particular movie. And we must be ready always to turn off the inappropriate. We and our kids were enjoying a wonderful series of a family show, when in the second season, there popped up out of nowhere a totally inappropriate scene with sexual content! Another time, it was a lewd relationship that surfaced in an otherwise wholesome show. Both times, we reluctantly had to discontinue watching. It is a huge example to our families when we turn things off.

Following the lead of an older, more experienced family of cousins, Mark and I decided we couldn't allow our kids to do sleepovers. It was just too risky to chance an image on an unmonitored screen or device to impose itself on them. Though our kids might have occasionally grumbled, we knew we had to be firm. Many a youngster has had a first look at pornography at a sleepover. So we have insisted that in the dark of night, parents need to be the guard.

Mark and I insist that in our home that we keep *all* computers and screens in the family room only. At first, I found it hard to make a place for all the family's media in the family room where it was visible and accountability could be enforced. I loved to do computer time in my bedroom! But I decided it was more important to me to protect my loved ones with my example. Mark and I set up a table desk in the family room pathway where all electronics could be set up. Once a friend came over and innocently started setting up a computer in another room to have our tech-y son help him fix it. "No," Mark corrected them, "Move these into the family room area only." What's more, we counseled with our kids and made it a strict family policy that the only internet usage even on phones was to be in that room with an adult present. Our sixteen-year-old, somewhat begrudgingly at first, would bring his cell phone in there to use. Because the family policy had been explained to him well, he complied. I was so grateful that the younger ones saw his example. It was totally worth the safety of our family to do all computer time there!

My friend felt pressure to put a second TV in the basement of her home. "No," she insisted, with lion-like firmness, "I can't monitor what the kids turn on down there. Our only TV must be in my view!" It was that important to her. Gradually, the other members of her family respected that righteous desire as well.

3. Handheld Devices

At one point, we discovered that as our kids got older, their games switched from a large screen to a handheld screen. It was much harder to monitor. We had to make an effort to talk to our kids about what they were playing and be aware of just what they were filling their minds with. On a long drive, we have made an exception to our usual limits on the time we play games, but it used to be that these games were a handheld Yahtzee or Tetris game, whereas now it is their phone or iPod that provides the games now being played in the back seats. These are much harder to monitor. Mark and I knew that many family talks about what we were filling their minds with was essential. We talk about games that are violent and those that are destructive of property. We don't want them to get used to anything even virtually inappropriate. So they have found more appropriate games.

There are more and more risky apps available. Most are anonymous and secretive. "Short term posts that can be deleted immediately can lead to bullying or inappropriate content," we are warned. "Don't ban apps just for the sake of banning apps or you may have a revolution on your hands. But be aware of what apps your youth are using, how it's affecting their gospel study time, school time, mutual time, and family time."[3] Many families I know are limiting their teenagers to flip phones all the way through high school, proving they can be successful without internet access constantly and thus limiting the danger. Others feel that now that missionaries have smart phones on their missions, teenagers need to learn the discipline to manage cell phones while they are in our workshop homes. The Spirit will guide us to do what is best for our children.

"The best way to avoid risky apps or dangerous entertainment is to have a healthy relationship with your youth. Talk to them about the apps they use and advise them to make good decisions when it comes to their activity online."[4] Along with our parental vigilance, the filters have to become internal.

4. Choice of What They Take into Their Minds

Internal control is by far the best! If a child knows from early on that he or she is a child of God, it follows that what he or she chooses to allow inside will be more God-like. There is a wonderful song that teaches kids to be careful about what they take into their minds and selves. "Stand Up, Walk Away!" teaches about closing books, turning off TV, and having the courage to walk out of a bad movie. My kids learned actions to it years ago and still love to sing this catchy song. What a valuable message it has about filling our minds with goodness: "Whatever you do, becomes you!" this marvelous song teaches.[5]

Remember Elder Boyd K. Packer's advice to have a song picked out and ready for use when an evil thought threatens?[6] Having a tool ready helps them be strong and ready whenever they face what is outside our fortress homes. We can sing the hymns at home, so they know some. Then we can pick a favorite one for ourselves and ask them theirs!

Another wonderful tool we like to use is called "following the eagle." From the time my kids were very little, I taught them about "the eagle." Whether it is a billboard, a picture on media, or a person dressed immodestly comes to view, they can use this technique! "When you see something bad," I taught them, "In your mind, turn it immediately into an eagle—one that is flying quickly past. Follow that eagle with your head and turn quickly away from the bad scene. Then, you can regroup and get the thought quickly from your heads, as you watch that eagle fly away! Or you can focus on the new thing in your view! It will especially help you when you are a missionary!" Periodically, I remind them and ask if they are following the eagle. "I sure am!" they will affirm. It is a valuable tool to have ready! (If only King David had known about following the eagle!)

5. The Rod of Iron: Holding Tight to the Word of God

"If we think we can solve pornography with only filters on devices, we are chopping only branches off a tree, and never getting to the heart," commented my friend, a mother of five. Handheld devices are the biggest culprit, and even those without internet capacity can access pornography through roundabout means, such as Facebook. We must "lead our children to deep conversion."[7]

Great power and protection comes from reading the scriptures—especially the Book of Mormon—together. If our family will hold tight to the iron rod, we will all better find our way through the dark mists and avoid the fiery darts. We will develop abiding testimonies as well as protection from the world. There are great promises that come from reading the Book of Mormon:

> I feel certain that if, in our homes, parents will read from the Book of Mormon prayerfully and regularly, both by themselves and with their children, the spirit of that great book will come to permeate our homes and all who dwell therein. The spirit of reverence will increase; mutual respect and consideration for each other will grow. The spirit of contention will depart. Parents will counsel their children in greater love and wisdom. Children will be more responsive and submissive to the counsel of their parents. Righteousness will increase. Faith, hope, and charity—the pure love of Christ—will abound in our homes and lives, bringing in their wake peace, joy, and happiness.[8]

What is the doctrine that we can teach specifically about pure thoughts? "He hath said that no unclean thing can inherit the kingdom of heaven" (Alma 11:37) and "watch yourselves, and your thoughts, and your words, and your deeds, and observe the commandments of God, and continue in the faith" (Mosiah 4:30). We can be cleansed through Christ. We must also teach our children that planning to sin now and repent later is making a mockery of our beloved Savior's Atonement. Rather, we must constantly be trying our best, quickly repenting of mistakes.

6. The Big Talks and the Little Talks

We must talk and listen. We need to ask our children regularly about their exposure to things and their use of electronics. A scheduled interview will be a huge deterrent from slipping into the inappropriate. Along with the formal asking, we must do the casual asking too. Listen carefully. And, as the church website directs, watch for changes in behavior that might be red flags.[9] It is imperative that we teach our children about intimacy, so they will get a wholesome view and not a worldly view. (See "The Special Talks" in chapter 8.)

M. Russell Ballard counsels fathers and sons—which definitely applies to mothers and daughters as well,

> Dare to have the "big talks" with your sons. You know what I mean: talks about drugs and drinking, about the dangers of today's media—the Internet, cyber technologies, and pornography—and about priesthood worthiness, respect for girls, and moral cleanliness. While these should not be the only subjects you talk about with your sons, please don't shy away from them. Your boys need your counsel, guidance, and input on these subjects. As you talk about these very important matters, you will find that the trust between you will flourish.
>
> I am especially concerned that we communicate openly and clearly with our sons about sexual matters. Your sons are growing up in a world that openly embraces and flaunts early, casual, and thoughtless promiscuity. Your sons simply cannot avoid the blatant sexual imagery, messages, and enticements that are all around them. . . . Be positive about how wonderful and beautiful physical intimacy can be when it happens within the bounds the Lord has set, including temple covenants and commitments of eternal marriage. Studies show that the biggest deterrent to casual sexual activity is a wholesome attitude that connects such personal relationships with genuine commitment and mature love.[10]

Mark and I had been interviewing our kids quite regularly when Mark asked me, "I want you to ask me regularly about my cell phone usage too." So I agreed that on the first Sunday of every month, I would ask him. Then I told Mark, "Once a month, I want you to ask me if I am living a transparent life." Our marriage is important enough to us to have the safeguard of accountability.

7. Warm Parenting Style

We should examine our parenting style, to make sure we parent our children with both accountability and warmth. Kids desperately need limits and to be accountable, and they just as desperately need our kindness and tender support. Steve Bahr and John Hoffman, two BYU sociology professors, in a study on parental impact on teenage drinking, found that

- Teens with Authoritative parents, who are warm as well as structured, were least prone to heavy drinking.
- Teens with Authoritarian parents, who were cold and strict, were twice as likely to heavily drink.
- Teens with Indulgent parents, who provided warmth but no accountability, were triply prone to binge drinking.
- And teens with Neglectful parents, who were inattentive and unsupportive, were four times as likely to heavily drink.

We learn from this that we must cultivate a parenting style of warmth and caring, while maintaining limits and accountability to provide the least risk of alcohol addiction for our children.[11]

8. Wholesome Love

One of the greatest deterrents to pornography is wholesome family love at home. We parents would do well to shower our family members with hugs and kisses and to fill our homes with words of endearment, praise, and encouragement. We can express love in many different ways, giving our children evidence of our love and sacrifice for them. What's more, we must show them our wholesome love for each other: let them see Dad sweep Mom off her feet in a huge hug and see Mom plant a juicy kiss right on Dad's lips. We should use words of endearment and praise to each other in front of them, thus letting them see that marriage is sweet and good.

Once, when I found that I was dwelling too much on the negative in the world, I began to add time to our schedule for having fun together and creating happy memories. I began to smile at the kids a lot more. Rather than leave them alone, I tried to take them with me more often and to turn something as mundane as getting gas into an adventure There is a lot of good in the world, I reassured the kids, and we can focus more on finding the good in this world to talk about.

Mark and I had already climbed into bed one night when one of our kids showed up in our room. There was really no reason; she just stood there at the doorway. Soon, her younger brother came in, too—only he pounced on the bed. Annoyed, I shooed him off, and whisked the kids off to bed. But later, as I thought about it, I remembered what security had come to me as a child, in my own mom and dad's room. Mark and I both knew that we had carried on many a great conversation in their bed with a child cozily in between us. "You know," I commented to Mark, "rather than shoo them away, I should have told them a story from my childhood or just let them lie here a minute." I knew that I should already have known that—we'd had many great conversations with a child there. But we parents must constantly be learning and relearning and listening to the Spirit. I hoped that the kids would stop by my bedroom before bed again soon and I would do better to fortify them with peace and love, even if I were tired.

Along with being fearless as a lion about what we will allow in our homes, we must be diligent about the expressions of warmth, kindness, and love to all members of our fortress homes.

Dear Mom and Dad,

I may grumble about them, but I am so grateful for your limits. It shows me that you really care and you want my happiness. I am going to grow up to have a wholesome marriage and family, thanks to you!

Love, Me

Fortifications from Our Fortress Home

I heard a mom say, "I want to just lock all my kids up in the temple!" She was anxious to keep them safe from the evils of this sometimes-forbidding world. Of course, we can't do that. But there is much we can do to build a fortress-like home and fortify them when they must leave it:

1. Fortify Our Children with Prayer

The scriptures encourage us to pray always, for "the effectual fervent prayer of a righteous man availeth much" (James 5:16). Do we realize just how powerful and necessary are the family prayers we offer for our children each morning? Prayer is a marvelous tool, for God is willing and able to bless us, but He never forces blessings upon us. He waits for us to ask.

We felt that it was imperative to teach our young children to have their own personal prayer every morning. Most of them remember their nighttime prayer well but struggle to remember the morning prayer, especially when things are busy. We came up with different ways: one child immediately fell to his knees as soon as he awoke; one child connected his morning prayer with putting on shoes; and another child said theirs along with making the bed. Soon, it was a daily habit, a guard in place.

Our family devised a couple of acronyms to help our kids remember to pray during the day:

- TP = Test Prayer. It reminds our kids to pray before taking a test, in order to have extra help to recall the answers they had studied.
- RTP = Remember to Pray. I have written the letters inconspicuously on a child's lunch sack, until it became a habit to quietly pray over the food before eating lunch. One of our daughters shared the acronym with her close girlfriends, who then helped each other remember to bow silently and quickly for a blessing over their school lunch.
- BIGWUP = Barbara, Instead of Getting Worried, You Pray. This was an important help for a daughter who was inclined to worry a lot. It helped her give the worries to God and instead ask His help during the day.

2. Arm Them with Scripture Power

There is power in the words of the Lord in the scriptures. Even a few verses from the Book of Mormon or Bible will shield our kids with the spiritual armor they need to face the world.

Our family has a pretty good habit of reading scriptures together in the mornings. On extra hectic mornings, we may read just a single thought, but most mornings we each get a turn to read several verses. But Mark and I wanted to coax our kids to start reading on their own as well. We started with our own examples, and if the kids often didn't see us reading, we would try to say, "I want to share with you something cool I read in the scriptures today!" At one point, we both moved our personal scripture study to the kitchen table, in order to set a better example to our children.

Then, when a certain child was ready (meaning when they were a fairly good reader and the time seemed right), Mark or I would ask him if he would like to read the scriptures together at night. These times are now choice memories. (See "Love of the Scriptures" in chapter 4.)

3. Empower Them with Music

Music can fill their minds with goodness. Our family decided to sing a hymn each morning before we read. I'm always so delighted to hear that hymn being hummed or sung later on in the morning! This tells me that the music stays in their minds through the day. As mentioned earlier, one son was going to have to leave extra early for football, so I had the three football players in the carpool sing a hymn each morning. Thankfully, after explaining to them my desire to fortify them before facing the locker room, these husky boys were willing to each take a turn to pick a hymn and to sing!

For one stretch of time, we decided to get an email with the list of the songs that would be sung in church that week from the ward music chairman to sing them with the family through the week. We would talk about the words and what they meant. By the time Sunday came and the hymn began at church, the children would look at me with triumph and mouth, "We know this song!" More and more, I hear them humming them!

4. Investigate Their Lives during Dinnertime Conversation

Sometimes it's hard to get the entire family together for a sit-down dinner, but it is such a valuable time. Parents often play undercover detective at dinner, trying to uncover the things the kids have been taught or exposed to that day. We try to phrase questions in such a way as to help them open up about what they are learning. I have learned the hard way, however, not to jump too harshly on a child when a falsehood or poor attitude had been taught. I have learned to back up a little and think about an effective way to present the truth and a wholesome philosophy. My plan is to talk it over with Mark and then bring it up at an upcoming family home evening or scripture time or even dinnertime. This way, our student will not get defensive but will consider the truths we try to teach effectively by the Spirit.

We have also found that dinnertime is a good time to talk over world events. Mark and I talk about the elections coming up. We try to talk about what is happening in the world, in a way that the children can understand. We always reassure our children that we would do everything to keep them safe and that the Lord will protect us when we do what's right. Whenever possible, we want our kids to see these things from our perspective first, before they hear other worldly views. (See "Teaching Them First" in chapter 8.)

Of course, parent interviews are another amazing way to find out what our kids are going through, to keep channels open. (See "Parent Interviews" in chapter 15.)

5. Fortify Each Child with a Priesthood Blessing

It's a rough world away from our house, and our children soldiers need all the help they can get. We would do well to get Dad or Grandpa or a friend to help give each one extra help from a priesthood blessing. Right before a new school year is a great time to do it.

My mother always wrote down the words to priesthood blessings, so I do too. Later on during the year, especially if things are getting tough, one of the kids and I may look over these notes to help us make a decision. Mark has always taught our kids the need to claim the blessings they receive by praying for them and helping them happen. The Lord gives us blessings, but He won't force us to accept them. We do our part by working toward them and asking for them to be fulfilled.

6. Give Them a Wholesome Family Example

A family that tries their best to keep commandments, follow prophets, and establish a Christ-centered home will be the best fortification. Deep down, our children want goodness. They feel secure in a family circle with wise boundaries (see "Set Boundaries Confidently," Chapter 9) and love in abundance. A fortress filled with wholesome family life will be their best defense, and as they join us in asking and receiving help from the Lord, they will want the same in their lives and families too.

One summer morning, I was up very early getting our teenage son off to work. As I glanced at the doorway, I had the impression that a guardian angel was standing there. He was dressed as an ancient soldier, with a hood and a cape. Startled at first, I discovered that I felt at peace. As I thought about it, I realized that our home is really our fortress, and it needs a strong guard to protect it from the evil of the world.

Dear Mom and Dad,

I am so glad you care about me enough to keep me safe from the bad things in our world. Though I may complain, I feel your love through the fortifications you set up and stick by.

Love, Me

Hope and Help for Those Caught in Addiction

If we were to discover that a family member had been viewing pornography, would all be lost? Even with the greatest filters in place and the best fortifications at home, pornography addiction can occur. But thankfully, because of our Savior's Atonement, there is always hope and help. His enabling power and the gift of repentance are ours. But how can we help our loved ones access these, get the help they need to get past it, and fill their lives with hope?

1. Avoid Overreacting

I was a brand-new mom with a little girl. In a college course, I had been learning about the addictive behaviors associated with anorexia and bulimia, when one day, out of the blue, my little toddler stuck her finger down her throat and made herself throw up! Trying hard not to overreact on the outside, I was panicky on the inside! Is my little baby going to have a problem with these terrible disorders?! I called my professor up! His reply was direct: "You can make this into a problem," he told me, "if you blow it out of proportion. This is likely an accident, a one-time occurrence, but if you feed it, it will much more likely to happen again!"

Chagrined and humbled, I realized that I had already learned the principle to water only what you want to grow. I just needed to apply it here and in many other mothering situations.

We must be careful to not overreact. If we react with "shock, anger, or rejection," teaches Linda S. Reeves, our children will "be silent again," and our chance to help them apply the Atonement has passed.[12]

2. Desire for Change

In order for healing from addiction to occur, a person must get to the point where he wants to change. I have learned that really, we who love a person caught in addiction cannot pray for that person to change, since each person on this earth has the precious right to exercise his own agency. Instead, we can pray for two things: one, that their eyes would be opened, and two, that their heart would be softened. These two prayers apply to many situations that come up.

Eyes can be opened, as in Mosiah 27:22, where we read, "they began to fast, and to pray to the Lord their God . . . that the eyes of the people might be opened to see and know of the goodness and glory of God." Hearts can be softened, such as in Mosiah 23:28: "Therefore they hushed their fears, and began to cry unto the Lord that he would soften the hearts of the Lamanites, that they would spare them, and their wives, and their children."

3. Access the Atonement

"Young people and adults, if you are caught in Satan's trap of pornography, remember how merciful our beloved Savior is," teaches Sister Reeves. "Do you realize how deeply the Lord loves and cherishes you, even now? Our Savior has the power to cleanse and heal you. He can remove the pain and sorrow you feel and make you clean again through the power of His Atonement."[13]

I was reading the Book of Mormon when I came across a wonderful scripture about bondage. It occurred to me that bondage is like addiction, and the Lord was giving us a key to freedom from addiction:

> And were it not for the interposition of their all-wise Creator, and this because of their sincere repentance, they must unavoidably remain in bondage until now.
>
> But behold, he did deliver them because they did humble themselves before him; and because they cried mightily unto him he did deliver them out of bondage; and thus doth the Lord work with his power in all cases among the children of men, extending the arm of mercy towards them that put their trust in him. (Mosiah 29:19–20)

We are taught to be humble and to cry mightily unto the Lord. Notice that the Lord tells us this works *in all cases*! The power of His Atonement covers all. "There are a number of very helpful Book of Mormon scriptures that describe the process of deliverance in which the Lord delivers His people" taught therapist Jonathan G. Sandberg. "Pay close attention to your part in the process of deliverance (see Mosiah 7:33; Mosiah 29:19–20; 3 Nephi 4:30–33). You may wish to also look up all the scriptures in the Topical Guide under "deliver, deliverance.""[14]

4. Give Strategies for Coping

Professor Sandberg relates, "Over many years clients have told me again and again that the most helpful talk they have seen about pornography is James M. Harper, 'Secret Shame: Isolation from Self,' a talk given at a BYU Cyber Secrets conference. This talk helps us understand that pornography is used as an escape from difficult or unpleasant emotional experiences. Most often pornography use is not an issue of hypersexuality, per se, but an issue of ineffective coping strategies for the difficulties of life. Most men I have worked with who look at pornography do it to cope because they do not have other healthy coping skills. Unfortunately, the use turns into a cycle of shame and acting out, as described by Dr. Harper. Please listen to the talk if you want to understand more and begin to heal."[15]

Other tools for coping include talking it out, especially with the Lord. Journaling is another wonderful coping mechanism.

One of the best substitutes for pornography is using the computer and extra time to do family history and indexing. It is a fulfilling task, with great promise. I remember vividly when our bishop was inspired to promise our congregation that if we would do family history work, the righteous desires of our hearts would be granted. It was a wonderful, powerful blessing, one that we could "take to the bank!" "What I the Lord say unto one, I say unto all!" (D&C 92:1)

5. Use Addiction Recovery Programs and Church Sites

The Church has many sites to help families that deal with addiction.[16] In addition, many stakes of Zion have wonderful senior missionary couples assigned to run the Addiction Recovery Program. These lovingly help people through the twelve-step program out of addiction. In addition, there are both in-person meetings and phone meetings for individuals who struggle with addiction and for their family members and friends.[17]

6. Conquer Bad Habits

Our family had a discussion about overcoming bad habits. One daughter told us that she learned some of the best counsel for overcoming bad habits and addiction on her mission from *Preach My Gospel*, the missionary handbook. It has some of the best counsel for overcoming addiction:

> Through baptism and confirmation people receive the gift of the Holy Ghost, which will strengthen their ability to overcome these challenges. But baptism and confirmation may not fully do away with the emotional and physical urges that go along with these behaviors. Even though a person may have some initial success, further emotional healing may be necessary to completely repent and recover.[18]

Preach My Gospel goes on to teach the miracle of spiritual healing as found in Psalms 147:3 that only God can accomplish. It lists the basic steps of the emotional healing process, such as "seeking forgiveness from others who have been harmed, and learning to forgive one's self" and "understanding that the Lord will always love His children—even when they make a mistake and yield to old cravings. Repentance and the road to recovery are always available."[19]

It emphasizes the truth that a person must begin to "do healthy things." Like the Savior's parable of the empty house, that fills with even greater evil spirits, we must all not be idle but fill our time with better choices (Matthew 12:38–39).

Another family member texted her comments about bad habits: "The only thing that has worked for me was replacing the bad habit with a new habit. That and praying for help. We don't have power to do it alone."

We must teach our loved one that they are a child of God, of infinite worth. We can give them tools to overcome addictive behaviors, help them want to avoid the ugly and negative, and fill their brain with the finest and best. If we are honest, each of us struggles with addictive behaviors in one form or another, though some may be much less visible than others.

Isn't it wonderful that the infinite Atonement of Jesus Christ, who descended below all things through His infinite Atonement, is available to all, to release us from the bondage of addiction?

Dear Mom and Dad,

Thank you for helping me through my difficult challenges and giving me tools to cope. You have taught me how to apply our Savior's Atonement in my life, and for this, I will be thankful forever!

Love, Me

Courage to Stand

My great-great-grandmother Agnes Haley Love Flake is one of my heroes. Raised in a life of luxury as a Southern belle, she was ostracized by her family and friends when she joined the Mormon faith. At the end of her life, she found herself and three children living in an adobe hut with a settlement of Saints in California. Her brother, traveling to check out the gold rush, found her there struggling as a washerwoman to support her family. He offered to bring her family back to Mississippi, where she could have a plantation of her own, and where the kids could be raised in wealth and sent to fine colleges. All she would have to do is to give up her new religion. "You don't think you are asking much," she told him. "No, not at all," was his reply. "It is my lifeblood," was her answer. "I will work my fingers to the bone to give this gospel to my children." Her brother left, urging her to write to him when she changed her mind. "You'll never receive that letter" was her reply. Because of this woman's courage, my family has a heritage of faithfulness and conviction.[20]

Another place where people take a difficult stand on their religious convictions and face enemies is the Book of Mormon. It recently struck me that there are two places where this is extra poignant. The first is the people in the city of Ammonihah. These are contemporaries of Amulek, probably taught the gospel by him and Alma. They are the wives and children of believers who had been stoned and cast out of the city by the unbelievers. I picture them standing by the place of martyrdom—likely with a view of a deep hole of burning flames. "Are you a believer?" they were asked, with the fear and torture of a fiery death for them and their little ones resting on their answer. What courage it would have taken to defend their perhaps new faith! Thankfully, after all that faith and courage, a loving God received them up to Himself in glory.

The second group was the people who lived just before the coming of the Savior. They had heard Samuel the Lamanite and believed his prophesies of the coming of the Lord. Now they had to answer also as to whether they were believers or unbelievers. A "yes, I believe" answer meant imminent death for them too, the very next day—death for them and their children and entire families. At the time they gave their answer, they did not know that the sign would be given that night—not until their prophet Nephi prayed long and then reassured them. What courage it would have taken to say, "Yes, I am a believer."

Will we ever have to stand up at the peril of our lives? Likely not. But will we have to stand up for our convictions, our religious freedom, and our faith? Likely yes. Will we and our children have the courage to stand up and not falter? "Let us have the courage to stand up and be counted as true, devoted followers of Christ."[21]

How do we develop the courage to take a valiant stand for what we believe?

1. Teach Courage through the Example of Truly Great Heroes

William Tyndale is a new hero of mine. Against all current thought, he believed that everyone should have access to the scriptures. So, he spent his life hiding from the authorities and translating the scriptures from Greek and Hebrew into English. He did this knowing full well that the penalty would be death by burning at the stake. But he pressed on with great courage and conviction and did end up paying with his life.[22] Tyndale "sacrificed, even to the point of death, to bring the word of God out of obscurity."[23]

Faith and courage grow when we learn about courageous people. "I invite you to qualify yourselves as did the two thousand stripling soldiers by being valiant in courage."[24] We can tell our children the stories of the great people in the scriptures. We can help them feel how Daniel felt when he chose to continue to pray day and night, with the penalty of hungry lions awaiting that decision. Or how Shadrach, Meshach, and Abednego felt, facing a fiery furnace seven times hotter than usual, for refusing to bow down to an idol. "If it be so, our God whom we serve is able to deliver us from the burning fiery furnace, and he will deliver us out of thine hand, O king," they replied. "But if not, be it known unto thee, O king, that we will not serve thy gods, nor worship the golden image which thou hast set up" (Daniel 3:17–18). By telling our children these true stories, we will give them an example of faith and courage. Holding those who have taken such a stand as their heroes will help our kids develop courage to stand up too.

A word of caution: These examples of great people include facing death by fire. In fact, there is a wonderful movie I saw recently about Joan of Arc, another great hero who had the courage to face a martyr's death by fire. But I realize that if I had watched this—or anything related to fire—as a little girl, I would have had bad dreams and worried about her for days! We must be careful about the movies we allow our young ones to see; a book about a hero is much better, since kids can visualize just what they can handle. Some children are more sensitive, and we must use the Spirit to help us know the best approach for teaching and inspiring each child.

Of course, our very best hero is the Savior. Can we help our children see the wonderful sacrifice he made and the terrible price He willingly paid for our sins? He loved and healed all He met, even when exhausted Himself. He faced that night in Gethsemane, knowing that He would have to bear every fear, every sickness, every trouble or trial anyone has ever faced. We cannot teach our children too much of our beloved Savior, His strength, His loving kindness and mercy.

My daughter had an incident at a school that required some courage and used the Savior's teachings.

> Callie was in my class, and my desk was next to hers. I was aware that she was somewhat different than the majority, and we didn't have a ton in common, but we'd grown up in the same neighborhood and ward, and I was her friend. One day, I specifically remember passing though the doorway of our classroom as a boy in our class asked me in a tone of disgust, "You're friends with *her* (referring to Callie)?" "Yes!" I said emphatically. I knew this might be socially unacceptable in this boy's eyes, but I abhorred that he would say such a thing—perhaps with Callie in earshot! Callie needed friends, and I was one of them, I told myself confidently. I remember feeling proud at the time that I didn't bow to the peer pressure to reject her, even in word.[25]

2. We Can Teach Courage by Talking about Current Issues and the Principles Involved

How blessed we are to have prophets who are standing on a tower and see afar off. May we listen carefully and then talk to our families about their counsel. We must arm our families with their words and warnings. We must help them understand the negative trends and the need to take a stand *against* them and to stand *for* families and religious freedom.

I was reading an article recently about a city that was named "the happiest city in the world." Reading further, I found that it was very socialistic, that the article maintained that happiness meant that someone else worried about all your needs being met. The happiest people, the article states, have a government "social system takes care of most people's needs" and that "keeps people from doing what will make them unhappy."[26] I brought this up to my family: Is it really happiness to have someone else make all your decisions and meet all your needs? Isn't that Satan's way, to give no choices nor freedom, but to force righteousness? This discussion made us all think. I need to be better at knowing current events, because when we do, we can talk them over with our families. We can use them to springboard conversation about the issues and the need to take a stand for righteousness and freedom. Courage starts with talking and teaching and is cemented with example. And when we talk to them first, before they get a worldly slant on things, they are more likely to have a gospel perspective. (See "Teaching Them First" in chapter 8.)

3. We Can Teach Them Courage Coupled with Civility

Courage does not necessarily mean to be loud and obnoxious—sometimes it takes great control and discipline to give a soft answer. Reason is usually more effective than emotion. Rather than "I can't see R-rated movies because my religion tells me I can't," one could take a stand by simply saying, "I'm just going to sit this one out." Another phrase our family uses to take a stand and not offend is "Does this movie bother anyone else?" Phrased as a question, it doesn't judge anyone, it simply helps others who may feel similarly to have a way out also.

"Offend only as a last resort" became my daughter's motto when she was working in a group that had many worldly ideas. She had to use the Spirit to help her reason and discuss mostly without having to offend someone. Mark is a great example of speaking to others calmly, even when situations become intense (when I get too worked up). We must teach our children that while standing firm, we must still be civil. "The gospel of Jesus Christ teaches us to love and treat all people with kindness and civility—even when we disagree."[27]

There are ways to take a quiet stand without offending. One time, my son went on a group date with friends out to the desert to watch a movie. It was one he hadn't seen before. There came on the screen a scene he was uncomfortable with, and though it took courage, he whispered to his date his discomfort. They decided to simply go for a walk while the others finished the movie. Another son and his date just slipped out of the theatre during a similar situation. It always takes courage, but others will appreciate the quiet stand we take.

4. We Teach the Most by Example

Our kids learn courage when we show it. We can also be a voice for religious freedom in our communities. When baccalaureate, the religious service traditionally held around high school graduation, was becoming more and more irreverent and almost anti-religious at our school, I decided I needed to take a stand. I was met with derision from faculty, but gradually I grew to understand them. I realized that they couldn't sponsor a religious service or a lawsuit may result. It was when we worked together to form a student-led interfaith club to sponsor baccalaureate instead, that things began to work. The result was a non-denominational religious service that represented many religions. This way it could even allow prayer! It took many years and much prayer, but the result was sweet, and hopefully my children saw an example of taking a stand on our right to religious freedom of expression.

We can't always be with our kids and we have no idea what they may face. But we can arm them with correct principles and model the courage to live them. We can help them form deep-rooted testimony and the conviction to stand up for their beliefs like the examples of heroes and of us! May we help them develop Christlike courage and conviction, holding tight to their beliefs and being ready to take a stand.

Dear Mom and Dad,

I am often fearful in our tumultuous world. Can you help me step by step to develop courage? I want to be like Nephi and all the courageous heroes you tell me about, and I want to be like you!

Love, Me

Chapter 17

Kick It like a Football

*A*s our children learn to drive, start to date, and hit more and more milestones, we start to realize that our time with them is limited. Have we taught them enough? Will they have a successful life ahead? While not denying them the struggles they need to grow and be strong, much like a chick breaking through the shell, we still need to support, encourage, and love them to pieces—all without hovering too close!

Missionary Prep

It must be a challenge to be a new missionary. There is no mom and dad to get you out of tough spots. There is little that you are used to in your daily life. And there is so much rejection to deal with! Here are some ideas we have used to help our pre-missionary sons and daughters be successful:

1. Teach Life Skills

Our kids fix their own dinners often on Saturday nights when Mark and I go out. I'll leave them a box of macaroni and a can of chili (they like it mixed) or an idea of something basic to make. They are hungry, and this is a good chance to learn a little cooking. Sometimes we have them make part of a big dinner as well—we like working together in the kitchen.

I was reluctant to have my kids do their own laundry at first. It took away my control of the laundry room! But it turned out to be a great thing. They took charge of seeing that they had clean clothes at the time they needed, and all I had to do was provide the detergent and a laundry schedule. These and other life skills sure give them a head start later.

2. Names and Social Skills

One of our missionaries wrote home and challenged his younger brothers to learn to memorize a whole bunch of names at once! This was a skill he found that he needed, especially on a new transfer, that they would be glad they practiced ahead! Any chance to make conversation and connect with people also helps develop valuable skills for missionaries to gain before serving. They have to make good impressions and earn people's trust quickly.

Another people skill is to offer a second sentence. "How are you?" is routine. I am pretty good at smiling at someone and asking how they are. However, I struggle with a second sentence, and that's the one that brings the emotional connection. One seventeen-year-old son, on the other hand, was amazing at having just the right thing to say. Once I asked him how he could remember details about a person and thus have just the right words to help someone feel good about themselves? "It's easy, Mom!" he answered, "You just have to love that person, then you'll have the words to say." "Oh!" was my astounded reply. Love brings the promptings of the Spirit to help you connect! The answer is more love!

3. Give Them a Goal

Kids will see themselves as missionaries one day if we plant the goal in them early. In the *Ensign* magazine one month, I found a bookmark-sized cutout with the prophet's picture on it that read,

"I Will Prepare (to Be a Missionary)." It listed several things to do daily to prepare. I cut it out and laminated one for each family member. It was to go above the light switch or on the bulletin board in their rooms, to remind them daily of this goal.

With nine sons, missionary work was on my mind early. When they were still very young, I started a Missionary Wall. I asked for family missionaries to send me a postcard from where they were serving. These went up, with a picture of a set of missionaries and of the Savior. Grandma and Grandpa brought home trinkets from their missions. The wall grew and soon included pictures of our sons and daughters as they served their own missions. The goal was constantly in front of our kids, without a word said.

4. Give Them an Away-from-Home Experience

Three of our missionaries went on their missions right after high school. But all three of them had spent time in previous summers away from home. One son worked on a ranch in New Mexico. He and a friend had to fend for themselves as they did the ranching, living out of an ice chest that was refilled weekly. It was a great chance to manage their own time and be their own boss. Two other sons worked a demolition project for several weeks out of state. Another lived in Maryland on a sales job for a couple of months. They all had to learn to problem-solve and to make decisions on their own.

Two more sons and two daughters did at least one semester away at college out of state before serving. They had to manage their own money, get themselves to classes and church, and cook for themselves too. All these kids had a chance to deal with homesickness—a very real thing—before a mission, instead of during it.

5. Let Them Use Their Agency

All teenagers need a chance to learn to make their own choices. If Mom and Dad have made all the decisions for them, later, on their own, they sometimes go to the opposite extreme and choose to use this new freedom to the extreme. I knew of a teenager who had a strict 8:30 p.m. curfew all through high school, so when she got on her own, she chose to stay up very late every night, just because she could! She had never learned for herself to choose a wise bedtime. Others chose to eat lots of junk, formerly not allowed. Others exercised their choice not to go to church. Parents need to teach correct principles and let kids govern themselves at least a little, while they still live at home.

One idea is to teach them what a good opportunity mission prep class would be, then let them choose whether to go. Forcing them would not bring as good results. But we can teach them how important it is to prepare to serve the Lord, and to learn from others so they don't have to make all the mistakes. And we can pray for their eyes to be opened and their hearts to be softened. Showering with love softens hearts. And it's certainly okay to praise them afterward for making such a good choice!

6. Take Care with Using Instant Rewards

Sometimes kids are raised with an instant reward for every good thing they do: a dollar for every "A," a candy bar for bringing their scriptures to church, an allowance for helping around the house. The problem with these instant rewards is there is nothing that teaches them about intrinsic rewards—or doing things for a much later reward. Our teenagers need to know how to wait. They need to learn the skill of giving themselves a pat on the back for something good they did.

On a mission, there are usually no instant rewards. Sometimes, testimonies grow very slowly and require lots of waiting. A missionary who has practiced and practiced before conquering a hard skill or who has worked long and hard to reach a sports goal has learned to wait for long-term rewards.

7. Have Them Work

We all know that missionary work is work! How good it is when we encourage our kids do some hard physical work, like chopping down a big tree, changing a tire, or painting a large room. All these things need to be taught, of course, and we can do them alongside, but gradually our kids will do more and more work on their own, and the feeling of satisfaction is itself a great reward. We can have our children wash windows and mop floors. They can fix bikes and maintain an engine. There is a learning curve, but they will gradually conquer these skills. Taking care of pets is great work, because there is responsibility built in. Managing their own money is a great life skill to learn early as well.

Another advantage of expecting hard work is that our kids have less time being entertained. Missions do not provide much entertainment, and we do our kids a disservice when we allow them a lot of it. It is a sorry life that expects to be amused much of the day.

8. Provide Roommates

Even when we have plenty of bedrooms in our homes, having siblings share is good practice for a mission. Companions are not always easy to live with, like brothers or sisters may not be. Even bunking up with a baby or a toddler can be quite a lesson in getting along with others! Even though we could have allowed our three youngest to have their own room, we chose to turn one into a study room, so that the boys could share. We challenged the older brother to let his younger sibling see him study the scriptures and pray. They learned about setting good examples and working out situations that came up.

9. Exact Obedience

With our youngest children, Mark and I realized that we were getting casual about exact obedience. An older son returned from his mission about that time, with such a zeal for exact obedience as a road to happiness. In fact, he had started calling his little white book of missionary rules the "book of blessings," instead of the book of rules. I realized that his younger siblings needed to learn now to follow exact obedience. Doing so would bring success and happiness on their missions, at their future jobs and in their lives!

Our missionary son went on to tell us about his experiences as a leader of other missionaries. "You can't micromanage missionaries," he told us. "You teach the doctrine, and you require accountability." We had slipped into reminding them daily about their duties, rather than teaching them and requiring accountability! We set up a time to teach exact obedience, its need, and its blessing.

"What is it you really want?" we asked our kids in this special family council. "What do you *really* want?" I asked again, and waited. "Eternal life in the top third of the celestial kingdom" was the good answer one of them gave. We then had them turn to Doctrine and Covenants 130:20–21 and read, "There is a law irrevocably decreed in heaven before the foundations of this world, upon which all blessings are predicated—And when we obtain any blessing from God, it is by obedience to the law upon which it is predicated." To receive the blessings, we have to follow the law that goes with it. If we want good health, we must live the laws that govern good health, like the Word of Wisdom. If we want eternal life, we must live the laws that lead us there.

"What did the stripling warriors really want?" was the next question we posed. "They were in a war, and facing threats on their lives constantly. What did they really want?" "To live!" was what we decided upon. "So what did they do to receive that?" In Alma 57:21 we read, "they did obey and perform every word of command with exactness; yea, and even according to their faith it was done unto them." Not one was killed in the battles with seasoned warriors, because they had faith in what they had taught, and because they were exactly obedient.

Missionaries want many blessings daily, such as safety, finding people to teach, the Spirit to help them teach, and ways to be opened up for them to bring others closer to Christ. In order to receive these blessings, they have to learn and perform exact obedience to the many rules. The more exact the obedience, the more blessings they are entitled to.

Mark and I decided we'd better teach exact obedience in doing chores, limiting screen time, plugging in cell phones on time, and keeping commitments.

10. The Savior's Role

A missionary who already knows how to repent and access the Atonement of Jesus Christ will have such an advantage. They will know where to turn when things go wrong and hope is dwindling. In their need, they will draw close to the true source of answers and peace.

11. Real Joy

If our teenager gets a taste of the joy of sharing the gospel, they will long to feel it again on a mission. As a family, we can invite and reach out to neighbors and help our kids see lives change from the gift of the gospel. As we reach out to others and try to always be an example of a believer, they will more likely develop that attitude too. The more we teach our families to love the Lord and His children, the more they will want to serve Him on a mission for the right reasons, and for real joy.

Of course, they are developing their own testimony. From the time they are tiny, we help them build theirs by the seeds of testimony planted each day. Their personal daily devotion is what will help the most. "And faith, hope, charity and love, with an eye single to the glory of God, qualify him for the work" (D&C 4:5).

12. Temple Preparation

One of our leaders urged us to prepare our young adults for the temple as much or more so than we prepare them for a mission. Temple ordinances are a pinnacle of life, a huge blessing to help us through trial. "We are endowed with a gift of power and knowledge from on high . . . [that] helps us in our daily lives and enables us to build God's kingdom."[1]

We can prepare our children for their own temple experience by example. They watch us go to the temple, but do they see our joy or hear our testimony and choice experiences? I have caught myself being grumpy when I get home from the temple, because I see the dirty kitchen the kids left or have to get back to the grind after my peaceful experience. Instead, I need to share that peaceful glorious experience! As I get ready to go, I need to show them my anticipation of a great experience rather than just my rush to "make the session." I have learned to stop and tell the kids that we were able to seal a whole family together, one of our very own relatives! I have tried to tell them a little more background about the family names we serve and translate to them the joy I feel. And when the kids finally turned twelve, we made it a great and reverent occasion when they got to go inside the temple for the first time to do baptisms for the dead.

The first temple endowment experience should be a highlight of this missionary prep season. Temple preparation classes are usually offered in our wards and branches, and we must support these for our young adult. In addition, we can enlist the Spirit to help us carefully prepare each of our children for the temple experience, tailored to their needs, using church books and resources[2] to know what we can appropriately share. The best prep of all is our attitude toward our temple experiences. Having loved ones and friends around them on their special first experience of this ceremony is an important gift of support and love.

May we give our children every chance for joy and success as a missionary. May we start young to give them tools they will need and use then and thereafter!

Dear Mom and Dad,

Wow! I am so grateful for all you have taught me! I can hit the ground running when I am called to serve, because of your wisdom.

Love, Me

Raising Young Adults:
Backing Off, Being There

As a young adult, I remember coming home for holidays and being filled with relief. "Everybody loves me here, just as I am," and "I don't have to play any games or try to be anybody special. I can be just me." How I loved to come home where I could rest and feel loved.

Now I am the one raising young adults, and it can be tricky. They are growing in their independence, but they still need us. As our kids leave the nest, Mark and I try to provide them a warm home where they can regroup and be showered with love, interest, and lots of acceptance. Once again, the answer is more love—combined with wisdom and expectation. Here are some ways to balance being there with backing off:

1. We Must Expect a Lot and Let Them Decide

Having watched our children grow up, and knowing their flaws and mistakes so well, we *might* resist letting them grow up and leave us. They have big steps to take and major decisions to make at this stage of their lives. Don't we parents have opinions on them all! But we must encourage independence. Rather than walking them through each step, we can ask, "What is your decision?" or "What have you felt when you prayed about this?" "What have you decided to do next?" Especially when they are this age, we must resist hovering! (See "Hovering or Letting Them Fly" in chapter 10.)

I felt strongly that one of my daughters should go to college before she went on a mission. She had just graduated from high school! I just knew that this daughter needed to deal with independence and homesickness before she served. But the age change for missionaries had just happened, and immediately her response had been, "This is for me!" She could think of little else but serving a mission. I had to back off and let it be her decision. She put in papers and received her call—and was able to fit in a semester of college before her report date! (I think it was my prayers!) It had been hard for me to back away, but I was glad that the timing worked out for her best good.

2. We Must Not Deny Them the Struggle

"Be careful with easy," cautions Elder Stanley G. Ellis:

> Before this calling I was a financial consultant in Houston, Texas. Most of my work was with multimillionaires who owned their own businesses. Almost all of them had created their successful businesses from nothing through lots of hard work. The saddest thing for me was to hear some of them say that they wanted to make it easier for their children. They did not want their children to suffer as they had. In other words, they would deprive their children of the very thing that had made them successful.
>
> By contrast, we know a family who took a different approach. The parents were inspired by J. C. Penney's experience where his father told him when he turned eight years old that he was on his own financially. They came up with their own version: as their children graduated from high school, they were on their own financially—for further education (college, graduate school) and for their financial maintenance (truly self-reliant) (see D&C 83:4). Happily, the children reacted wisely. All of them are college graduates, and several also completed graduate school—all on their own. It wasn't easy, but they did it. They did it with hard work and faith.[3]

While being supportive and watchful, we must let our children struggle to grow more and more self-governing. This way, they will become more dependent on the Lord rather than on us.

Our daughter really struggled her last semester of college. She was working, along with all the demands of student teaching. On a gloomy February day, when she found herself with sleep deprivation, no time to eat well, and hurt feelings from girls in her cohort that weren't very nice, she called Mark on a Sunday night to tearfully ask him about her car troubles. She was so close to getting her degree, but it all seemed so daunting. The next morning, he and a son drove the eleven hours to help with the car and bring moral support. Her struggle made her degree mean all the more to her, but the timely support from home also meant so much.

3. We Should Still Connect Often

Our young adults still need our regular connection. Most of my older kids really respond to texting. A random text tells them I am thinking of them and they can respond to it when they can. When one daughter was feeling depressed, we started a game of "I love (random things)!" All that day we texted back and forth, "I love tennis shoes! They are so comfy and bouncy!" "I love it when sidewalks are clear but there's still snow all around." "I love it when Mr. and Mrs. Duck come back and meander around campus." This game gave us a reason to focus on good things and share them.

I have discovered that sharing a song with one of my older kids shows him my love best. I am constantly on the lookout for nice new songs that I could send to him. Another son loves long talks on a Sunday evening. Another likes to chat on his commute home from work. A daughter needs a cheery phone call almost every day. The Spirit will help us see the best way to connect with a child who is on his own now but still needs the support from home.

4. We Must Be Careful with Advice

Mark and I have learned over and over to advise sparingly! We have seen that it is better to wait until they ask for our counsel and advice than to offer it unsolicited. When they ask, they are so much more receptive! When we do give suggestions, we can't insist they do what we think. We try to follow up by expressing confidence in them, with "You'll make the right decision."

A counselor once told me that the best message our young adults need from us is this: "You have everything it takes to accomplish what is before you." Rather than conquer the details of their problems, we can reassure them that they can figure this out! "I'll be praying for you!" is a huge way to give support. Further, I like to pray that my struggling kids will feel my prayers for them.

I learned the power of many prayers one time when our family was in a pageant. We were halfway through the rehearsals for this huge outdoor pageant based on the Savior's life and resurrection with a cast of close to five hundred people. One family who had a major role suddenly had a young son who became seriously ill and was sent to intensive care. This family was in such a quandary, because both parents were needed in the pageant, as was the grandmother, who was the director! I observed this and wondered, "Why would the Lord allow this child to get so sick right then? Why did He allow this timing for such a trial, right during this pageant?"

My answer came when I heard the testimony of the grandmother. She rejoiced at the timing! Not only had they experienced many people reaching out to cover the bases, but also the support from so many. She told us, "When else could we have had five hundred prayers for our little boy?" Wow! It was marvelous that our entire cast had been praying fervently for this boy and his family! These prayers not only helped him to heal, but they also brought our cast together in a close bond, bringing the Spirit in rich abundance to our performances.

I have thought about this a lot. Many prayers do make a difference. When someone in our family is struggling—usually a young adult—we will often have a family fast, if they are willing. There is such power in joining together in fasting and prayer. Or if they prefer to keep it to themselves and Mark and me, we still fast, but we also enlist the prayers of all temple-goers by putting their name on the prayer roll. Rather than unsolicited advice, even more effective is faith and prayers.

5. "Just Save the Relationship"

Marjorie Pay Hinckley was the one who coined this catch phrase, referring to our interactions with our children.[4] "Just save the relationship" applies poignantly to our young adult children. Keeping them connected to us is paramount, regardless of their choices.

"Watching our adult children make choices that we cringe at is hard to watch," wrote my friend in a Facebook comment. "We have often bit our tongue till it bleeds. But our RELATIONSHIP is more important than us 'being right.' If we have no relationship with our adult kids, we have no influence. . . . And if we have a relationship with them, we can still set an example, and teach, and occasionally offer some advice."

To save the relationship, we must listen to the Spirit for the best responses. "I often got caught up in the emotion of a situation," this Facebook friend wrote, "But I can honestly say, that when I STOPPED to listen to Spirit—when I stopped to give myself time to say a prayer—the outcome was ALWAYS better. Often the outcome was my first instinct, but other times it was so out in left field it truly did not come from me! But the random decisions from spiritual promptings, were the right thing to do."[5]

6. Trust Them to God

When my missionary son was going through some trial, Mark reminded me, "The Lord can take better care of him than we can!" I had to entrust my precious son to the Lord. I could pray and write encouraging letters, but then I had to back away and let him grow. My friend put it this way, "We have learned that they are Heavenly Father's children first! We need to trust in His timing and wisdom. Our job is to love them and continue to invite them to be with us."[6]

As time goes on, how wonderful it is when our young adults marry! That is our payday! But it is important then to back off even more. The Savior teaches us that our children shall "leave father and mother and shall cleave to [their spouse]" (Matthew 19:5).

It might be hard to step back, but we must help them transfer their loyalty to their new spouse. While maintaining our connection, we cannot let it interfere with their most important connection. We must respect their time with their new spouse. In fact, we can encourage them to talk to their new best friend about issues they might bring up. Rather than find fault with the spouse, we must support them and this new forming family—using the Spirit as our guide.

When our young adult has left our home, we can still be at the crossroads. By letting them come home to rest and feel totally loved and accepted, and by making connections often and expressing our confidence in them, we can be instruments in God's hands. Crises will come, but our best answer is often the reassurance, "It's going to be fine." The Spirit will help us know how to springboard them to a successful life ahead.

Like the brother of Jared carried in his hands the stones he had carefully molten up the mountain to talk to the Lord about them, we can carry the names of our precious children who we have carefully tried to mold up to the Mountain of the Lord, His temple. Like this man of faith asked the Lord to please "touch these . . . that they may shine forth," we too can ask our Savior to touch the hearts of our young adults and make them grow in light and truth. (Ether 3:1, 4) We will see the hand of the Lord in their lives as we trust them to Him.

Dear Mom and Dad,

You have given me a great upbringing and now, at last, I get to try my own wings. I know I will make poor judgment calls at times, but thanks for allowing me to stumble and to practice getting up and brushing myself off. Thanks for still being there when I need you but encouraging me to be independent. And thanks for your confidence in me.

Love, Me

Chapter 18
Love as Our Savior

Our Savior's love and our love for Him are the very best reasons for doing what we do. When we talk of Christ and His love for each family member, keeping Him foremost in their minds, we not only change motivation, but we also mold character.

Why We Do Things

"Because I said so!" may not be the best reason for kids to do things. In 2 Chronicles 25:2, we read about Amaziah, king of Judah. "And he did that which was right in the sight of the Lord, but not with a perfect heart." The previous verse tells us his mother's name, Jehoaddan. My guess is that she taught him to choose the right, that she "trained up" her son "in the way he should go." But he failed to learn the best reasons for doing good and right. How can we help our children get past just doing the actions and help their hearts be in it? How can we help them develop the best motivations for what they do?

Do you know a child—or a teen—who loves to ask, "Why?" "Why do we go to church?" "Why do we say prayers?" "Why do we make our beds? They'll just get slept in again!"

We might just feel at times driven to exclaim, "Just because!" as our answer. But there's a better one! Dallin H. Oaks, in his landmark talk "Why Do We Serve?" gives us better and better reasons to do good things, and the best one. In ascending order, he gives lesser to the higher motivations:

1. Earthly reward: "If I do this, I'll get a treat!"
2. Good Companionship: "Maybe someone will notice what a good thing I am doing" or "I really like being around these people."
3. Fear of Punishment: "I might get in trouble if I don't!"
4. A Sense of Duty: "I really should do this."
5. Hope of Eternal Reward: "This will help me get to heaven someday."
6. The Pure Love of Christ: "I serve because I love the Lord."[1]

Doing good for *any* reason is good! Those who come to the service project for the refreshments still come! But we can gradually train our kids to do good for better and better reasons. We can guide their motivation for the good things. Elder Robert D. Hales taught, "Spiritually mature obedience is 'the Savior's obedience.' It is motivated by true love for Heavenly Father and His Son."[2]

One Monday night, Mark and I taught a family night lesson using this talk by Dallin H. Oaks. He reminds us, "If we love [the Savior], we should keep his commandments and feed his sheep"[3] (John 14:15 and John 21:16–17). It matters what we are thinking when we do good. Mark and I listed all the reasons mentioned for doing good, and talked about each one, for example, that the first two are somewhat selfish, the second two are a little better, but the very best one is the last. We taught our kids that the best reason to do anything good, is because we love the Lord!

"Let's try it!" we challenged them, and together, we brought up things they do, and talked through together how that thing could be done because we love the Lord! It was a fun challenge, and a good concept to think about, and to try to apply. Here's some we came up with:

"Why do we have to go to school?" "Because we love the Lord, and He has given us our wonderful brains, and He would want us to learn all we can with them."

"Why do we have to practice the piano?" "Because we love the Lord, and He gave us our talents to use and to serve in His kingdom."

"Why do we have to do chores?" "Because we love the Lord! He gave us families and He expects us to do our part in our families."

"Why do we have to be nice to that person who is mean?" "Because we love the Lord! He made that boy and loves him too, and he asks us to 'love our enemies,' and to 'do good to them that hate you'" (Matthew 5:44). We found that it works every time!

Changing our motivation for why we do things changes our very character. "The Lord requireth the heart and a willing mind" (D&C 64:24). Not only should we be willing to do good, but we also need to make sure our hearts are in the right place as we do good. The Savior said to those who reminded Him of the many good things they had done: "Ye never knew me" (Matthew 7:22, 23). These people had done their good works to serve their own purposes and ego. If our motivation is to become more God-like, however, we will know Him better, and be more like Him. It's something family members can help each other to do!

If it's ever hard to love, we can simply pray to be filled with it, as we are taught in Moroni 7:48, "Wherefore, my beloved brethren, pray unto the Father with all the energy of heart, that ye may be filled with this love, which he hath bestowed upon all who are true followers of his Son, Jesus Christ."

Periodically, in informal settings, we still talk about our motivations: "Why are we going to church today?" or "Why are we helping Grandma?" Sometimes we start out with "because we are supposed to" or "because she needs our help," but increasingly through the years, we land at "because we love the Lord." It is my hope that we will internalize these teachings and improve our motivations, to become more Christlike. We hope to get pure motivating love into our lives and hearts.

Dear Mom and Dad,

Sometimes I like to ask why. Thank you for taking the time to talk with me about my best reason for doing good things. As I grow older, I am learning better and better motivations. I want to be like you, and I want to love the Lord.

Love, Me

We Talk of Christ

Most of my children have had to read *The Scarlet Letter* by Nathaniel Hawthorne in high school. One time, I read it too and found it hard to get through. Toward the end, I discovered the real reason why. Here was this book all about repentance, filled with extremely pious people, but they left out the most important thing. There was absolutely *no mention of our Savior*! All this expounding religion, and no mention of the Lord's Atonement in our behalf to let us repent and gain forgiveness. There was plenty about paying consequences and even overcoming them, but no gratitude for or even acknowledgment of our Savior's tremendous part.

We have to be the ones who talk of Christ, "that our children may know to what source they may look for a remission of their sins" (2 Nephi 25:26). In fact, for them to know and use that source to save their lives, "we talk of Christ, we rejoice in Christ, we preach of Christ, we prophesy of Christ, and we write according to our prophecies" (2 Nephi 25:26). He must be part of our daily conversation. We must give Him credit and have Him as our guide.

If one of our children is ever in a bind, we want them to know immediately where to turn for help. There is always available to each of them a loving Savior who knows them entirely and loves them completely and is ready with succor when invited. May we teach this to each of them and give them this champion, this ally, the best of heroes.

I recently came across this inspiring quote, "Christ is the center of our home, a guest at every meal, a silent listener to every conversation." What a supreme goal—to have our Savior be the focal point of our lives, to have Him as the Ultimate Hero. How can we keep Him at the forefront in our homes?

1. Pictures for a Christian Home

Once, when my son-in-law was living with us, he told me that he worked such long hours at discouraging work, so he wanted to see a picture of the Savior. "They are up all over," I pointed out to him. But he longed to see a picture of Jesus in his regular path from the top of the stairs to the bathroom. I thought that was a commendable wish, so we rearranged the pictures on the wall and put a prominent one in the hallway. I wanted there to be no doubt that ours was a Christian home, one that honors the Savior Jesus Christ, so I put up pictures of Him in every room.

Each of our children got to pick his or her favorite picture of the Savior to frame and put up in his room. To make it even more special, we found a place that made small plaques—much the same size as a missionary tag. We had them print on these: "I am His disciple" to go at the bottom of each picture. It was our hope that these would reinforce to us who we are in relation to Him.

2. Teach His Commandments

Jesus said, "If ye love me, keep my commandments" (John 14:15). In order to keep the commandments, our children need to know them well. The Ten Commandments are the basis of good society and good homes. But His higher commandments were also dictated by Christ himself in the Sermon on the Mount, showing us an even higher way to live.

One family home evening, Mark and I had each of our children choose two commandments to teach the family. They read them, and then talked about living them. We then taught them that a couple of the commandments contain a built-in promise. For example, the commandment to honor our father and mother promises us that our days will be long upon the land. I told them of a high school friend who had not listened to parents and had been killed in an accident. Mark then shared times when he was protected after being obedient.

Another commandment, to remember the Sabbath day to keep it holy, promises: "the fullness of the earth is yours" (D&C 59:16). Mark and I shared the story of an ancestor who made the decision to travel on Sunday in order to catch up with the pioneer group. Unfortunately, just after they arrived, this ancestor's wagon was broken when horses were spooked, setting them back an entire week! We also reminded the kids of an experience within our own family. We had been blessed to find a lost rocket at the high school by waiting to retrieve it until after the Sabbath. On Sunday night, a heavy wind arose, and blew the rocket out of a tree, so we could find it on Monday! Conversely, a friend told me her most memorable Sabbath was when after much prayer, the third hour meeting was cancelled, and the Relief Society went to give a much-needed cleaning to a sister's house. The Christlike service made her Sunday! "Ye shall keep the Sabbath, for it is . . . a sign" that we love God (Exodus 31:14, 17).

Once, our stake president encouraged the members of the stake to frequently review with their children the teachings of Christ in the Sermon on the Mount, for it is the higher law, the way we want to live to qualify for the celestial kingdom. So, on the days Mark had to go to work early, I would deviate from our family's regular scripture study and teach our family from Matthew chapters 5–7 or 3 Nephi chapters 12–14. Not only would we read them, but I would also share my insights, stories about living these principles and messages from a New Testament class I had taken. Our kids became very familiar with the Beatitudes, letting your light so shine, turning the other cheek, and building your house upon a rock. Not only shall we not kill, Christ teaches, but we should not even hate others, and so forth. As we followed our stake president's counsel and became well-versed in the teachings of the Savior, we found an increased desire in our family to live by those teachings and follow Him.

3. Tie Good Feelings to Our Savior

We must be careful not to make God into someone who is disappointed in us. Rather, wait to bring Him up when we can couple it with praise. Never say, "The Lord did not like the way you treated your brother," but instead, "The Lord must be so proud of you because you were sharing." We want to show our children a loving, merciful God who suffered in order to allow us repentance. The message we must teach is, "He died so we can try again and again to do better," along with, "We are trying to be more and more like Him so we will be happy! We want to be comfortable in His presence when He comes again."

4. Do the Lord's Work

When we serve, we are doing the work the Lord would do if He were here. "He's not here with us physically; He needs our hands!" is what we can help our children internalize.

Whenever we pick up a flyer for a neighbor on vacation or take in their garbage can, whenever we pick up trash along the sidewalk or at the park, whenever we take a little child by the hand or build a tower of blocks with them, we are being the Lord's hands. When we help Mom or Dad, brother or sister, Grandma or Grandpa, a neighbor, or the one at school who has no friends, we are doing the Lord's work.

Years ago, I had decided that our family could do service by visiting a local nursing home on a regular basis. We didn't know any of the residents there, so I asked a person in charge to give us names of those who needed visitors. She suggested Cheryl. Not knowing what to expect the first time, and thinking this must be an elderly lady, we headed for "her" room, all little kids in tow.

We entered a darkened room, with a curtain pulled most of the way to block the bed. When we ventured closer, we were in for quite a surprise. The first thing we saw was a huge black and red Elvis picture, on what looked like velvet. Surrounding Elvis was quite a variety of pictures of girls scantily dressed or in swimsuits! And on the bed was a man, Cheryl, a fairly young man for a nursing home—maybe in his early fifties—watching a movie. Trying not to glance around too much, we swallowed and introduced ourselves, made a little small talk, and quickly left.

Afterward, I struggled with a dilemma. Somehow, we'd been told that this man was a Christian and he needed visitors. What about the bad pictures? Do I subject my little children to this borderline pornography? What would the Savior do? *No really*, I asked myself again, *what would He have done?* I struggled over and over. I came to the conclusion that the Savior wouldn't have rejected him nor refused to visit him, even with the pictures around.

I talked to my kids and told them my struggles. Could we go and visit this man who needed us, without looking at the pictures ourselves? Could we communicate to him that he was important and that we could like him despite his surroundings? We tried it. We came, me and all seven of my children at the time. We looked only at him. We didn't stay long, but we tried to show him we cared. After our visits, I would check with my kids to see if they were able to not look at the bad pictures, and they said yes.

Then, at one point, we decided to make him a gift of a picture of the Savior. So we did! "We noticed that you like pictures, so we brought you one." Well, for the next several visits, our picture wasn't up—he told us it was at his sister's or something when we asked. But gradually, he would point out to us a picture of the temple or mention that he had watched conference. Gradually, the worst pictures came down. Then at last, the picture of Jesus went up! It was a great victory.

We learned how very weak Cheryl was. Upon learning that lifting small weights helps a bedridden person feel so much better, I brought him some tiny cans, but there was no way he could lift even those! He began talking to us about the prophet or our missionary. And soon, there was not one bathing suit picture up in his room! We started to notice a light in his eye that wasn't there before. It was a great learning experience for us on how light can replace darkness.

Then one day, we learned that Cheryl had died. How wonderful that he was free at last from pain and weakness.

5. Invite Him in Our Homes and Our Lives

In my very favorite movie, *The Woman Who Willed a Miracle,* we meet Joe and May Lemke, an older couple who raised a foster baby. This baby boy, Leslie, had his diseased eyes removed, suffered cerebral palsy, and had severe brain damage as well. Despite his vegetative state, for years they daily talked and sang to him, massaged his limbs, and took him outside into the nearby lake. Then one night, the miracle they had prayed for happened. Leslie began to play the piano beautifully. In fact, despite His limitations, he could play anything he heard! The Lemkes soon set out to share this miracle and let him perform for others.

In the introduction to their performances, author Shirlee Monty would say, "Most people assume there are three people in the Lemke family but they are wrong. Actually, there are four: May, Joe, Leslie, and Jesus Christ.

"I've been in homes where Jesus Christ is a Sunday guest and others where He's invited only on holidays. In some homes, He's somewhat akin to the family doctor. He's called in only when there is an emergency.

"Sometimes he's more like a college student. There are pictures and mementos all over the house but you really don't feel His presence. He's obviously away for a while.

"But the Lemke home is different. Jesus Christ is as much a part of that family as May or Joe or Leslie. He's introduced to every guest and included in many conversations. May might say, 'You know, I was talking to Jesus the other day . . .' or she might say, 'Isn't it amazing what Jesus has done with that boy?'"[4]

What a wonderful ideal to strive for, to have Him be a part of our lives that much! We must talk of Him, enjoy His creations, access repentance and forgiveness through Him and make Him our model and mentor. We must study His word until it becomes a part of us, using the Bible and the Book of Mormon as two witnesses of Him that point us to Him. We can praise Him with music and song. We strive to have His very image in our countenances (Alma 5:14). May we give each of our children a true champion to emulate, the very best of heroes. As we bear testimony to them of His part in our lives, both formally and casually, they will sense our love for Christ and want it for themselves.

One of our greatest goals as parents is for our children, from toddlers to young adults, to be able to feel the Spirit. When we invite our Savior into our homes and lives, the Spirit is present. We are promised that if we always remember Him and keep His commandments, we will always have His Spirit to be with us (see Moroni 4:3). And when that peaceful feeling is there, we have the chance to point out to our children that this wonderful calm and peace they are feeling is the Holy Ghost. They will learn to recognize this, our Savior's Spirit, in their lives, and they will feel His love. As we parent with love, we reflect the Savior's love for our little ones and help them look to Him.

Dear Mom and Dad,

I am so glad that Jesus died for us, so we can try again, over and over. Thanks for teaching me that this life is the workshop—thanks to His Atonement. And thanks for loving me so I know He loves me.

Love, Me

In conclusion, can I share a story? It was Christmastime, and I was feeling bogged down with all there was to do and lots of little children to care for. I remember feeling that I was not doing very well in my mothering and "wife-ing," and specifically, I was afraid. My fear was that the Lord expected too much of me too fast and that I just couldn't measure up! Then, I turned on the television and Handel's *The Messiah* was being performed. The words jumped out at me, "He shall feed His flock like a shepherd . . . and *gently lead those that are with young.*" *Those with young*, I thought. *That's me!* I was with my young children, and He was going to lead me gently. He wasn't going to require too much of me too fast, but He was going to see me through this, step by step. I know that our kind and merciful Messiah, Jesus Christ, will lead us gently and patiently, allowing us to try again and fail, and try again. How I love Him, and how I love you.

Notes

Introduction

1. Massimo De Feo, "Pure Love: The True Sign of Every True Disciple of Jesus Christ," *Ensign*, May 2018.
2. Joseph F. Smith, *Teachings of the Presidents of the Church*, 299.
3. Russell M. Nelson, "Revelation for the Church, Revelation for Our Lives," *Ensign*, May 2018.

Chapter 1

1. Dorothy Law Nolte, "Children Learn What They Live."
2. Ralph Waldo Emerson, "Social Aims" (1875).
3. Dieter F. Uchtdorf, "Happiness, Your Heritage," *Ensign*, October 2008.
4. Karen Kleiman, "Try Some Smile Therapy," Psychology Today, Aug. 1, 2012, https://www.psychologytoday.com/blog/isnt-what-i-expected/201207/try-some-smile-therapy.
5. Uchtdorf, "Happiness, Your Heritage."
6. Pearce, Virginia H. editor. *Glimpses into the Life and Heart of Marjorie Pay Hinckley* (Salt Lake City: Deseret Book, 1998).
7. Shane M. Bowen, "The Atonement Can Clean, Reclaim and Sanctify our Lives," *Ensign*, November 2006.
8. Maxwell Maltz, *Psycho-Cybernetics* (New York: Perigree, 2015).
9. Attributed to Abraham Lincoln.
10. Gary Chapman, Ph.D. and Ross Campbell, M. D. *The Five Love Languages of Children* (Chicago: Northfield, 1977).
11. See M. Russell Ballard, "Fathers and Sons: A Remarkable Relationship," *Ensign*, November 2009.
12. Richard Feloni, *Business Insider,* September 19, 2014.
13. "The Family: A Proclamation to the World," *Ensign* or *Liahona*, November 2010, 129.
14. Personal text conversation.
15. American lullaby, Gladys Rich.
16. Wade Horn, Ph. D., "In the Absence of Fathers—A Story of Elephants and Man," June 20, 2012, http://chsfsc.org/in-the-absence-of-fathers-a-story-of-elephants-and-men.
17. Ross and Campbell, *The Five Love Languages of Children* (Chicago: Northfield, 1997).
18. C. Terry Warner, *Bonds that Make Us Free* (Salt Lake City: Shadow Mountain, 2002).
19. Relief Society Lecture, February 2018.
20. Robert D. Hales, "Our Duty to God: The Mission of Parents and Leaders to the Rising Generation," *Ensign*, May 2010.
21. "The Family: A Proclamation to the World."
22. Spencer W. Kimball, *Marriage and Divorce* (Salt Lake City: Deseret Book, 1976).

Chapter 2

1. E. Iarskaia-Smirnova and P. Romanov, "Institutional Child Care in Soviet Russia: Everyday Life in the Children's Home 'Krasnyi Gorodok' in Saratov, 1920s–1940s," in Kurt Schilde, Dagmar Schulte (eds) *Need and Care—Glimpses into the Beginnings of Eastern Europe's Professional Welfare* (Opladen and Bloomfield Hills: Barbara Budrich Publishers, 2005), 91–122.
2. Kendra Cherry, "The Story of Bowlby, Ainsworth, and Attachment Theory: The Importance of Early Emotional Bonds," Feb. 19, 2018, www.verywell.com/what-is-attachment-theory-2795337.
3. Saul McLeod, "Attachment Theory," 2009, www.simplypsychology.org.
4. Lawrence Thomas, *The Family and the Political Self* (Cambridge: Cambridge University Press, 2006).
5. Phillip Jackson, *Life in Classrooms* (New York City: Holt, Rinehart, and Winston, Inc., 1968).
6. Dr. Mary Ainsworth in John Bowlby, *A Secure Base: Parent-Child Attachment and Healthy Human Development* (New York: Basic Books, 1988).
7. Yudhigit Bhattacharejee, "The Science of Good and Evil," *National Geographic*, January 2018.
8. Dr. Urie Bronfenbrenner in Jill Stamm, *Bright from the Start* (New York: Gotham Books, 2007).
9. B. Hart & T.M. Risley, *Meaningful Differences in the Everyday Experience of Young American Children* (Baltimore, MD: Paul H. Brookes Publishing Company, 1950).

10. Jill Stamm, *Bright from the Start* (New York: Gotham Books, 2007).

11. John Bowlby, *A Secure Base: Parent-Child Attachment and Healthy Human Development* (New York: Basic Books, 1988).

12. William Ross Wallace, "The Hand That Rocks the Cradle," *Beautiful Gems of Thought and Sentiment* (Boston, MA: The Colins-Patten Co., 1890).

13. Ezra Taft Benson, "To the Mothers in Zion," address given at a fireside for parents, Feb. 22, 1987, 8–12.

14. Dr. Urie Bronfenbrenner in Jill Stamm, *Bright from the Start* (New York: Gotham Books, 2007).

15. Personal email, January 27, 2018.

16. David L. Hill, MD, FAAP, *Between Us Dads: A Father's Guide to Child Health* (Itasca, IL: American Academy of Pediatrics, 2012).

17. Christina Steinorth, *Cue Cards for Life: Gentle Reminders for Better Relationships* (Nashville, TN: Hunter House, 2013).

18. Rob Kemp, "The Importance of Father-Child Bonding," Feb. 8, 2011, www.thenational.ae/lifestyle/family/the-importance-of-father-child-bonding-1.467546.

19. Christina Steinorth, *Cue Cards for Life: Gentle Reminders for Better Relationships* (Nashville, TN: Hunter House, 2013).

20. Russell M. Ballard, "Fathers and Sons, a Remarkable Relationship," *Ensign*, November 2009.

21. Michael Austin, *Fatherhood—Philosophy for Everyone: The Dao of Daddy* (Hoboken, NJ: Wiley-Blackwell, 2011).

22. Elizabeth Weiss McGolerick, "The Importance of the Father-Daughter Relationship," Feb. 9, 2017, http://www.sheknows.com/parenting/articles/821928/the-importance-of-the-father-daughter-relationship.

23. Michael Austin, *Fatherhood—Philosophy for Everyone: The Dao of Daddy* (Hoboken, NJ: Wiley-Blackwell, 2011).

24. Ron Huxley, "Importance of the Father/Child Bond," accessed 4/10/18, www.familycorner.com.

25. D. Todd Christofferson, "Fathers," *Ensign*, May 2016.

26. Dieter F. Uchtdorf, "Perfect Love Casteth Out Fear," *Ensign*, May 2017.

27. Ibid.

Chapter 3

1. William Wordsworth, "Ode on Intimations of Immortality from Recollections of Early Childhood," 1798.

2. Joy D. Jones, "Value beyond Measure," *Ensign*, November 2017.

3. From song written by Calee Reed, 2012.

4. John Pielmeier, "Gifted Hands," Sony Pictures, September 8, 2009.

5. *For the Strength of Youth* (booklet, 2011).

6. Vicki Jo Anderson, The Other Eminent Men of Wilford Woodruff (Cottonwood, AZ: Zichron Historical Research Institute, 1994).

7. History of the Church, 6:305, 2.

8. Lectures on Faith (1985), 38, 42.

9. Jeffrey R. Holland, "The Grandeur of God," *Ensign*, November 2003.

10. Ronald A. Rasband, "By Divine Design," *Ensign*, November 2017.

11. From her Facebook post 7/18/2017.

12. Jorg Klebingat, "Approaching the Throne of God with Confidence," *Ensign*, November 2014.

13. Personal email correspondence.

14. Linda K. Burton, "Is Faith in the Atonement of Jesus Christ Written in our Hearts?" *Ensign*, November 2012.

15. Sally Deford, *Friend*, March 2013.

16. Dieter F. Uchtdorf, "Come, Join with Us," *Ensign*, November 2013.

17. Dieter F. Uchtdorf, "Perfect Love Casteth Out Fear," *Ensign*, May 2017.

Chapter 4

1. Russell M. Nelson, "A Plea to My Sisters," *Ensign*, November 2015.

2. Kevin S. Hamilton, "Continually Holding Fast," *Ensign*, November 2013.

3. "A Letter to Church Members from the First Presidency," *Church News*, 27 Feb. 1999, 3.

4. Thomas S. Monson, "Consider the Blessings," *Ensign*, Nov. 2012.

5. Boyd K. Packer, "These Things I Know," *Ensign*, May 2013.

6. John H. Groberg, "The Power of Family Prayer," *Ensign*, May 1982.

7. Ibid.

8. "Lesson 18: Prayers Are Answered in the Best Way." Primary 2: Choose the Right A Manual, 1995.
9. "Did You Think to Pray?" *Hymns*, no. 140.
10. Anne G. Wirthlin, "Teaching Our Children to Love the Scriptures," *Ensign*, May 1998.
11. Joseph B. Wirthlin, "Growing into the Priesthood," *Ensign*, November 1999.
12. Colleen Menlove, "A Voice of Gladness for Our Children," *Ensign*, November 2002.
13. Gordon B. Hinckley, regional conference in Montevideo, Uruguay, 10 Aug. 1997.
14. Attributed to Mark Twain.
15. Melvin J. Ballard, *Conference Report*, April 1929, 68.
16. Ezra Taft Benson, "To the Young Women of the Church," *Ensign*, November 1986.
17. Joseph Walker, "More than Hemlines and Haircuts," *Ensign*, February 1992.
18. Susan Bednar, "Reverencing Womanhood" (Brigham Young University–Idaho Six Stake Fireside, September 16, 2001), http://www2.byui.edu/Presentations/Transcripts/MiscellaneousAddresses/2001_09_16_Bednarsusan.htm.
19. David O. McKay, as quoted in Harold B. Lee, "Be Loyal to the Royal Within You" (Brigham Young University devotional, September 11, 1973), speeches.byu.edu.
20. Bednar, "Reverencing Womanhood."

Chapter 5

1. Attributed to Mark Twain.
2. Listen to this song at http://valuesparenting.com/joy-school/sample-lessons/lesson-3-3.
3. Herbert W. Armstrong, "The United States and the British Commonwealth and Prophesy," The Worldwide Church of God, 1980.
4. Russell M. Nelson, "Reflection and Resolution," BYU fireside, January 7, 1990.
5. "The Living Christ," *Ensign*, April 2000.
6. "The Family: A Proclamation to the World," *Ensign*, November 1995.
7. James E. Talmage, *Jesus the Christ* (1981).
8. Russell M. Nelson, "The Sabbath Is a Delight," *Ensign*, May 2015.

Chapter 6

1. Irving Berlin, "Count Your Blessings (Instead of Sheep)," in *White Christmas*, directed by Michael Curtiz, 1954.
2. Linda and Richard Eyre, *Teaching Your Children Joy* (New York, NY: Touchstone, 1994).
3. Dieter F. Uchtdorf, "Grateful in Any Circumstances," *Ensign*, May 2014.
4. Corrie Ten Boom, *The Hiding Place* (Bantam, 1974).
5. Boyd K. Packer, "Little Children," *Ensign*, November 1986, 16.
6. The First Presidency Message, *Ensign*, June 1999.
7. Jeffrey R. Holland, "A Prayer for the Children," Ensign, May 2003.
8. Gordon B. Hinckley, "Each a Better Person," *Ensign*, November 2002.
9. Julie B. Beck, "Nourishing and Protecting the Family," Women's Conference, May 1, 2009.
10. M. Russell Ballard, "Let Our Voices Be Heard," *Ensign*, November 2003.
11. M. Russell Ballard, "Finding Joy through Loving Service," *Ensign*, May 2011.
12. "Let Us Oft Speak Kind Words, *Hymns*, no. 232.
13. James E. Faust, "A Christmas without Presents," *Ensign*, December 2001.

Chapter 7

1. Chris Medina, *What Are Words*, Feb. 21, 2011, 19 Entertainment, track 4 on *What Are Words*, 2011, CD.
2. Jessica Grayless, "Running the Extra Mile," *The New Era*, March 2013.
3. Sally Deford, "If the Savior Stood Beside Me," *Friend*, March, 2013.
4. Barbara M. Joosse, *I Love You the Purplest* (San Francisco: Chronicle Books, 1996).
5. Gordon B. Hinckley, "The Continuing Pursuit of Truth," *Ensign*, May 1986 (emphasis added).
6. Richard G. Scott, "How to Obtain Revelation and Inspiration for Your Personal Life," *Ensign*, May 2012.
7. Peter B. Rawlins, "A Serious Look at Humor," *New Era*, August 1974.
8. Ibid.
9. Jennifer Grace Jones, "No Corrupt Communication," *Ensign*, August 2013.
10. Ibid.
11. Peter B. Rawlins, "A Serious Look at Humor," *New Era*, August 1974.

12. Paul Coughlin, "Parental Sarcasm Is No Joke," *Focus on the Family*, May 2008, as quoted in Jones, "No Corrupt Communication," *Ensign*, August 2013.
13. Jennifer Grace Jones, "No Corrupt Communication," *Ensign*, August 2013.
14. Rebecca Rice Berkin, "Open Mouth, Insert Car," *New Era*, October 2006.
15. Peter B. Rawlins, "A Serious Look at Humor," *New Era*, August 1974.
16. Gordon B. Hinckley, "The Continuing Pursuit of Truth," *Ensign*, May 1986.

Chapter 8

1. Rosemary M. Wixom, "Stay on the Path," *Ensign*, November 2010.
2. Examples include Clark B. Hinckley, *Christopher Columbus: A Man Among the Gentiles* (Salt Lake City, Deseret Book, 2014) and Chris Stewart and Ted Stewart, *Seven Miracles that Saved America: Why They Matter and Whey We Should Have Hope* (Crawfordsville, Indiana: The Shipley Group, 2009).
3. Russell M. Nelson, "A Plea to my Sisters," *Ensign*, November 2015.
4. Bonnie L. Oscarson, "Rise Up in Strength, Sisters in Zion," *Ensign*, November 2016.
5. Ibid.
6. See *Illustrated Stories from the Bible*, and *The Old Testament for Latter-day Saint Families*.
7. Gillian Strickland, "The Reading Mother," in *The Best Loved Poems of the American People*, sel. Hazel Felleman (1936), 376, as quoted in "If Ye Are Prepared, Ye Shall Not Fear," *Ensign*, November 2004.
8. Arizona Interfaith Movement, www.AZIFM.com
9. "Family Conversations: What's the Best Thing Parents Can Do to Protect Children from Negative Sexual Influences," LDS Media Library, www.lds.org/media-library/video/family-conversations.
10. Ibid.
11. *A Parent's Guide* (booklet, 1985), 11.
12. Ibid., 12.
13. Ibid., 15.
14. Janeen Brady, "Safety Kids," Brite Music Enterprises, 1983, http://www.britekids.com/products/safety-kids-1-personal-safety.
15. *A Parent's Guide*, 23.
16. Ibid., 30.
17. *For the Strength of Youth* (booklet, 2011).
18. *A Parent's Guide*, 39.
19. Ibid., 36–37.
20. Ibid., 36.
21. Ibid., 42.
22. Ibid.

Chapter 9

1. Clay Olsen, "What Teens Wish Parents Knew" as found in "Protection from Pornography—a Christ-Focused Home," *Ensign*, April 2014.
2. Jeffrey R. Holland, "Place No More for the Enemy of My Soul," *Ensign*, May 2010.
3. Kimberly Reid, "Finding Help," *Friend*, February 2012.
4. Anne G. Wirthlin, "Teaching Our Children to Love the Scriptures," *Ensign*, May 1998.
5. "Can You Prevent ADHD?" *WebMD*, no date, https://www.webmd.com/add-adhd/childhood-adhd/preventing-adhd#1.
6. Perri Glass, "Health Views," *New York Times*, May 10, 2011.
7. Ibid.
8. Perri Glass, "Fixated by Screens, but Seemingly Nothing Else," *New York Times*, May 9, 2011, http://www.nytimes.com/2011/05/10/health/views/10klass.html?_r=0.
9. Spencer W. Kimball, "Strengthening the Family—The Basic Unit of the Church," *Ensign*. April 1978.
10. Joseph F. Smith, *Gospel Doctrine*, 389.
11. *Teachings of Presidents of the Church: Gordon B. Hinckley* (2016), 171.
12. Boyd K. Packer, "Little Children," Ensign, Nov. 1986, 17.

Chapter 10

1. James E. Faust, "The Greatest Challenge in the World—Good Parenting," *Ensign*, October 1990.
2. George Albert Smith, "Latter-day Prophets Speak: Strengthening the Home," *Ensign*, October 2001.

3. James E. Faust, "The Greatest Challenge in the World—Good Parenting," *Ensign,* October 1990.
4. Joseph Smith, as quoted by John Taylor, *Millennial Star,* Nov. 15, 1851, 339.
5. Jan Karron, *A Light in the Window* (New York: G.P. Putnam's Sons, 1995).
6. Boyd K. Packer, "Little Children," *Ensign,* November 1986, 17.
7. Fred Rogers, as quoted in Richard Crum, *Relentless* (Springville: Bonneville Books, 2011).
8. *Dictionary.com,* s.v., "betimes," accessed May 19, 2018, http://www.dictionary.com/browse/betimes.
9. Boyd K. Packer, "Little Children," *Ensign,* November 1986, 17.
10. Brigham Young, *Journal of Discourses,* 9:124–25.
11. Jan Karron, *A Light in the Window* (New York: G.P. Putnam's Sons, 1995).
12. Ezra Taft Benson, "To the Mothers in Zion," 1987, 8–12; see also Ezra Taft Benson, *Come, Listen to a Prophet's Voice* (Salt Lake City: Deseret Book, 1990), 32–36.
13. Joseph Smith, as quoted in John Taylor, *Millennial Star,* November 15, 1851, 339.
14. Richard G. Scott, "The Power of Correct Principles," *Ensign,* May 1993.
15. Ibid.
16. M. Sue Bergin, "The Hazards of Helicopter Parenting," *BYU Magazine,* Spring 2013.
17. Ibid.
18. Ibid.

Chapter 11

1. D. Todd Christofferson, "The Doctrine of Christ," *Ensign,* November 2017.
2. Dieter F. Uchtdorf, "Be Not Afraid, Only Believe," *Ensign,* November 2015.
3. David A. Bednar, "The Tender Mercies of the Lord," *Ensign,* May 2005.
4. Richard G. Scott, "I Have Given You an Example," *Ensign,* May 2014.
5. Brent L. Top and Bruce A. Chadwick, "Raising Righteous Children in a Wicked World," *BYU Magazine,* Summer 1998.
6. Gordon B. Hinckley, "Great Shall Be the Peace of Thy Children," *Ensign,* November 2000.
7. Stephen W. Owen, "Repentance Is Always Positive," *Ensign,* November 2017.
8. *Primary 3* (1994), lesson 10, https://www.lds.org/manual/primary-3/lesson-10-repentance.
9. *For the Strength of Youth* (booklet, 2011).
10. Stephen W. Owen, "Repentance Is Always Positive," *Ensign,* November 2017.
11. Linda and Richard Eyre, "The Repenting Bench: A Great Way to Bench Squabbles," *Deseret News,* July 24, 2011.
12. Ross Campbell and Gary Chapman, *The Five Love Languages of Children* (Chicago: Northfield Publishing, 1997).
13. Dale G. Renlund, "Repentance, A Joyful Choice," *Ensign,* November 2016.
14. Stephen W. Owen, "Repentance Is Always Positive," *Ensign,* November 2017.
15. Personal email correspondence.
16. Richard G. Scott, "Finding Forgiveness," *Ensign,* May 1995.
17. D. Todd Christofferson, "The Divine Gift of Repentance," *Ensign,* November 2011.
18. "Baptism," https://www.lds.org/children/resources/topics/baptism.
19. "The Holy Ghost," Gospel Topics, lds.org.
20. *Teachings of Presidents of the Church: Lorenzo Snow* (2012), 76.
21. Personal email correspondence.
22. Carol Lynn Pearson and Lex de Azevedo, "My Turn on Earth," musical production, 1977.
23. Leonard D. Greer, from Kimball Stake Conference, Mesa, Arizona, January 2018.
24. Dale G. Renlund, "Latter-day Saints Keep on Trying," *Ensign,* May 2015.
25. D. Todd Christofferson, "Give Us This Day Our Daily Bread," CES Fireside for Young Adults, January 9, 2011, Brigham Young University, https://www.lds.org/broadcasts/article/ces-devotionals/2011/01/give-us-this-day-our-daily-bread.
26. Gordon B. Hinckley, "We Have a Work to Do," *Ensign,* May 1995.
27. Dale G. Renlund, "Latter-day Saints Keep on Trying," *Ensign,* May 2015.

Chapter 12

1. Boyd K. Packer, "Little Children," *Ensign,* November 1986.
2. Patricia P. Pinegar, "Peace, Hope, and Direction," *Ensign,* November 1999.
3. M. Russell Ballard, "Family Councils," *Ensign,* May 2016.

4.   *Oxford Dictionaries*, s.v. "synergy," accessed June 20, 2018, https://en.oxforddictionaries.com/definition /synergy.
5.   M. Russell Ballard, "Counseling with our Councils," *Ensign*, May 1994.
6.   Jennifer Lyn Pond, "Our Successful Family Council," *Ensign*, December 2017.
7.   Ibid.
8.   M. Russell Ballard, "Counseling with our Councils," *Ensign*, May 1994.
9.   Russell M. Nelson, "Revelation for the Church, Revelation for Our Lives," *Ensign*, May 2018.

Chapter 13

1.   Garry Flake, "A Deal Is a Deal."
2.   James E. Faust, "Instruments in the Hands of God," *Ensign*, November 2005.

Chapter 14

1.   See also Bahr & Loveless, "Family Work," *BYU Magazine*, Spring 2000, retrieved from https://magazine .byu.edu/article/family-work.
2.   Mormon Channel, "Interview with Sister Julie B. Beck," Episode 5, *Conversations*.
3.   Kenny Kemp, *My Dad Was a Carpenter: A Father, A Son, and the Blueprints for a Meaningful Life* (Acme Publishing, 2008).
4.   John Bytheway, *Tour de Family: Doing Your Part to Help Your Family Succeed* (Salt Lake City: Deseret Book, 1997).
5.   Robert D. Hales, "Provident Providers," *Ensign*, May 2009.
6.   David A. Bednar, "Bear Up Their Burdens with Ease," *Ensign*, November 2014.

Chapter 15

1.   Brad Wilcox, "Can Your Child Really Talk to You?" *Ensign*, September 1995.
2.   Gordon B. Hinckley, "Each a Better Person," *Ensign*, November 2002.
3.   Wilcox, "Can Your Child Really Talk to You?"
4.   Personal email correspondence.
5.   Personal email correspondence.
6.   Gary Chapman, PhD, and Ross Campbell, M.D., *The Five Love Languages of Children* (Chicago: Northfield, 1997).
7.   Jennifer Graham, "How to Cheat-proof Your Marriage, According to Science," *Deseret News*, April 14, 2017 (emphasis added).

Chapter 16

1.   Julie B. Beck, *BYU Women's Conference*, April 29, 2010.
2.   See Danielle Kennington, "Crash & Tell," *Friend*, June 2011.
3.   Collin Bishop, "7 Risky Apps All Parents Should Know About," *LDS Living*, http://www.ldsliving.com/7 -Risky-Apps-All-Parents-Should-Know-About/s/75855.
4.   Ibid.
5.   Janice Kapp Perry and Joy Saunders Lundberg, "Stand Up, Walk Away!" Prime Recordings, 2009.
6.   Boyd K. Packer, "Inspiring Music Worthy Thoughts," *Ensign*, November 1973.
7.   Linda S. Reeves, "Protection from Pornography: A Christ-Centered Home," *Ensign*, May 2014.
8.   Marion G. Romney, "The Book of Mormon: Keystone of Our Religion," *Ensign*, May 1980.
9.   "Spouses and Families," *Overcoming Pornography through the Atonement of Jesus Christ*, accessed June 20, 2018, http://overcomingpornography.org/spouses-and-families.
10. M. Russell Ballard, "Fathers and Sons: A Remarkable Relationship," *Ensign*, November 2009.
11. M. Sue Bergin, "Understanding and Improving Your Parenting Style," *BYU Magazine*, Fall 2010.
12. Linda S. Reeves, "Protection from Pornography: A Christ-Centered Home," *Ensign*, May 2014.
13. Ibid.
14. Jonathan G. Sandberg, "Healing=Courage+Action+Grace" (Brigham Young University devotional, January 2014), speeches.byu.edu.
15. Ibid.
16. "Spouses and Families," *Overcoming Pornography through the Atonement of Jesus Christ*, accessed June 20, 2018, http://overcomingpornography.org/spouses-and-families.

17. The Church of Jesus Christ of Latter-day Saints, "Family Services Addiction Recovery Program," https://addictionrecovery.lds.org/home.
18. *Preach My Gospel* (2004).
19. Ibid.
20. Osmer D. Flake, *William Jordan Flake: Pioneer, Colonizer*, 1933.
21. N. Eldon Tanner, as quoted in Gary E. Renlund, "Be Valiant in Courage, Strength, and Activity," *Ensign*, November 2012.
22. Michael S. Wilcox, *Fire in the Bones: William Tyndale—Martyr, Father of the English Bible* (Salt Lake City: Deseret Book, 2015).
23. D. Todd Christofferson, "The Blessing of Scripture," *Ensign*, May 2010.
24. Gary E. Renlund, "Be Valiant in Courage, Strength and Activity," *Ensign*, November 2012.
25. Personal email correspondence.
26. Dan Buettner, "These Are the World's Happiest Places," *National Geographic*, November 2017.
27. First Presidency letter, January 10, 2014.

Chapter 17

1. *Preach My Gospel* (2004), 86.
2. One such example is *The Holy Temple* by Boyd K. Packer.
3. Stanley G. Ellis, "Do We Trust Him? Hard Is Good," *Ensign*, November 2017.
4. Virginia H. Pearce (ed.), *Glimpses into the Life and Heart of Marjorie Pay Hinckley* (Salt Lake City: Deseret Book, 1999).
5. Personal Facebook post, March 23, 2018.
6. Ibid.

Chapter 18

1. Dallin H. Oaks, "Why Do We Serve?" *Ensign*, November 1984.
2. Robert D. Hales, "If Ye Love Me, Keep My Commandments," *Ensign*, May 2014.
3. Oaks, "Why Do We Serve?"
4. Shirlee Monty, *May's Boy: The Rest of the Story* (CreateSpace Independent Publishing Platform, 2012).

Acknowledgments

*I*t was only our second date when Mark and I started talking about children. From the time he was little, he had told everyone he wanted to grow up to be a dad and to have thirteen kids. But he never held it over me. In fact, each time we were ready for another baby, he urged me to visit the doctor to make sure I was healthy enough. So, we got to have many years of raising children—lots of chances to keep trying! We made plenty of mistakes but got to try something different on the next one! Through it all, it was teamwork and more love.

Thank you with all my heart to

- Mark, my life and my love, thank you for an amazing life and for everything.
- My kids, M & N, B & S, J & K, D & L, C & T, G & K, R & D, J & D, E, Q, K, T, and R, who lived it and who loved me through it!
- My grandchildren, K, A, A, B, L, J, J, E, S, R, C, J, A, S, M, M, B, A, O, M, R, M, R, C, J, and C, who drew such amazing pictures!
- Cara Holladay and her husband, Tim, who have been my support from the start.
- Marie Ricks, who believed in me and urged me forward.
- Sabrina Hulse, who was tireless with her help.
- Melvin Richardson, who gave me so much time and invaluable service.
- Elizabeth Carroll, who listened, read, and edited.
- Joe Free, for his generous website help and his countdown.
- Mom, Rauna, Erin, Dania, Miriam, and Joann, who read and helped edit.
- My sisters, who gave me their ideas, and my brothers, who urged me to write.
- My mother and father, Jay and Lavona, who helped me find my gifts and loved me patiently as I developed them.
- Jessica and Kaitlin at Cedar Fort, who were always so positive.

It was my dear dad, Jay Richardson, who championed the phrase *The Answer Is More Love.* He lived it as his motto, and it became mine too. As far as we can tell, the phrase was coined by a Jesuit Priest, Gene Jakubek, in his book of the same title, published in 1968. Thanks, Dad!

About the Author

*M*arlene Ellingson loves to help families, and along with earning a bachelor of arts, summa cum laude in family living from BYU, her best qualification is her own experience! She grew up second of eleven children in a loving family in Arizona. Currently, she and her husband, Mark, are raising their close-knit family of thirteen children—nine boys and four girls, one set of twins—in Mesa. Eight of these are married, two are at college, one is on a mission, and two are still living at home.

Parenting with the Spirit: The Answer Is More Love is her first book about love as a means to empower children, build faith, and create peaceful family dynamics. A sought-after speaker, writer, and educator, she has taught these ideas with anecdotes from real families at many parenting workshops for over nine years, as well as in her family support blog. She has also taught co-op preschools for thirty years, elementary school art and music appreciation for twenty-eight years, and scripture-based homeschool through the years to her children and grandchildren. Marlene has also been a voice for religious freedom in her community, recently spearheading an eight-year effort to establish an interfaith high school baccalaureate.

When asked why so many kids, Mark and Marlene like to explain that on their second date, they decided they both wanted a large family. They were blessed with easy pregnancies and wonderful children! With so many kids—and each one so different—they were also blessed with lots of trial and error. (They know thirteen different ways to potty-train a child!) They learned firsthand the need for promptings from the Spirit and that more love is the best approach to any family challenge.

Marlene loves reading, sewing, and swim aerobics. She enjoys half-marathons with her family—they run the race and she takes their pictures! Her favorite pastime is to interact with her twenty-six (so far!) grandchildren.

Whenever she reads books with ideas and helps, Marlene likes to jump immediately to the true stories, so she put plenty of them in her book! She hopes to share Christian principles and ideas that lift discouraged mothers and fathers. Though all parents fall short at times, they can point their children to the perfect mentor, our Savior Jesus Christ, by listening to His Spirit. Marlene would love your comments at www.theanswerismorelove.com.

Scan to visit

theanswerismorelove.com